Jewish Philosophy and the Academy

Jewish Philosophy and the Academy is a publication of
The International Center for University Teaching
of Jewish Civilization, Jerusalem

Continuing support for the workshop on Jewish Philosophy has been provided by the Lucius N. Littauer Foundation, and by the Memorial Foundation for Jewish Culture.

Jewish Philosophy and the Academy

Edited by
Emil L. Fackenheim
and Raphael Jospe

Published in Conjunction with the International Center
for University Teaching of Jewish Civilization

Madison • Teaneck
Fairleigh Dickinson University Press
London: Associated University Presses

Associated University Presses
440 Forsgate Drive
Cranbury, NJ 08512

Associated University Presses
16 Barter Street
London WC1A 2AH, England

Associated University Presses
P.O. Box 338, Port Credit
Mississauga, Ontario
Canada L5G 4L8

The paper used in this publication meets the requirements of the American National Standard for Permanence of Paper for Printed Library Materials Z39.48-1984.

Library of Congress Cataloging-in-Publication Data

Jewish philosophy and the academy / edited by Emil L. Fackenheim and Raphael Jospe.
p. cm.
"Published in conjunction with the International Center for University Teaching of Jewish Civilization."
Includes bibliographical references.
ISBN 0-8386-3643-8 (alk. paper)
1. Philosophy, Jewish. 2. Philosophy, Jewish—Study and teaching (Higher) 3. Rosenzweig, Franz, 1886–1929. 4. Lévinas, Emmanuel. 5. Holocaust, Jewish (1939–1945)—Causes. I. Fackenheim, Emil L. II. Jospe, Raphael.
B154.J49 1996
181′.06—dc20 95-37533
CIP

PRINTED IN THE UNITED STATES OF AMERICA

To

HERBERT and STEPHANIE NEUMAN

devoted friends

committed to the pursuit of knowledge

Contents

Introduction

RAPHAEL JOSPE

WE are a pivotal generation in the history of Jewish philosophy in the academy. In 1915, when Harry Austryn Wolfson was appointed to the faculty of Harvard University to teach Hebrew literature and philosophy, there were no universities in the Land of Israel,[1] and the centers of *Wissenschaft des Judentums* were located in central Europe. Despite the limited but important research and teaching of Judaica at a small number of rabbinic seminaries and other Jewish institutions in the United States, Wolfson had no colleagues holding chairs in Jewish studies, let alone Jewish philosophy, at any of America's prime universities.[2]

Within Wolfson's lifetime (he died in 1974), major universities were established in Israel, the Nazis largely succeeded in making much of Europe free of both Jews and Jewish culture, and in North America, especially in the last decade of Wolfson's life, there was rapid and radical expansion of Jewish studies, with full-time chairs or part-time positions funded on literally hundreds of campuses.

Our generation lives, then, at a unique historic junction. We are the last to be taught by the giants of European *Wissenschaft des Judentums* after World War II, and the first to experience the great expansion of Judaica scholarship in Israel and abroad since the 1960s, most recently, in Eastern Europe and the former Soviet Union. New libraries and facilities (including the Jewish National and University Library in Jerusalem, with such resources as its manuscript collection and its Institute for Microfilmed Hebrew Manuscripts) have revolutionized our access to previously unknown or inaccessible primary materials.[3]

It is appropriate for us, therefore, to reflect on the state of Jewish philosophy in the academy in the last decades of the twentieth century. Philosophy being what it is, reflection on Jewish philosophy in the academy cannot be limited to the practical aspects of the question—pedagogy, curriculum, texts, and so on—nor even to the "political" aspects of the question, namely the academic setting of Jewish philosophy in departments or programs of Jewish studies, philosophy, religion, all of which are of greatest importance and all of which profoundly affect the ways in which Jewish philosophy is and should be taught in the university. Philosophers, however, prefer to contemplate the metaquestions that underly the practical issues and give them direction and meaning.

One cannot, then, teach philosophy without philosophizing, and as Emil Fackenheim points out in the first chapter of this volume, "What is philosophy?" is itself a philosophical question. For us, then, the obvious first question is "What is Jewish philosophy?"[4] (a term which some regard as an oxymoron).

Of course, most of us do not regard the respective legacies of Athens and Jerusalem to be mutually incompatible or exclusive, despite the obvious differences between these two cultures, with their diverse ways of thinking and fundamentally different ways of life.

Harry Wolfson's famous thesis suggested that all of Western philosophy following the Greeks and Romans, whether in Jewish, Christian, or Islamic cultural garb, was "Philonic." Greek and Roman philosophy was pagan, independent of revealed scriptural religion. It was Philo, the Jew of ancient Alexandria, who was the most important Western philosopher after Plato and Aristotle, because he attempted to bridge the gap between Athens and Jerusalem, to harmonize philosophy and revealed religion. All subsequent religious philosophy in the West was a Philonic attempt to relate philosophy and revelation, until Spinoza tore down that seventeen-century-old structure, by liberating philosophy from Scripture. By breaking with medieval tradition, Spinoza paved the way for modern philosophy. In short, according to Wolfson, it was Philo who made possible medieval philosophy, and it was Spinoza who made possible modern philosophy.

Emil Fackenheim suggests in the first chapter that, if we are indebted to Socrates for the philosophical method, beginning with a sense of wonder at reality, we (especially we, whose wonder after Auschwitz is "mingled with a new horror") are indebted not only to Athens but also to Jerusalem—not only to philosophers like Socrates, but even more to the prophets of Israel like Isaiah, for the ethical content of their teachings. The method is Greek; the message is Jewish. In this respect, "Jewish philosophy" is no oxymoron; it is, rather, both an intellectual and a moral challenge.

This dual challenge shapes the diverse essays in this volume, and provides an implicit, if not always overt, thematic coherence as we explore dimensions of Jewish philosophy and the academy. Philosophy's encounter with Scripture, beginning with Philo, led to the rise of a new philosophic literary genre: Bible exegesis, which enables the religious philosopher to understand revelation philosophically and, simultaneously, to reconcile philosophic doctrines with the teachings of religion. Furthermore, as Raphael Jospe proposes in the second chapter, it provides the religious philosopher with an occasion, a platform "both for teaching philosophy within a religious community and for demonstrating the rational validity of religion within the philosophic community."

The ethical focus of much of Jewish philosophy is explored in the third chapter by Andrey Smirnov, who examines the question from the perspective of distance, both disciplinary (he is a specialist in Arabic-Islamic philosophy and mysticism) and geographic (he is a member of the Russian Academy of Sciences in Moscow). Philosophy, he argues, is the quintessence of the spirit of a people. The Jewish spirit, as he sees it, is typified by "the historical and ethical character of experiencing being. . . . A distinctive feature of Jewish philosophy is the injection of ethics into being."

In the modern period, however, the traditional categories and definitions (philosophic and religious alike) tended to break down. In the fourth chapter, Gershon Greenberg characterizes Jewish thought (note the use of the more neutral and vague term "thought" instead of "philosophy") in the nineteenth century by the kabbalistic metaphor of *shevirat ha-kelim,* "the shattering of the vessels."[5] The Emancipation in the eighteenth century had shattered the premodern, traditional "vessels" of Jewish life, the cohesive unity of autonomous Jewish communal life and the belief in the revealed Torah as absolute truth. "With the Emancipation . . . the common source that enclosed the dialectic was removed." However, Greenberg concludes, the fragmentation of philosophic outlook in the nineteenth century, in turn, eventually permitted flexible and diverse responses to the calamities of the twentieth century.

The first part of this book, "Jewish Philosophy and the Curriculum," thus examines some of the fundamental questions relating to teaching Jewish philosophy: the place of Jewish philosophy in the academy; the Philonic paradigm of philosophic encounter with revealed Scripture and the philosophic literary genre Philo innovated, namely philosophic exegesis of the Bible; the ethical character or focus of much of Jewish philosophic concern; and the breakdown, in the nineteenth century, of many of the traditional and classical definitions—religious, political, and philosophical—a nineteenth-century fragmentation that made possible twentieth-century flexibility.

Logically and chronologically, this leads us to the second part of the book, in which we consider the presentation of two contemporary Jewish philosophers in the academy, Franz Rosenzweig in the first decades of the twentieth century, and Emmanuel Levinas in its last decades.

What about Martin Buber, who surely is the most popular contemporary Jewish philosopher, especially among non-Jews? Emil Fackenheim has noted "that Buber's thought is being de-Judaized in the very process of being received as philosophy."[6] However popular Buber's philosophy may be (often in academic settings other than departments of philosophy), the contemporary Jewish philosopher taken most seriously as a philosopher in philosophic circles is Emmanuel Levinas. And yet, many in these philosophic circles would question—like Levinas himself—whether there is anything particularly "Jewish" about his philosophy, and thus whether there is any meaningful connection between his purely philosophical work and his more overtly Jewish works. The essays in the second section of this volume question that judgment, even that self-judgment, by attempting to present Levinas in a Jewish context (in relation to Franz Rosenzweig) and by pointing to the Jewish content of his thought (the emphasis on ethics and justice, rather than on being).

In the fifth chapter, Richard Cohen proposes a resolution of an apparent paradox in Levinas's *Totality and Infinity.* Levinas states in the preface that "We were impressed by the opposition to the idea of totality in Franz Rosenzweig's *Star of Redemption,* a work too often present in this book to be cited"—and then never mentions the *Star* again. In a careful contextual study of this passage, Cohen argues for the *Star*'s "presence in absentia," namely, that Levinas, while indebted to phenomenology, was enabled by Rosenzweig to make a more subtle critique of phenomenology (which ultimately destroys itself), and to have a greater appreciation for ethics and justice, of which philosophy should ultimately acknowledge itself to be a mode.

In the sixth chapter, Johanan Bauer argues to the contrary, viewing Levinas not as Jewishly indebted to Rosenzweig (as Cohen proposes), but as a Jewish critic of his predecessor. For Levinas, Bauer suggests, Rosenzweig's conception of God's "eternal becoming" blurs the significance, so central to prophetic monotheism, of God's radical difference from the world. Once again a metaphor of Lurianic kabbalah (the *tzimtzum,* the self-contraction of the infinite) may intrude into philosophy, as Levinas conceives of creation as *décalage absolut,* as a shifting of the infinite to make room for separate being.

Both Cohen and Bauer thus place Levinas within the context of

Jewish philosophy, Cohen seeing Rosenzweig's Jewish influence on Levinas, and Bauer seeing Levinas as a Jewish critic of Rosenzweig.

The Jewish context and content of Levinas's philosophy are further explicated in the seventh chapter by Ephraim Meir, primarily on ethical grounds: Levinas replaces concern for being with concern for the other. The life of "difficult freedom" is characterized by such responsibility. The ethical, which replaced the ontological, now leads to the metaphysical, for in responsibility for the other, the individual approaches God. At the same time, Levinas maintains (like Maimonides, in the last chapter of the *Guide of the Perplexed*), that what one knows of God must be expressed ethically.

Can Levinas's notion that phenomenology destroys itself, and that ethics can effectively replace ontology, be sustained? In the third part of this volume, the uses of Jewish ethical and political thought are examined.

Gillian Rose, in the eighth chapter, argues, in effect, that philosophic ethics has destroyed itself, and that "Kant's emphasis on the priority of practical reason or subjective freedom . . . has itself undermined ethics," given "the disjunction between morality and law . . . [between] the moral discourse of rights and the systematic actualities of power in modern societies and states." The crisis, Rose claims, is not just in Judaism but in modern philosophy itself, and it follows from the idea of freedom. Aharon Lichenstein's Orthodox view of *lifnim mi-shurat ha-din* (the superogatory category, "beyond the measure of the law") as a "supralegal but not optional" morality of aspiration, balances, according to Rose, "universal and local factors in any specific case" and thus provides a flexible, "noncategorical" imperative. In contrast, Rose sees Eugene Borowitz's Reform attempt to expand the halakhah by the Kantian categorical imperative as no less absolute and uncompromising. However, neither position proves able to remedy the status of women, discussed so extensively in much of halakhic literature, a problem that "will continue to explode any surety it is made to stand for on the way."

Whereas Rose argues that modern ethical theory destroys itself, Michael Morgan holds, in the ninth chapter, that modern political theory destroys itself. Jewish reflection on modern liberal political thought cannot save it. Leo Strauss therefore opted for a return to "common sense," to the political insights of the ancient Greeks and to the ethical teachings of the classical—that is, prephilosophic—Jewish sources, despite the fact that Athens and Jerusalem are in a state of fundamental tension. The conflict between the biblical and philosophic concepts of the good life cannot be resolved, but must be acknowledged and lived. Given this incompatibility between the practical activism of the biblical vision, of "obedient love," and the Greek ideal of theoretical contemplation, of "autonomous understanding," Strauss concludes that modern liberal democracy, committed as it is to a modus vivendi, and making no pretensions of being "expressivistic" of one ideal conception of the good life, is the best attainable structure. In such a framework, the real tensions between Athens and Jerusalem are not eliminated, but lived. One wonders, then, together with Morgan, why, for Strauss, the term "Jewish philosopher" had to be an oxymoron, and why he could "be either a Jewish thinker or a philosopher, but not consistently both," in a dynamic tension.

The limits, if not the bankruptcy, of modern ethical and political thought are brought out most clearly by the Holocaust, that crime of humanity and by humanity against humanity, perpetrated by the country that produced the most brilliant modern philosophers. The fourth part of this volume, accordingly, explores philosophical perspectives on the Holocaust.

In the tenth chapter, Emil Fackenheim points out that there has been much more research on the "small question," *How* did the Nazis murder the Jews? than on the "big question," *Why* did they murder the Jews, and why did they persist in the murder while the Third Reich was collapsing? "The covering law theory of historical explanation," he says, "has reached its limits." Fackenheim proposes that the German people's respect and need for a *Weltanschauung* was met by the Nazis.

Steven Katz extends Fackenheim's argument. In the eleventh chapter, Katz shows that Hitler's *Weltanschauung* was no mere political ideology; it was cosmic in its pretensions: transcendental metaphysical principles became incarnate in history through race. In a closely reasoned argument, Katz shows that the fate of women provides the test case of the uniqueness of Nazi ideology. In other historic tragedies, utilitarian considerations prevailed. Hundreds of thousands of Armenian women and children were taken into Turkish harems—a miserable fate, but they were not exterminated. In the nineteenth-century African slave trade, economic considerations mitigated in favor of keeping slaves alive, not killing them, and women in particular were valued for the profits accruing from their offspring. The Nazi *Weltanschauung,* however, required the extermination of all Jews; it was unmoved by utilitarian considerations. Children and pregnant women were the first to be selected for death.

The historic uniqueness of the Holocaust is an acutely painful subject for Jews. But do the historical facts warrant the philosophic conclusion that the Holocaust is qualitatively, and not merely quantitatively, unique?[7]

Ze'ev Mankowitz examines, in the twelfth chapter, various approaches to the question of the Holocaust's historical uniqueness. For Elie Wiesel and Emil Fackenheim, the Holocaust's uniqueness is metahistorical. For Richard Rubenstein, its uniqueness lies in its perpetration; the Holocaust became possible when it was removed from the hands of hoodlums and put into the hands of bureaucrats. For Steven Katz, the Holocaust is unique in its intentionality, that is, in its being the outgrowth of a consistent *Weltanschauung*. For Lucy Dawidowicz, its uniqueness also lay in its consequences, the success of the Nazis in destroying much of Jewish civilization, especially in Eastern Europe. Mankowitz is not satisfied with these answers. He does not dispute the distinctions between the Holocaust and other twentieth-century mass atrocities, but he questions what moral difference these academic distinctions make. "Murderous self-realization," he argues, "is universal; it is not unique."

If the Holocaust represents one pole of twentieth-century Jewish life, the pole of powerlessness and vulnerability as a result of the Jewish people's lack of national status (homeland and state), the other pole is the Zionist return to and rebuilding of the Land of Israel, a process culminating but not terminating in the restoration of Jewish national sovereignty in the State of Israel.

This process, which Emil Fackenheim brilliantly termed "the Jewish return into history," in turn requires philosophic assessment, presented in the fifth part of this book. In the thirteenth chapter, Daniel Elazar surveys issues creating tensions in the Israeli society and polity that require that the original social contract of the Jewish state be renegotiated. All too often (and this is certainly understandable, given Israel's virtually constant struggle for survival and security), these issues are at most dealt with on a short-term, pragmatic basis of political expedience, without sufficient attention being paid to the tradition of Jewish political philosophy and its relevance to the moral issues of power and powerlessness, both in Israel and in the Diaspora.

The Jewish return into history, inescapably, means a Jewish return to power, which in turn inevitably raises questions about the uses of that power.[8] Elazar concludes that "moral judgments only begin to be meaningful when there is a sufficient level of moral choice. The Jewish people were not more moral when they were powerless; they were simply outside the realm of moral decisionmaking as a people—when they did not have political power, when they were less than fully human."

In the fourteenth chapter, Emil Fackenheim continues the philosophic reassessment of the "Jewish return into history" by characterizing the great German-Jewish philosophies of the early twentieth century as "stateless Jewish philosophies," a moral luxury the Jewish people can no longer afford. Jewish powerlessness and power are typified, for Fackenheim, by the two seminal events that brought to fruition the Jewish struggle for national independence in Israel: The United Nations General Assembly Resolution 181 of 29 November 1947 (the "Partition Resolution"), and the Proclamation of Independence of the State of Israel on 14 May 1948. The first, Fackenheim notes, was an action by the United Nations, in which the Jewish people was still the passive object of charity. The second, however, was a decisive act of collective self-determination, by which the Jewish people returned into history.

Whereas 14 May 1948 was, according to Fackenheim, a Jewish encounter with the political, 7 June 1967, the day on which Jerusalem was reunited in the Six-Day War, was an encounter with the theological. Jewish political philosophy, then, must come to terms with "the four pillars of Zionism"—the Land, the State, the Law of Return, and Jerusalem.

The Jewish return to statehood in the Land of Israel was thus a profound historical step, a return into history. The enactment of the Law of Return was a profound moral step, rendering universal both the Jewish participation in the building of Israel, and, at least potentially, the Jewish right to the benefits and protection of the Jewish state. The Jewish return to Jerusalem was a profound religious step, for all Jews—whether they are (supposedly) "secular," "nonreligious," or overtly "religious"—who identify with the age-old yearning for Zion.

The five parts into which the essays in this volume are organized present various—by no means exhaustive—dimensions of the challenges posed to, but also by, Jewish philosophy in the academy. To these five parts we have appended a conclusion, in which Emil Fackenheim offers us a philosophical retrospective. Fackenheim's impassioned and eloquent demand that philosophy confront ethical reality speaks for itself. So does his retrospective.

* * * * *

The editors wish to express their gratitude to Professors Moshe Davis, Nehemiah Levtzion, Zev Harvey, and Aviezer Ravitzky for their consistent support and encouragement; to Priscilla Fishman for her invaluable editorial assistance; to Professor Norbert Samuelson for his perceptive advice; to Matelle Godfrey for her cheerful help at all times.

Notes

1. The foundation stones of the Hebrew University of Jerusalem were laid on Mount Scopus on 24 July 1918, but the first lecture (by Albert Einstein) was not delivered until 1923, and the university only opened in 1925.

2. Salo Baron was appointed to teach Jewish history at Columbia University in 1930.

3. Cf. Emil Fackenheim, "Jewish Philosophy in the Academy," *Midstream* 33 (August–September 1987):19–22, and his subsequent exchange with Gershon Weiler in *Midstream* 34 (April 1988): 63–64. Also cf. the related articles by Raphael Jospe, "Jewish Philosophy: Texts, Translations and Teaching," *Jewish Studies* 34 (1994): 17–19 and "Teaching Jewish Philosophy: The Continuing Workshop in Jewish Philosophy," in *Teaching Jewish Civilization: A Global Approach to Higher Education,* ed. Moshe Davis (New York University Press, 1995), pp. 155–59.

4. Cf. Raphael Jospe, *What is Jewish Philosophy?* 2d ed. (Ramat Aviv: Open University, 1990), which attempts to survey a representative spectrum of opinion on this question.

5. Much has been written about this doctrine of Lurianic kabbalah. Cf. Gershom Scholem, *Major Trends in Jewish Mysticism* (New York: Schocken, 1965), pp. 244–86, ch. 7, "Isaac Luria and His School."

6. Fackenheim, "Jewish Philosophy in the Academy."

7. Paradoxically, for some Orthodox Jews the Holocaust is not at all unique. It is treated in terms of the classical Jewish theological framework of human sinfulness and just divine retribution, just as Jews had traditionally responded to the earlier catastrophes of the destruction of Jerusalem: "On account of our sins were we exiled from our land." And yet, most Jews today find the traditional response existentially and morally inapplicable to their situation, to the point of obscenity: what crime could merit such a "punishment," of what crime were one and a half million children so guilty as to deserve their fate, and do not all such obscenities imply the ultimate obscenity, that Hitler was God's just agent?

8. More than eight hundred years before the restoration of the Jewish state, Judah Ha-Levi questioned whether Jewish morality is a true virtue, or whether it is merely a function of Jewish powerlessness. When Ha-Levi's Jew takes pride in Jewish meekness and powerlessness (thus practicing the virtue preached by the Christians and the Muslims), he is rebuked by the (as yet) non-Jewish Khazar king: "That would be so, if your humility [*tawaduᶜ*] were voluntary; but it is involuntary, and if you had the power, you would kill" (Judah Ha-Levi, *The Kuzari* 1:114).

Jewish Philosophy
and the Academy

Part One
Jewish Philosophy and the Curriculum

Jewish Philosophy and the Academy

Emil L. Fackenheim

1

A book whose subject is the teaching of philosophy is best begun with an exemplary teacher of philosophy. In the West, there is surely none to compare to Socrates: he taught Plato. But who taught Plato's teacher?

The story is told in Plato's *Apology*. When a curious person asked the Delphic oracle to reveal the wisest of humans, the reply was: Socrates. Incredulous when hearing this, but unwilling to dismiss the oracle, Socrates embarked on a venture that was to be of great consequence. He sought out people he considered wiser than himself, asking them questions he himself could not answer. "What is art?" he asked of artists. "What is the state?" he asked of statesmen. What did he find? The people he visited were good at their pursuits, the artists at art, the statesmen at statecraft; they were at a loss, however, to answer his questions. Either they had thought all along that they knew but, on being asked, did not; or, more typically, they had never given thought to what yet was so great a part of their lives.

Socrates' venture had three results. First, the Delphic oracle had been right after all, for while he too did not know, any more than the artists and statesmen, he at least *knew* that he did not know. His was—to use a term that came into use much later—a *docta ignorantia,* a learned ignorance.

Second, and more important, Socrates discovered that he was a philosopher. For whereas only the gods were wise, he strove after the wisdom of which the gods were in possession. This striving was inspired by love, nay, it *was* love: "lover of wisdom" is what "philosopher" means. How does this love originate? Socrates wondered about what nonphilosophic opinion either ignores or takes for granted. He discovered that philosophy, the love of wisdom, begins with wonder.

His venture had yet a third result. In going about, a "gadfly," asking artists, statesmen, and others questions they had not asked, and that they would rather have left unasked, he had aroused a good deal of hostility, and for this he eventually paid with his life. He paid that price, however, without regret. Would the unexamined life have been worth living? Not for Socrates. And if to this day he has remained the paradigm of a teacher of philosophy, it has been for what he taught, not only with his life but also with his death.

Who then taught Socrates? A great many centuries later—philosophy was by then well on its way—Augustine wondered about time. "If nobody asks me what time is," he confessed, "I know. But if someone does ask me, I do not know." But who did the asking? Surely it was Augustine himself, and what is surely true of him is indisputably true of Socrates.

Who *did* teach Socrates? None other than Socrates himself. To go further, if Plato was not merely to learn about other people's philosophy but was himself to become a philosopher, then all Socrates could really teach him was to teach himself, to ask his own questions, to do his own wondering. For Socrates, philosophy had begun with wonder. Plato reaffirmed it, as did Aristotle after him. This is one characteristic of philosophy that has never been successfully denied—that wonder is not a one-time beginning of philosophy, way back in ancient history. So long as there is and will be philosophy, the wondering must be done and redone.

But where does one go from there? If only the gods are wise, if they alone have achieved wisdom, this question is difficult to answer: different philosophers travel different roads. Hence, What is philosophy? is itself a philosophical question. Philosophers can often agree only on a circular definition: Philosophy is what philosophers are doing. Hence, too, and this is crucial to how the present volume has come into being, philosophy teachers cannot deal with the teaching of philosophy without also dealing with philosophy itself. The contributors to this volume, teachers of philosophy all, and banded together by a common concern for teaching, were drawn by that concern into philosophy itself and, as it has turned out, into the work of quite a few philosophers.

2

Philosophers ask what philosophy is. Of Jewish philosophy it may well be asked whether it exists at all or, perhaps more precisely, whether such existence as it does have is legitimate. This has often been denied by both Judaism and philosophy. For the purpose of the present volume, the objections coming from philosophers may be more relevant. But those coming from the Jewish side are not to be ignored.

On the latter side, the most clear-cut objections have always come from Orthodox Judaism, based as it is on halakhah, "the way" as prescribed by the 613 commandments divinely revealed on Mount Sinai. At worst, what could philosophy do to the Sinaitic Word except call into question, if indeed not deny altogether, the divine authority on which, Jewish orthodoxy claims, the Torah rests? At best, what could it do except endorse that Word, as if its authority required extraneous endorsements? Not accidentally, the greatest work in Jewish philosophy, Maimonides' *Moreh Nevukhim* (Guide of the Perplexed), was under Orthodox attack for well over a century, with here and there a *ḥerem* ("ban") hurled at it. Indeed, if Maimonides himself escaped Spinoza's fate—excommunication by an Orthodox rabbinic court—it was arguably because the author of the *Guide* also composed the *Mishneh Torah* (Repetition of the Torah), one of the most important codes of Jewish law, that remains influential to this day.

At length, however, not only Maimonides himself but also his *Guide* became pillars of Orthodox Judaism. It is thus not obvious that, even for Jewish orthodoxy, philosophy must be beyond the pale of Judaism.

But if Maimonides is not beyond the pale, Spinoza can hardly be within it. Moreover, that this view is not necessarily limited to Orthodox Judaism is illustrated by the Jewish but non-Orthodox philosopher Hermann Cohen. As a liberal proponent of free speech, Cohen was surely a principled opponent of the practice of excommunication. Yet, to judge by what he wrote on Spinoza, he must have thought that if the Amsterdam rabbinate had to single out a foe of Judaism, they got the right man. The liberal Cohen, no less than the Orthodox Amsterdam rabbinate, viewed Spinoza as an enemy of the Jewish religion.

Must a Jewish philosophy necessarily be religious? Ever since Moses Hess, Zionist thinkers have labored at reclaiming Spinoza as a Jewish philosopher. And, at this writing, a work that makes that unique heretic into the philosophical founding father of modern Jewish secularism is a best seller in Israel.[1] Thus questions about the concept "Jewish philosophy"—whether it is a legitimate discipline and if so, just what it is—do not have obvious answers from the Jewish side.

As is shown in the present volume, the question ought to be similarly open on the side of philosophy. This, however, is not always conceded in the academy, even now when the spirit of the age seems to call for "multiculturalism." The argument of the modern academy against a Jewish philosophy has long been firmly entrenched, so much so that few academics have ever found it necessary to take the trouble of spelling it out.

The entrenched argument may be presented as follows. The Socratic wonder with which philosophy begins is surely rational and, equally surely, so is the examination of life to which it gives rise. The hallmark of rationality, however, is detachment from partisanship, an objectivity that seeks a truth as universal as reason itself. How then can "philosophy" be qualified by the adjective "Jewish," when the latter seems to signify commitments that are subjective, partisan, particularistic—even tribal and parochial? Is there a Jewish mathematics or physics? Then how can there be a Jewish philosophy?

Arguments entrenched in the academy are rarely entirely without substance; a philosophical work is not Jewish by dint of the Jewish birth of its author. Books such as Edmund Husserl's *Logical Investigations* and Henri Bergson's *Creative Evolution* did not become works in "Jewish philosophy" until they were defined and ostracized as such by Adolf Hitler's *Weltanschauung*. Few facts show quite as glaringly how utterly antiphilosophical that *Weltanschauung* was, and how disgraceful was the surrender to it of quite a few once respected professors of philosophy, not excluding some distinguished philosophers.

The works of Husserl and Bergson, then, are clear-cut cases of what Jewish philosophy is *not*. In contrast, the cases of Maimonides and Spinoza are not nearly so clear-cut. Why has the first traditionally been kept out of philosophy departments, whereas the place given to the second was always secure and unchallenged until the advent of the Third Reich? Have the academy and its philosophy departments kept Maimonides out because, so far as Judaism is concerned, he remains inside? And have they let Spinoza in because, so far as Judaism is concerned, he opts out? To press this question further, have the doors of the academy been wide open to Spinoza because, in opting out of Judaism, he "outgrows" or "transcends" a heritage that is "narrow" or "parochial"? Spinoza scholars have often written in this vein and, at times, have not hesitated to use these and similar words. *But is Judaism "narrow" or "parochial," and is to opt out of it to "outgrow" or "transcend" it? And is "Jewish philosophy" nothing less than a contradiction in terms—"Jewish" being "narrow" and "particularistic" and "philosophy" being "wide" and "universalistic"?* These questions, introductory to the concerns of the present book, will stay with us—through medieval, modern, and "postmodern" Jewish philosophy—to the end.

3

Once, modern academic curricula typically would leap from the last of the ancient philosophers—Neoplatonists, Skeptics, Stoics, and Epicureans—to the first of the moderns, including Descartes, Spinoza, Bacon, Locke, and others equally modern-minded. The entire Middle Ages was simply skipped. Implied in this practice was an argument as entrenched as the one already referred to, this one also so seemingly obvious as hardly to need the bother of being spelled out until, in more recent times, it was dislodged.

There was some substance to this argument as well. Medieval philosophy may be viewed purely as a developmental stage within philosophy or else, more comprehensively and also more profoundly, as an effort to relate philosophy, the work of a "reason" merely human, to "revelation," the more-than-rational, more-than-human act or acts of God. The latter task could not be considered by Socrates and other ancient philosophers, except for Philo of Alexandria, for it presupposes the exposure of philosophy to one of the religions of revelation—Judaism, Christianity, Islam. This exposure having become a fact, however, the theme appearing on the scene, not ever to disappear, may be summed up as "Athens and Jerusalem."

But "what indeed has Athens to do with Jerusalem?" This question, as asked by the Christian Tertullian[2] from the side of Jerusalem, is purely rhetorical. And when asked in the modern academy from the side of Athens—with "Athens" standing for *all* Western philosophy, modern as well as ancient—it is no less rhetorical.

The once entrenched argument may be spelled out as follows. What originality can be found in medieval philosophy when it very nearly remains within the confines of the Aristotelian-cum-Neoplatonic tradition? Furthermore, is medieval philosophy philosophical at all when sooner or later—in some cases sooner, in others later, but *always somewhere*—philosophical reason is fettered by the limits imposed by divinely revealed Scriptures, the Jewish Bible, the Christian Bible, the Qur'an? *Is* the Christian Thomas Aquinas a philosopher when he writes that "although the argument from authority based on human reason is the weakest, yet the argument from authority based on divine Revelation is the strongest"?[3] And *how much* of a philosopher is the Muslim Ibn Rushd ("Averroës" in Christendom) when he believes, and acts on the belief, that Aristotle is a gift of "divine grace" bestowed on humanity in order that it may "know what is knowable"? Is not, then, authority the great stumbling block for philosophy in the Middle Ages—one view of it being that of an Aristotle, the other that of a sacred Scripture?

With these two views of medieval philosophy prevailing, it comes as no surprise that, whichever is adopted, the question of a place for medieval Jewish philosophy in the academy simply did not arise.

The more recent academic welcome accorded to medieval philosophy shows its former exclusion, for all its superficial justice, to have been riddled with prejudice that may be called "modernist," "crypto-Protestant," or "neopagan." If truth and not originality is the goal of the "love of wisdom," is it self-evident or even plausible that such wisdom as is attainable had to wait for modernity, for the twentieth century, for the 1990s, or even for the year 2000? May it not be worth a philosopher's while to "reopen dusty old books" (Leo Strauss) in pursuit of truth, so that even Averroës is not beneath modern philosophical contempt when, typically, he does his philosophizing not in "original" treatises of his own but in commentaries on Aristotle? Averroës viewed the Stagirite as "*the* philosopher"; was this view necessarily due to slavish obedience to authority, rather than to serious, critical—nay, *self*-critical—thought?

A prejudice is "modernist" when it rests on the unexamined belief in the superiority of present wisdom over that of the past. It is "crypto-Protestant" when resting on the unexamined belief that, as a ground on which would-be believers in revelation may stand, a Luther-style "here I stand, I can do no other" is superior to a time-honored tradition.

Lastly, and in the present context most important, although no prejudice is implicit in the "paganism" of Socrates and his ancient followers (for an exposure to religions of revelation had yet to occur), prejudice *is* involved when, *after* such exposure, philosophers resort without examination to "*neo*paganism," as if the rejection or "overcoming" of revelation were a self-evident necessity for modern philosophers. Should they not ponder the fact that, of the great speculative philosophers of the earlier modern period—Descartes, Spinoza, Leibniz, Kant, Fichte, Schelling, Hegel—only Spinoza and Fichte rejected revelation and chose modern "autonomy"? Should they not also ask whether, of the more recent antispeculative philosophers, such foes of revelation as Marx and Nietzsche are truly better and more solid guides to modernity than the Christian Kierkegaard and the Jew Rosenzweig?

It was Rosenzweig who coined the terms "old paganism" and "new paganism," and this, note well, vis-à-vis revelation defined as the "incursion" of a "higher [i.e., divine] content" into a [human] "vessel" unworthy of it. *Simply in being,* revelation is an "insult" to "paganism," whether "old" or "new"; and, with the appearance of the theme "Athens and Jerusalem" on the scene, a pride "insulted" by the "incursion" of "higher content" stands in need of philosophic examination. With the demand for just that examination, the modern Jewish philosopher Rosenzweig storms, in the twentieth century, into the bastion of modern philosophy.[4] In different language and with a different emphasis, Kierkegaard had done likewise in the nineteenth century, leaving a significant mark, however, only in the twentieth.

With the exposure of the above three prejudices—modernist, crypto-Protestant, neopagan—the once entrenched argument for leaping from the last of the ancient to the first of the modern philosophers collapses; medieval philosophy must be given its academic due. With this established, are any grounds left for admitting medieval *Christian* philosophy and yet continuing to keep its *Jewish* counterpart out? Reason in Maimonides' philosophy may be "fettered" by the limits imposed by revealed authority, the characteristic medieval Jewish argument for authority being that no fewer than 600,000 Israelites witnessed the Sinaitic Revelation: that so many could not have been mistaken, and that an unbroken line of trustworthy witnesses leads from Sinai to the present. But then (as has been shown), with his reliance on "sacred" authority, reason in Thomas Aquinas's philosophy is equally fettered. With Aquinas given a secure place in the academy, what, other than surviving prejudice, is at work whenever Maimonides is ignored, or else reduced to background material for understanding the Angelic Doctor?

Just one argument for excluding Jewish philosophy deserves consideration and, in the present context, indeed requires it. In medieval (and almost all) philosophy, the scope of "reason" is universal. And, in both Christianity and Islam, the scope of "revelation" is also universal. (In contrast to both, "revelation" in Judaism is focused on, or even limited to, just one particular people.) What if, in medieval times, this shared universalism had given rise to genuine Christian and Muslim philosophies; would the academy still need to bother with the empirical study of *Jewish* philosophy in order to dismiss its claim to genuineness? Does the "universalism" of philosophy not of necessity clash with the "particularism" of Judaism? If Christians or Muslims can become philosophers and still remain Christians and Muslims, must not, in contrast to both, Jews aspiring to philosophy "outgrow" or "transcend" a background shown by that very universalist aspiration to be "narrow" or "parochial"? Indeed, precisely with prejudices against medieval philosophy as such removed, does not what once may have been riddled with prejudice purify itself into a well-founded judgment that there is not and can not be a medieval Jewish, nay, a Jewish, philosophy? Is the view not confirmed that Maimonides, who remains within Judaism, is ipso facto not a philosopher, whereas, in order to *become* a philosopher, Spinoza must opt out of it?

A point has now been reached for a look at what Jewish philosophers are doing; better still, at what Jewish philosophers were doing in the Middle Ages; best of all, at what was being done by that medieval Jewish philosopher whose bold "particularism" has never been matched, namely, Judah Ha-Levi. (Even in modern "tolerant" rather than medieval "intolerant" times, only Franz Rosenzweig ever comes close to it.)

In the eighth century, the Khazars, thought to have been a Tartar people, converted to Judaism. Judah Ha-Levi's *Kuzari,* written "in defense of a religion held in contempt," is based on this event. The work has the Khazar king consult, in turn, a philosopher, a Christian, a Muslim, and, dissatisfied with all three, speak last but at length with a rabbi—*last* because his religion, after all, is held in contempt, and *at length* because, step by step, he discovers that the contempt meted out to Judaism by Christians and Muslims is utterly undeserved. When speaking with the Christian and the Muslim (the philosopher is not relevant in this context), he begins to make three discoveries, subsequently to be confirmed in his dialogue with the rabbi. Both the Christian and the Muslim base their claims on the Scriptures of Judaism; both despise the very religion on whose Scriptures their own claims are based; and although, admirably, they are sincere believers in love, both human and divine, they are always at each other's throats. (Rediscovering the Khazar king's first discovery, subsequent thinkers were sometimes to speak of Christianity and Islam as "daughter religions" of Judaism.) With his three discoveries taken together, the king may be paraphrased as asking. "What universalism is this on the part of the 'daughters,' that does not extend even to the 'mother'; and what love is this on the part of the 'sisters,' that expresses itself in warfare between them?"

The Khazar king shows grave doubts about Christian and Muslim universalism. The rabbi, however, although an unabashed "particularist," gives striking proof of his universalism when he, the Jewish teacher, takes instruction from his pagan pupil. He has previously taught the latter that even though Jews are in exile and the Holy Land is in ruins, it is a Jewish duty to dwell amid the ruins rather than in comfort elsewhere. Having listened and learned, the pupil reprimands the teacher:

> If this be so, thou fallest short of the duty laid down in thy law, by not endeavoring to reach that place, and making it thy abode in life and death, although thou sayest, "Have mercy on Zion, for it is the house of our life" (*Kuzari* 2.23).

This reprimand occurs early in the dialogue between the two. Yet so deeply is the rabbi disturbed by it that the whole work ends with the teacher obeying the pupil. He sets out for the Holy Land. Apparently the Jewish teacher needed his pagan pupil to remind him of the teaching of his own religion that "Jerusalem can only be rebuilt when Israel yearns for it to such an extent that they embrace her stones and dust" (*Kuzari* 5.27).

A universalist in that he examines *everything* prior to his commitment to Judaism, the *Kuzari*'s pagan king thus endorses, far back in a medieval Jewish philosophical work, what has become in this postmodern age the most dramatic expression of a particularistic Jewish destiny.

The "postmodern" relevance of yet another text in the *Kuzari* may well be even greater. Here too the Jewish teacher takes instruction from the pagan pupil, and in this exchange the universalism inherent in Jewish particularism is wider still, in that its stance toward the two "daughters" of Judaism is positive.

Quite early in the dialogue, the king has touched what the rabbi admits is a weak spot in Jews. Whereas Christians and Muslims have saints who choose humility, poverty, and even degradation, Jews assuredly suffer humiliation, poverty, and degradation at the hands of enemies, but rarely if ever seek to convert necessity into virtue (*Kuzari* 1.113–15). Returning to the theme because of its importance later in the dialogue, the rabbi once again pays tribute to the saintliness of some Christians and Muslims, and once again concedes that the king rightly blames Jews for "bearing degradation without [spiritual] benefit." Yet he then states that "thoughtful men among . . . [Jews] could escape this degradation by a word spoken lightly"—the "word" of conversion to Christianity or Islam, "spoken lightly" because not from conviction. They could do it but, because of fidelity, they do not. If Christian and Muslim virtue is saintliness, Jewish virtue is fidelity (*Kuzari* 4.22, 23).

To become wholly up-to-date, this medieval Jewish philosophical teaching needs changing in but one respect. In order to opt out of Jewish history, its fate and its destiny, in the "postmodern" world, even a word spoken lightly is no longer required, nor is the possibility confined to the thoughtful. In "enlightened" societies Jews can simply drift away. In consequence, the "postmodern" world—which is also the post-Holocaust world—discloses this stark difference between Christians and Muslims on the one hand, Jews on the other: Christianity and Islam do not fully lose credibility so long as they have even a few saints; without fidelity, however, Jews cannot—never did, never will—survive at all.

4

The Jews among whom Spinoza grew up descended from Portuguese Marannos, forced converts to Christianity, and, as "new Christians," the bona fide of their conversion was subject to inquiry. From the standpoint of the Inquisitors this was consistent for, while forced to make a show of their new faith, these former Jews had inwardly remained true to their old one, so much so as to keep on practicing secretly—in view of the methods of the Inquisition, *very* secretly—such fragments of Judaism as circumstances permitted, and as they themselves remembered. Spinoza's ancestors had fled from the Inquisition but also, more profoundly, from *having to be* Christians. Hence, once having reached tolerant Holland, they had returned openly to their old faith. But scars of the past had remained, and affected their present consciousness.

This background helps explain the Amsterdam rabbinate's unwonted harshness toward the renegade in their midst. It was feared that, even in tolerant but not omnitolerant Holland, his presence among them threatened the repute, or even safety, of the refugee community. So some say. Others say that this background helps explain Spinoza himself:

> Everyone else in Europe was born into pre-determined categories of thinking, Jews into the categories of law and justice, Christians into the categories of sin and redemption. Here, however, there is for the first time a group of people without pre-determined categories of their own, a people with a ruptured consciousness. A people looked for the coasts—and Spinoza discovered a new world.[5]

This judgment is far removed from the academic prejudices hitherto encountered. ("Academic prejudice" may be a contradiction in terms, but often it is real enough.) If the Jew Spinoza had a "narrow" background, so did his Christian contemporaries. If the "new world" discovered by such as Columbus, Copernicus, and Galileo required philosophers among Jews to "outgrow" or "transcend" their "background," it made the same requirement of philosophical minded Christians, with respect to theirs. Indeed, what with his "ruptured" post-Marrano Jewish "consciousness," Spinoza may be said to have faced the "new world" more radically than, say, René Descartes or Francis Bacon. The modern *cogito* of the former is never made to clash with the premodern claims of revealed authority. And the latter's modern war on "four idols" is not extended so as to make premodern revealed authority into yet a fifth. In contrast to these Christian contemporaries, Spinoza's *Theologico-Political Treatise* includes a modern wrestling with premodern authority, and extends this wrestling—circumspectly, to be sure—to authorities that claim to be divinely revealed. Spinoza dares to publish the *Treatise*. His *Ethics* he prudently leaves unpublished for, to readers who understand both its teaching and what revelation implies, the work is incompatible not merely with revealed *authority* but with nothing less than the truth claim of *revelation itself,* whether Jewish, Christian, or Muslim.

Spinoza, Descartes, Bacon: these are three modern philosophers—one a Jew who "opts out," the other two Christians who "stay in." Descartes, Bacon, Moses Mendelssohn: these, modern philosophers all, "stay in"—the first two in Christianity, the third to emerge as the first modern philosopher to remain, not casually but most emphatically, within Judaism. However, it is worthy of note that, whereas the Christians avoid a clash with premodern revealed authority, the Jew expressly invokes that very authority:

> The [revealed] law [of Judaism] can perhaps . . . be changed according to the requirements of a particular time, place, and set of circumstances, but only if and when it pleases the supreme Lawgiver to let us know His will—to make it known to us just as openly, publicly, and beyond any possibility of doubt and uncertainty, as He did when [at Sinai] He gave us that law itself.[6]

Why and how are the "staying in" of Descartes and Bacon on the one hand, Mendelssohn on the other, not on a par? The fact of difference is undeniable. The two Christians, and many others after them, avoid a clash between the philosophy of the "new world" and the revealed authority of the "old." They do so—can afford to do so—quietly and perhaps even hypocritically. Why, in contrast, and in a work committed to the "new world"'s philosophy, does the Jew Mendelssohn explicitly *hark back* to the "old world"'s revealed authority? In order to "stay in" Judaism, why can he not afford his Christian counterparts' luxury—or hypocrisy—but *must* do his harking back? Mendelssohn, the first modern Jewish philosopher, must have known or at least suspected that premodern authority fails in the modern world. That it does in fact fail was to be shown no more clearly than in his own descendants, the most famous of whom was Felix Mendelssohn-Bartholdy, the Christian composer of the oratorio *Paul.* The simple but weighty answer is this: *Descartes, Bacon, and all their spiritual children, while entering a "new world," continue to live in* one *world. Mendelssohn's, to be sure, is no "ruptured consciousness": he is no Marrano and no son of Marannos. However, he and his children live in* two *worlds:*

> Even now, no better advice than this can be given to the House of Jacob: Adopt the mores and constitution of the country in which you find yourself, but be steadfast in upholding the religion of your fathers, too. Bear both burdens as well as you can.[7]

Such is the advice given by the first modern Jewish philosopher. Practicing what he preaches, he bears the two burdens, as a way of thought as well as of life. Mendelssohn's was a privileged position, dramatized by his "right of residence" in Berlin, a right rarely granted by Frederick the Great of Prussia to Jews in particular, despite his enlightened and broad-minded attitude toward matters religious in general. Yet Mendelssohn remained within Orthodox Judaism in both practice and belief.

Privileges were granted this Jew and praise showered on him, as a man. Among the philosophically minded, he earned the title "the German Socrates"; nor was this appellation without justice, for among his numerous contributions to German thought and letters is a work that argues for the immortality of the soul and is entitled *Phaedon.* Yet, untempted by the privileges granted him and the praise showered on him, he never ceased to think of himself as a Jew, practicing solidarity with his unprivileged fellow Jews and doing what he could to improve their social and spiritual condition. In due course this "new Socrates" was also thought of, by his own people, as yet another Moses—after the original one and Maimonides.

Mendelssohn, then, lived in two worlds. However, the philosophically minded who celebrated him and had discourse with him lived in one world. This was shown dramatically by the so-called Lavater Affair. A Swiss clergyman named Johann Caspar Lavater admired Mendelssohn for his wisdom and learning, and especially for the broad-minded views on Christianity he had expressed to him in private conversation. When Lavater published a German translation of a French Calvinist tract, he dedicated it to Mendelssohn and, forgetting or ignoring the private nature of their earlier conversation, publicly challenged him either to refute the work's argument in support of Christian truth, or else "to do what wisdom, love of truth and honor require, and what Socrates would have done had he read the treatise and found it irrefutable."[8]

That a person could be wise, noble, learned, enlightened, broad-minded, modern-minded, and still remain a convinced Jew rather than become a Christian, the theologian Lavater could not imagine. His philosophical contemporary, none other than the towering Kant (a lukewarm Christian at best) presumably *could* imagine Mendelssohn's not becoming a Christian—not a convinced one because of his rationalism, and not an opportunistic one because of his integrity. But Kant's views on Mendelssohn's Judaism were much the same as Lavater's, as is shown by his expressed hope for the "euthanasia" of Judaism. Even in the "dark" Middle Ages, Christian theologians would sometimes go to school with rabbis. Now that the "bright" Enlightenment had arrived, and along with it the first modern Jewish philosopher, the idea that admirers of his philosophy should be curious about his Judaism, and ask him to teach them some of it, did not occur even to Kant and certainly not to Lavater.

Presumably the "Berlin Socrates" would have had little trouble refuting the arguments presented in the book dedicated to him; were it not for the "affair," not even the name of its author—it was Charles Bonnet—would still be remembered. In publicly refusing to take up Lavater's challenge, Mendelssohn lists among several reasons the fact that he is part of "an oppressed people," and that for him to engage in public Jewish-Christian polemics would be to risk making things worse. A privileged Jew and an apostle of modern Enlightenment, Mendelssohn had, nevertheless, always viewed himself as sharing the exile of his unprivileged fellow Jews. Lavater's challenge proved that he had been right all along.

At the time, the Lavater Affair created a sensation. In retrospect it would be a tempest in the teapot were it not for one important result: it occasioned the first work in modern Jewish philosophy. At one time Mendelssohn had "wanted to refute the world's derogatory opinion of the Jew by righteous living, not by pamphleteering." He had refrained from Jewish-Christian polemics for the reason subsequently given to Lavater. This was before the "affair." After, and on account of it, he saw himself duty-bound, no matter what the risks, to write *Jerusalem*. Little wonder that, given these circumstances, the first work in modern Jewish philosophy could come nowhere near the militant particularism of the medieval *Kuzari*. Little wonder, too, that, in defense of the continued survival of Jews and Judaism in the "enlightened" modern age, it had to fall back for support on a revealed authority, which itself was no longer defensible. It is also perhaps not too much of a surprise—although better might have been expected—that, having read the work, Kant did not change his mind about Judaism.

The circumstances in which the first work in modern Jewish philosophy was written ought to give pause to modern and "postmodern" philosophers even now, for they like to think of their discipline as continuing the war on the idols of prejudice and "blind authority" begun by such as Descartes and Bacon, as being both critical and self-critical, universalistic, and in no way either partisan or parochial. Although this self-understanding is generally justified, one must ask whether general virtue has manifested itself in particular justice in a fair and evenhanded stance toward Christianity and Judaism. Such, however, is not the case among the great philosophers. Even as lukewarm a Christian as Kant manages to save quite a lot of Christianity by making Jesus into a great and possibly unique teacher of morality; to conduct a similar rescue operation for Judaism—say, by linking Mendelssohn with Isaiah—never enters his mind.

In this and some other respects, Hegel towers above the towering Kant. He enters into biblical—but only biblical—Judaism, deeply enough to achieve some remarkable insights. Whether or not "euthanasia" will befall Judaism, he strongly supports the emancipation of Jews. And since, in Hegel's view, a meeting of Jewish "East" and Greek-Roman "West" in the ancient world lies behind the modern world, much in Hegel's work raises the thought that a place might be left, or even required, for a vital Judaism in the modern world. The thought comes to his reader's mind, especially in our time. But it does not come to Hegel's mind. As he moves through the ancient, the medieval, and, at length, the modern world, the theme "Athens and Jerusalem" becomes an anachronism; and so, along with "Athens," does both "Jerusalem" and its manifestation in Judaism.

Hegel enters into the Judaism of his Old Testament. Kierkegaard's self-immersion in *his* Old Testament is so total as to make him proclaim that his "knight of faith" par excellence is Abraham, none other than the patriarch whose children's children are Kierkegaard's own Jewish contemporaries, whose God continues to be invoked in their prayers. Unlike Hegel (to say nothing of Kant), Kierkegaard is indisputably a Christian or struggling to become one. Equally indisputably, he is in and of modernity, for his Abraham is his own spiritual contemporary and not—to put the contrast as starkly as possible—that of Torquemada. Everyone's Abraham—he who sets out to sacrifice Isaac (Gen. 22:1–19)—is prepared to do what would make him a criminal were it not for the divine commandment. In obeying the commandment, however, Kierkegaard's Abraham is not serene and in much company, relying on a sacred authority that, whether human or divine, is infallible. He acts in "fear and trembling," and he is utterly alone, for in deciding whether what appears to be the will of God is in fact that will, whether in heeding it he is His obedient servant or a common criminal, he does not rely on infallible authority, human or divine; all he can rely on is his own solitary, all-too-human, all-too-fallible, "existential" commitment. This is Kierkegaard's "knight of faith"—the only Abraham that *can be* that knight.

Kierkegaard, then, as well as his Abraham, are of postauthoritarian modernity. An unparalleled pioneer of a modern Christian philosophy, his Christian focus on Abraham on the road to Mount Moriah rather than, say, on Paul on the road to Damascus, makes him, potentially, an unparalleled pioneer also in theological relations to Jews, whose thought is focused on the same event in their ancestor's life, most clearly so when on Rosh Ha-Shanah they read the biblical text in their synagogues.

The door is thus opened, directly to an encounter and a dialogue between the two commitments and, indirectly, to a Christian philosophy that "circumnavigates human existence" as a whole, and leaps into a particular Christian "immediacy" only after a universal philosophical "reflection" has done its work. (These are Kierkegaardian expressions.)[9]

Kierkegaard makes many forays in the direction of such a philosophy. Yet he only paves the way for it, and the justice he accords to Judaism remains limited. His Abraham turns out to be proto-Christian—a Christian-before-Christ; and when elsewhere he has Christianity "invent martyrdom," he either forgets the Maccabees or else makes them, too, into Christians-before-Christ.

Uneven justice to Judaism and Christianity is not confined to pre-twentieth-century, or to Christian, or to continental philosophers. Jean Paul Sartre is no Christian: yet his atheistic existentialism notwithstanding, he recognizes a Christian alternative but not, despite Martin Buber and Franz Rosenzweig, a Jewish existentialism. Martin Heidegger, no theologian himself, recognizes theology, but ignores all but the Christian; and of what may be his only notice of Judaism—it is of biblical prophecy—Buber is reluctantly compelled to write: "I have never in our time encountered on a high philosophical plane such a far-reaching misunderstanding of the prophets of Israel."[10]

Is uneven philosophical justice to Judaism and Christianity confined to the European continent? Crossing the Channel, one comes upon Cambridge philosopher John Wisdom's "Gods."[11] Like Kierkegaard, Wisdom is a Christian, a modern philosopher, and one whose thought is focused on an Old (rather than New) Testament figure. But there the resemblance ends, for Wisdom is a British empiricist, and while Kierkegaard's Abraham is his spiritual contemporary, Wisdom's Elijah is of the primitive, prescientific, religiously irrelevant past.

This is true at least of Elijah's act on Mount Carmel when, confronting 450 priests of Baal, he challenges them, as it were, to a duel. Accepting the challenge, the priests beseech Baal to accept their sacrifice, and pray all day without anything happening. But when Elijah, alone and abandoned by men, implores his God not to abandon him also, a fire falls from heaven to devour his sacrifice, and the people, overwhelmed by what has happened, exclaim "*Adonai*, He is God" (1 Kings 18:20–39).

Elijah's act is celebrated in Judaism but not in John Wisdom's modern-empiricist philosophy. In Judaism, Elijah risks all—the meaning of his life if not his life itself and, far beyond his own puny life, that of the Covenant between Israel and its God, at that moment all but extinct. In Wisdom's thought, in contrast, that act on Mount Carmel is merely an experiment to settle what god or gods exist; and what is risked by those performing or witnessing it is only what is risked, say, by scientists peering through a microscope. No wonder that Wisdom's Elijah belongs to the dead and irrelevant past. Wisdom rescues some of Elijah; not, to be sure, his Mount Carmel "experiment," but the "still, small voice" that subsequently speaks to him in the desert. But his rescue operation exacts this price: "The Kingdom of Heaven is within us, Christ insisted."[12]

How does Wisdom's Elijah compare with Kierkegaard's Abraham? Kierkegaard's is a genuine, painful struggle with a Christian text that is Jewish as well, which is why modern Jewish philosophers, themselves struggling with that text—no less genuinely, no less painfully—must also struggle with Kierkegaard, the modern Christian philosopher. Nothing resembling this struggle is necessary, or possible, with Wisdom, for he does not hesitate to play fast and loose with what is said in a biblical—but for him merely "Old" Testament—text.

Let us consider when the text's "still, small voice" speaks to the text's Elijah. The Mount Carmel duel is won, but its effect has not lasted; once more God's people have abandoned Him. His prophets are slain, and Elijah alone has survived the slaughter. More desperately alone than ever, he is overwhelmed at last by despair, left only with the wish that his God take his life. This is when the "still, small voice" speaks. What does it say? It issues a promise and a commandment. The promise: a remnant will survive. The commandment: Elijah must appoint a successor. Then Elijah, no longer alone or the last of the prophets, his faith and strength revived, goes forth to appoint Elisha (1 Kings 19:15–18).

That is what the "still, small voice" said, not what Wisdom makes it say—and never since Elijah's own time did it speak as clearly as just a year or so after Wisdom gave his lecture on "Gods." The year was 1945. At long last, the murder camps, endured by their victims for so long, were revealed to a horrified world. For Jewish survivors of the camps and Jews outside them, stunned by the revelation, the Covenant was all but extinct. Just then a voice—still, small, heard by some if not by others—began to issue a promise and a commandment: a new page was to be opened in the life of the Jewish people and of their ancient Covenant. There would be, would have to be, a rebirth of a Jewish state.

With continental philosophers, injustice to Judaism may be due to a priori prejudice. To what is it due in the case of John Wisdom? In his lecture, published in the 1944–45 *Proceedings* of the Aristotelian Society, Wisdom addressed himself to its circle of academics. He did not go outside his country to reflect on what was happening across the Channel, even as he was speaking. He did not even go outside his academic circle to inquire what Elijah's Mount Carmel "experiment" meant to observant—if nonacademic—Jews. And one dare not guess his reaction had he discovered that "*Adonai,* He is God," the confession that concludes the Mount Carmel incident, is also the confession that concludes the liturgy of the synagogue on Yom Kippur, the holiest day in the Jewish calendar.

To what can one ascribe the injustice to Judaism in Wisdom's religious empiricism? It is insular; and, if "empirical" has a richer meaning than what is seen by scientists peering through a microscope, his thought is insufficiently empirical.

The philosophers just cited are all significant enough to have generated schools or, at any rate, fashions. After Wisdom's "Gods," it was fashionable for a while among like-minded philosophers to invoke Elijah's "experiment," as if Wisdom's view of the biblical text could not be questioned. Similar orthodoxies are found in nineteenth-century Germany. Christian philosophers on the Hegelian right ignored the Jewish Hegelian Samuel Hirsch, while atheist philosophers on the Hegelian left ignored the Jewish Hegelian Moses Hess, or else invoked him—especially if they were Marxists—only for vituperation. Twentieth-century Kantians could not ignore Hermann Cohen, since for a while he was himself foremost among them.

But they did ignore the Jewish component in his philosophy that, as the philosopher aged, became increasingly prominent. Even across the Atlantic matters were not all that different, at least until the advent of the "postmodern" age. (There now is an openness to Emmanuel Levinas and also to the Jewish thought of Leo Strauss, a promising development.) While Martin Buber has long been one—perhaps the only—Jewish philosopher accepted in philosophy departments, his thought, in the process of acceptance, was largely dejudaized.

But the last, climactic words in the sorry tale of insufficient justice to Judaism in modern philosophy belong to Germany, for just as the greatest medieval Jewish philosophy stems from a debt to, and struggle with, Greek philosophy, so the greatest modern Jewish philosophy stems from a debt to, and struggle with, Lessing, Kant, Schelling, Hegel, Kierkegaard, even Nietzsche and even Heidegger—all Germans except for Kierkegaard, who himself is indebted to, and struggles with, Hegel and Schelling. It was a great story, but the following is its end. Franz Rosenzweig, critically ill and already near death, still took account of Heidegger's *Being and Time* and recognized its importance. Heidegger himself, though surviving Rosenzweig by a whole generation, took no notice whatever of the *Star of Redemption.* And as for Heideggerians, with the single and great exception of Karl Loewith, it took a unique catastrophe—German as well as Jewish—for them to take notice of Rosenzweig.

To be sure, the notice taken of him was magnificent when in 1985 a Rosenzweig conference was held in his native city of Kassel. It resulted in a massive two-volume work.[13] But whereas many German philosophers, Heideggerians and others, attended the conference, Jewish philosophers, except for a small remnant, had to be imported, and those few among them who were German-speaking were old, doomed to pass soon from the scene.

Modern German Judaism, and hence modern Jewish philosophy in Germany, started when Moses Mendelssohn translated the Jewish Bible, in order to teach German Jews to speak German. It ended when Buber and Rosenzweig translated the Jewish Bible once more, this time in order to teach Hebrew to German speakers. But when Buber completed the translation in 1961—Rosenzweig had died in 1929—German Judaism had been murdered, and with it the possibility of a future Jewish philosophy in Germany.

Hegel once speculated that the "World Spirit" might move from Germanic lands to America. This thought comes to mind when one considers the place and condition of future Jewish philosophy in the "postmodern" academy. Hegel also speculates that the World Spirit never returns to the place where it once has been. The thought comes to mind that, as regards a future Jewish philosophy, he may have been right about Germany, but wrong about the place where the Jewish contribution to the theme "Athens and Jerusalem" originated—Jerusalem itself.

5

Once, when modern Germany had Jewish philosophers, its academy all but ignored them. Now, "postmodern" Germany has philosophers who seek Jewish colleagues with Jewish commitments but, in Germany, they cannot find them. Perhaps they can meet a few in nearby France or England. For a rich encounter in the context of a vibrant Jewish life, however, they must travel beyond Europe altogether, to America or Israel. From Germany itself—once the land, if not particularly of poets, certainly and uniquely of philosophers—Jewish philosophers, as well as a German Judaism that might give birth to them in the future, are absent.

This fact requires philosophical attention. "Postmodern" is a term already much used in the previous pages, but hitherto only in quotation marks, for it was neither defined nor explored in its relevance, if any, for philosophy. From now on the quotation marks are omitted. In Germany, if nowhere else, a caesura separates modernity from what comes after, as well as modern philosophy from what comes after.

This is, of course, far from universally recognized in the German academy. Had Dietrich Bonhoeffer lived, his biographer Eberhard Bethge has written, he would have been astonished by how "seamlessly" Christian theology after 1945 resumed its business where it had left off in 1933. Munich philosopher Kurt Huber would have had the same reaction to much of post-1945 German philosophy. (Bonhoeffer was legally murdered by the Third Reich for his share in a plot on Hitler's life; Huber, for supporting the "White Rose," surely the purest student resistance movement ever.) But "seamless" continuation of academic business is not all there is; some Christian theologians and some German philosophers recognize a caesura and its imperatives, one of which is to do philosophical justice, if belatedly, to Judaism.

But the Jewish philosophical present is not in Germany, nor, so far as foreseeable, is its future. The one thing German philosophers can do to heed the imperative toward Judaism without going abroad is to retrieve Germany's own Jewish-philosophical past. Such a retrieval, far from confined to scholarship alone, may well have effects on the philosophical present, and may reverberate even in the philosophical future. This must be considered possible because of the greatness of past German philosophy.

Philosophical greatness—one name this brings to mind is that of Hegel. The philosopher died in 1831. Samuel Hirsch's *Religionsphilosophie der Juden* appeared in 1841, and Moses Hess's *Rome and Jerusalem* in 1862. Hegel's epigones ignored Hirsch and vituperated Hess. Had the master himself been alive—such was his greatness and his rectitude—one can visualize him reading Hirsch on the Hegelian anti-Hegelian religious right, and giving up his view of Judaism as an anachronism. One can equally visualize him reading Hess on the Hegelian anti-Hegelian atheistic left, and giving up his view of Jews as a people that, with the loss of the Bar Kochba war, had also lost, without possible recovery, national courage.[14]

Conceivably, a retrieval that related these and other Hegelian anti-Hegelian Jewish philosophers on both right and left far less to the epigones that were their contemporaries, and far more to the thought of the master himself, would have a major result for philosophy as a whole; it could also be a retrieval of Hegel himself. The several past academically recognized neo-Hegelianisms, not only in Germany but also in England, America, and elsewhere, all philosophically impressive, testify to the richness of Hegel's own thought. What if that richness were still unexhausted? What might emerge from yet another retrieval of Hegel, this time postmodern? Part and parcel of this would have to be, in our postmodern time, meting out the complete justice to Judaism that, in his modern time, Hegel tried but failed to impart to it. To be sure, a neo-Hegelianism of this kind could not make Jewish philosophy into a presence in postmodern Germany. But at least it might cease to be a sheer absence and become, as it were, the presence of an absence.

"Philosophical greatness" calls to mind Kant, and "presence of an absence" recalls, along with Kant, Hermann Cohen; for of the several neo-Kantianisms in modern Germany, none can compare with the one of which Cohen was the undisputed leader. That postmodern German philosophy needs a new back-to-Kant movement was revealed when Adolf Eichmann, on trial in Jerusalem, invoked the categorical imperative. Kant teaches the duty to treat all human beings with dignity, never only as a means, but always also as an end in itself. Eichmann invoked Kant in defense of his duty to annihilate human dignity along with human lives. A German retrieval of Kant is thus a postmodern imperative. This would be enriched by the simultaneous retrieval, itself imperative, of the Jewish aspects of Cohen's neo-Kantianism. Cohen restated Kant's ethics, but added one element that he could find neither in the master nor, indeed, in philosophy as a whole; he had to borrow from the prophets of Judaism the messianic hope. A rigorous philosopher, Cohen must have found this borrowing questionable, so far as method is concerned. He did it anyhow because—so he thought—it was a moral and religious necessity.

For the Jew in Cohen, the messianic hope was necessary; but for the philosopher in him it was possible only because it seemed empirically endorsed by history. The world was in fact moving in a messianic direction. The reader must bear in mind that Cohen wrote as he did just before the Great War brought his century of hope to an end, to initiate—a grim beginning!—the twentieth.

Rosenzweig, Cohen's disciple, cannot have been unaware of this new century; he drafted his *Star of Redemption* as a soldier in the Great War's trenches. In this awareness, as well as in other respects, perhaps the only work that merits comparison is Martin Heidegger's *Being and Time.* "All cognition of the All originates in death, in the fear of death," are the first words of the *Star. Being and Time* is informed throughout by a human *Dasein* that is authentic only if it is being-toward-death. Both these twentieth-century works, then, are far removed from Cohen's messianic hope. Yet while hope is totally absent from Heidegger's work, Rosenzweig's Jewish-philosophical work culminates with Yom Kippur and its Jewish testimony to the nations, to the victory of life over death.

A retrieval of Cohen and Rosenzweig by postmodern German philosophers is inevitably an inspiring source of strength. But, also inevitably, it is a source of melancholy, for the testimonies of Cohen and Rosenzweig, the one to hope, the other to life, shortly preceded a Germany that overwhelmed hope and life with despair and death. But then, a postmodern German retrieval of its own past philosophy, too, is inevitably permeated with melancholy. Melancholy could be avoided or evaded by the present German academy only if it cut itself off from its own past, and this is not possible. Nor, in view of the greatness of so much past German philosophy, is it desirable.

6

For German philosophy, the caesura created by the years 1933–45 may or may not be central. For Jewish philosophy its centrality is beyond dispute, and such is its abiding shock that normative responses have yet to emerge. Not accidentally, therefore, the two Jewish subjects whose postmodernity is also beyond dispute—the Holocaust itself and the State of Israel—appear in the present book in symposia, whose participants make no claim to normativeness for their views. Perhaps it is also no accident that the two post-Holocaust Jewish philosophers treated in this volume seem to move under the impact of the event in opposite directions.

Leo Strauss and Emmanuel Levinas are post-Holocaust in having lived through and beyond the years 1933–45. Neither is a Holocaust philosopher whose thought is focused on those years. "Progress or return?" is Strauss's question, and he set out on the way of return prior to 1933. Levinas, a much younger philosopher, went on his way only after 1945; by his own confession, however, his lifelong concern with "alterity" is inspired by Rosenzweig who died in 1929. Surely both thinkers would have gone on their way if the dread events had never happened. And yet, it is hard to imagine that, but for a radical failure of the modern world and its promise—manifest both in Nazism and in the feeble philosophical resistance to it—Strauss's return would have carried him so relentlessly beyond modernity to the Middle Ages (he held Maimonides to be a greater philosopher than Spinoza), and beyond the Middle Ages all the way back to Athens and Jerusalem. It is also hard to imagine that, but for the unprecedented failure displayed by humans, including philosophers, to be their brother's keeper, Levinas would have pushed alterity so hard in his endeavor to expose and oppose philosophical egotism.

It thus would seem that the caesura that separates the modern and the postmodern world moves both philosophers back to the theme "Athens and Jerusalem"—but in opposite ways. For if, ultimately, Strauss turns to Athens, and on this even his disciples are divided, it is because Athens requires only reason, whereas Jerusalem requires a faith that may be inaccessible. And if, ultimately, Levinas lets Athens be instructed by Jerusalem, it is because a Jerusalem that teaches the duty to be a brother's keeper never needed instruction about "alterity."

Perhaps this move in the same direction in opposite ways may be illustrated by two images of Socrates. Strauss's Socrates, discoursing as he does on immortality to the end, is the teacher of eternity to the end, of the need to return to the eternally True, the eternally Good, the eternally Beautiful—in view of what has happened, above all to the eternally Good. For Levinas, the Socrates who is about to drink the cup of hemlock is different. The flaw this post-Holocaust thinker finds in Heidegger at the end of a tradition, carries him back to Socrates with whom it begins. Levinas's Socrates is the husband and father who sends away his wife and children, all weeping, so as to spend his last hour with fellow philosophers, discussing philosophy.

A caesura for German and Jewish philosophy: are the years 1933–45 a caesura also for philosophy at large? This question is itself large, and requires for consideration a scope that is the broadest possible. An exciting recent discovery: the most ancient grave ever found is estimated to be one hundred thousand years old. How do archaeologists decide that it is a grave? By bones. So long as prehistoric bodies were simply left lying where they had dropped dead, animals would devour the flesh, leaving archaeologists to find scattered bones. The bones of this body, however, were not scattered. Whose body is it? A member of the Neanderthal species, which may or may not be the ancestor of *Homo sapiens*. The latter species had yet to evolve. But its precursors already knew the awe of death, the difference between life and death, and thus had developed the respect due to the dead.

With this discovery civilization may be said to have begun, and to have continued ever since, with the burial of relatives, friends, and strangers. Even enemies so many and so hated as to be denied individual burial were still given mass graves, their bones left in peace. But something unprecedented and unique occurred at Auschwitz when, what was usable in the bodies of the victims having been used, their bones were ground into dust, to be cast into the rivers.

No Socrates a hundred thousand years from now will be able to wonder at this fact, for archaeologists, if any, will find no bones. However, a Socrates in this age, knowing what has happened, would be forced into a new wonder. Like ancient Athens's Socrates, his philosophy would begin with wonder. But the age-old wonder would be mingled with a new horror.

7

Let us conduct an experiment in the philosophical imagination. Let Socrates cross the Aegean, arrive in Jerusalem, and, after his long and arduous journey, at length meet the prophet Isaiah. The meeting would give Socrates much cause for wonder. His own Delphic miracle was mysterious enough; its mystery is dwarfed, however, by a God whose thoughts and ways are as high above those of humans as heaven is above earth (Isaiah 55:8–9). The one who hears the oracle and tries to fathom it, is restrained from going astray by his *daimonion;* the other, who is to hear the thoughts of a God high above earth, is nothing better than a "man of unclean lips" (6:5). How can the gap between that God and that man be bridged? This would be the core of the wonder that Socrates did not experience in Athens but would have experienced had he visited Jerusalem. What would he have made of the fact that, with Isaiah's lips cleansed by angels at divine command, with the touch of a glowing stone taken from the fire (6:6–7), the Word of God who is Mystery itself becomes Commandment so far removed from all mystery and ambiguity as to be universally compelling?

The Athenian philosopher and the Jerusalemite prophet never met. But, after them, Athens and Jerusalem met often enough. One look at the postmodern world suffices to prove the need for a new meeting. As for the postmodern academy that is heir to Athens, will it continue its tradition of dismissing Jewish heirs of Jerusalem as being limited by parochialism? Let the academy face up to the fact that from Isaiah, and not from Socrates, came this commandment and this promise:

> And they shall beat their swords into plowshares and their spears into pruning hooks. Nation shall not lift up sword against nation, neither shall they learn war any more. (Isaiah 2:4)

Notes

1. Yirmiyahu Yovel, *Spinoza v-kofrim aherim* (Tel Aviv: Sifriat Poalim, 1988). Published in the United States as *Spinoza and Other Heretics,* vol. 1, *The Marrano of Reason;* vol. 2, *The Adventure of Immanence* (Princeton: Princeton University Press, 1989; paperback edition, 1991).
2. *On Presrciption against Heretics.* ch. 7. On this subject, see E. Gilson, *Reason and Revelation in the Middle Ages* (New York: Scribners, 1946), ch. 1.
3. *Summa Theologica* I Qu. 1 art. 8.
4. See "Atheistische Theologie," in *Kleinere Schriften* (Berlin: Schocken, 1937), p. 285. The essay is an attack on a theology that is "atheistic" in its appeasing paganism through hostility to Revelation. "Atheistische Theologie" was written in 1914, soon after Rosenzweig's celebrated decision against converting to Christianity and for remaining a Jew; he had rediscovered revelation in Judaism.
5. Carl Gebhard in the preface to his German edition of Spinoza, *Theologico-Political Treatise* (Leipzig: Meiner, 1922), pp. xivff.
6. *Jerusalem and Other Jewish Writings,* trans. and ed. Alfred Jospe (New York: Schocken, 1969), p. 104.
7. Ibid.
8. *Herrn Carl Bonnets . . . philosophische Untersuchung der Beweise für das Christentum . . . herausgegeben von Johann Caspar Lavater* (Zurich, 1769), pp. 4–5. Cited in Alexander Altmann, *Moses Mendelssohn* (Tuscaloosa: University of Alabama Press, 1973), p. 209.
9. For a brief statement on Kierkegaard as a modern theologian of revelation, see my *What Is Judaism?* (New York: Collier Books, 1987), pp. 26–27.
10. *Eclipse of God* (New York: Harper Torchbook, 1957), p. 73.
11. *Logic and Language,* ed. Antony Flew, (Garden City, N.Y.: Doubleday Anchor, 1965), pp. 194–216. The essay appears in several anthologies.

12. Ibid., 213.
13. *Der Philosoph Franz Rosenzweig (1886–1929)*, 2 vols., ed. Wolfdietrich Schmied-Kowarzik (Munich: Alber, 1988).
14. The reader may find the grounds for so exalted a view of Hegel in my *The Religious Dimension in Hegel's Thought* (Chicago: University of Chicago Press, 1982); *Encounters between Judaism and Modern Philosophy* (New York: Basic Books, 1973), ch. 3; and *To Mend the World* (Bloomington: Indiana, 1994), ch. 3.

Biblical Exegesis as a Philosophic Literary Genre: Abraham Ibn Ezra and Moses Mendelssohn

RAPHAEL JOSPE

THE philosophic literature of the Jews, like that of the non-Jews, includes various genres. All too often we tend to focus in our teaching on systematic or other prose works, to the exclusion and neglect of alternative literary forms of philosophic expression.

In the Middle Ages, as well as in modern times, Jewish thinkers have utilized diverse literary genres to present their philosophy. The Platonic form of dialogue was adopted by the medieval Solomon ibn Gabirol, Judah Ha-Levi, and Shem Tov ibn Falaquera, and by such moderns as Samson Raphael Hirsch. Like their non-Jewish colleagues, various Jewish authors also wrote philosophical novels. Some of the leading philosophers were also among the greatest Hebrew poets of the Middle Ages. The polemical literature of Jews, Muslims, and Christians is often based not merely on scriptural and moral considerations, but also on attempts to employ philosophic argumentation against the rival religious community. As Daniel Lasker has put it, according to the medieval philosophical polemicists, philosophy may not be able to prove a religion, but it may be able to disprove one.[1]

As we consider the various problems that texts and translations present in the effective teaching of Jewish philosophy, we need to pay particular attention to an especially difficult literary genre Jews employed to expound their philosophic views, namely Bible exegesis. The problems of researching and teaching this genre of philosophic literature are great, given the frequently elliptic style of many of the exegetes as well as the inherent complexity of the subjects, combining as they do philosophic discussions with considerations of biblical language and grammar, as well as frequent explicit or implicit references to the vast body of rabbinic law and lore (halakhah and aggadah). Moreover, since this is not a systematic genre of philosophic exposition, it is almost inevitable that one must scan a vast body of commentaries to find an author's position on a given point.

Unless one is teaching advanced students who are familiar both with Hebrew and philosophic literature, one is accordingly forced to engage in a Herculean task of translation, in which virtually every phrase requires explanation, explication, and cross-references to other passages. To complicate matters further, only a tiny fraction of this literature has been translated into English and other modern European languages. Moreover, the existing translations are often incomplete and inaccurate, and sometimes even slanted, in order to censor passages that apparently were ideologically provocative or sexually explicit.

Nevertheless, if we want to understand what various Jewish philosophers had to say, we must study all of their writings, and not merely their overtly philosophic or systematic works. In some cases we may find ideas discussed in exegetical works that are not discussed in a philosopher's other works. In other cases, we may find that an author wrote for diverse audiences (Jewish and non-Jewish, for example, or the intelligentsia and the general population) in different works.

It seems to me that Bible exegesis as a philosophic literary genre, or at least as a literary device for expounding philosophic ideas, follows necessarily from the very nature of Western religious philosophy. I emphasize *Western* religious philosophy and not just Jewish philosophy, because the fundamental problem of "faith and reason" is formally, and often substantively, identical in the three Western religious traditions that base themselves on claims of historic revelation in inspired Scripture. If one is committed to both scriptural faith and reason as sources of truth, then those two different aspects of truth must be interrelated, and the need to understand them in terms of each other, or at least consistently with each other, becomes an obvious philosophic as well as religious imperative.

Philosophic exegesis of the Bible is, then, at the same time a way of understanding Scripture philosophically and a way of reconciling philosophic doctrines with the requirements of revealed religion. Philosophic exegesis, furthermore, provides an occasion both for teaching philosophy within a religious community and for demonstrating the rational validity of religion within the philosophic community.

Given the inherent tension of faith and reason underlying all Western religious philosophy, it is no accident that the exegetical genre of philosophic literature begins with Philo Judaeus of Alexandria, the first "Jewish philosopher" and, according to the well-known thesis of the late Harry Wolfson, the first and archetypal Western religious philosopher.

> As for Philo, he is not only in the midst of a general philosophic tradition, but he is also the founder of a new trend within that tradition—a trend which continued without any interruption for about seventeen centuries, terminating ultimately with Spinoza.[2]

Philo's pioneering efforts at philosophical exegesis of Scripture also led him to adapt Greek allegorization of their sacred mythology to Jewish Scripture.

> In the proper study of the relation of Scriptures to reason, therefore, Scripture has to be interpreted in the light of what is most evidently true in reason, and reason has to be corrected in the light of what is most evidently the true teachings of Scripture.[3]

According to Wolfson, it was a Jew, Philo, who built the system of religious philosophy, which a Jew, Spinoza, would tear down. Before Philo, philosophy did not have to come to terms with Scripture; after Spinoza, philosophy freed itself of Scripture. The interim is, in Wolfson's view, medieval philosophy in Judaism, Christianity, and Islam. Wolfson's thesis is borne out by the fact that many medieval philosophers, such as Aquinas in Christianity and Ibn Rushd in Islam, saw fit to cite and relate to scriptural passages in their philosophic works. The need to confront Scripture philosophically is thus a common problem for the three Western religious philosophical traditions.

In the case of Judaism, it also gave rise to a genre of philosophic Bible exegesis. This exegesis need not be purely philosophical and, in fact, often deals with other aspects of the Bible, including linguistic, grammatical, and literary analysis of the text, as well as the attempt to draw moral and religious lessons from biblical teachings. Whatever else we may find, the philosophic treatment of the Bible, in passages expected and unexpected by us as we read the biblical text through modern eyes, gives us greater insight into the thought of Jewish philosophers as they confronted the Bible, and as the Bible gave them the occasion to expound their philosophic perspectives.

I should like to examine a few selected passages in the Bible commentaries of two very different Jewish philosophers, Abraham ibn Ezra (Spain, twelfth century) and Moses Mendelssohn (Germany, eighteenth century). Mendelssohn was thoroughly familiar with the corpus of medieval Jewish Bible exegesis, including that of Ibn Ezra, who is one of the medieval philosophers frequently cited or referred to in Mendelssohn's Bible commentary, *Beʾur*. Despite Mendelssohn's modernity in his other writings, such as *Jerusalem,* his Bible commentary is traditional in style, approach, and content. It is one of the paradoxes of history that, because of religious and family developments after him (for which he certainly cannot seriously be blamed and much of which was totally at odds with his own values), it was suspect in traditionalist circles and generally ignored; conversely, because his Bible commentary was written in the traditional mode and in the Hebrew language, it was generally ignored in liberal circles, which would often have been at odds with his stance had they been able to read his words. Whereas the behavior, including apostasy, of Mendelssohn's children rendered their father's commentary suspect in the eyes of traditionalists down to our own day, it is perhaps a sign of greater human empathy and religious tolerance in the Middle Ages that Abraham ibn Ezra's commentaries have always been included in traditional rabbinic Bibles and studied in the most Orthodox of circles, notwithstanding his son Isaac's alleged conversion to Islam and despite the fact that, unlike Mendelssohn's very conservative approach, Ibn Ezra included radical philosophic doctrines in his commentary.

A comparison of several points in these two commentaries will therefore be instructive as we attempt to understand the thought of two different and fascinating figures in the history of Jewish philosophy, and will serve as an indication of Jewish intellectual concerns under radically differing circumstances. It will also illustrate the need to consider Bible exegesis as an integral component of Jewish philosophical literature over the centuries.

The cases studied here are frequently familiar to specialists in the field. However, they may exemplify the kinds of problems often encountered in teaching this genre of Jewish philosophic literature and incidentally, in some cases, will make texts available for the first time in English.

We begin with a comparison of Abraham ibn Ezra and Moses Mendelssohn on the question of the biblical text. This question, at first glance, would appear to be of general intellectual and historical, rather than purely philosophical, interest. However, the attitudes toward the biblical text reflect a larger philosophic stance and should be understood consistently in that light.

For Abraham ibn Ezra, as we shall see, revelation is essentially a rational process, and not merely a historic event. Reason therefore led him to question traditional assumptions regarding the revealed text. For Moses Mendelssohn, on the other hand, revelation is an indisputable historic fact (as had been argued by Saʿadiah Gaʾon and, more importantly for Mendelssohn, by Judah Ha-Levi). What was revealed at Sinai was a particular divine legislation, not universal rational principles or religious truth. Therefore, the biblical text was accepted as historically given and was not subjected by Mendelssohn to Spinoza's rationalist critique (with which Mendelssohn was thoroughly familiar).

The question of the biblical text, then, is perhaps the prime test case for philosophic exegesis of Scripture, for it forces the philosopher-exegete to deal with the very meaning of revelation and its relation to reason—problems that have been fundamental to Western religious philosophy since Philo.

Ibn Ezra and Mendelssohn on the Biblical Text

In several areas of philosophic import, it is evident that the modern Jewish philosopher, Moses Mendelssohn, whose status in Orthodox circles has been suspect for the two centuries since his death, in many respects affirms completely traditional or "Orthodox" views, whereas the medieval Jewish philosopher Abraham ibn Ezra, whose Orthodoxy is not generally questioned by the Orthodox themselves, affirms, or at least manifests tendencies toward, radical doctrines.

The first of these areas is the question of the integrity of the biblical text itself, which Mendelssohn seeks to defend at length. The *ʾOr La-Netivah,* the introduction to Mendelssohn's Bible commentary, clearly sets forth his concerns in this regard. Although Mendelssohn did not write the entire commentary himself (Shlomo Dubno wrote most of the commentary to Genesis and Ḥertz Weisel wrote the commentary to Leviticus), Mendelssohn edited the entire book, adding parenthetical notes to the work of Dubno and Weisel; we may accordingly regard the entire commentary as reflecting Mendelssohn's views and approach to the Bible.[4]

The entire Torah, Mendelssohn states, was written by Moses himself, including the last few verses describing Moses' death and burial. The text that Moses wrote is the text we have today, unchanged and complete. Those minor differences which are found among the various manuscripts are insignificant and do not affect the meaning of the text.

Mendelssohn then expounds on the view that Hebrew is the original human language, indeed the divine language of creation, and on other features of biblical Hebrew and the Hebrew alphabet, including the masoretic notes *(taʿamei ha-miqraʾ)* that punctuate the text.[5]

Mendelssohn explains that he translated the Torah into "proper" German for the sake of his sons (p. 12b).[6] The commentary was intended "to explain Scripture in language that would be easy for any reader to understand" (p. 13a). It would, inter alia, summarize the views of the classical commentators, among them notably Abraham ibn Ezra, "who was fluent in all the sciences," and would thus explain why he translated passages as he did. (It is no accident that Mendelssohn, the first modern Jewish philosopher, translated Scripture into the dominant philosophical-scientific language of his day—German—as did the first medieval Jewish philosopher, Saʿadiah Gaʾon, who authored an Arabic Bible translation and commentary.) The *Beʾur,* then, together with the translation it accompanied, was intended for mass education, and was entirely traditional in content and format, despite the novelty of Jewish translation of the Torah into German.

Alexander Altmann wrote:

> The employment of a pure and refined German, albeit in Hebrew characters . . . was an innovation. . . . The rendition of the Tetragrammation . . . as "the Eternal One" *(der Ewige)* had an alien ring. . . . The new edition of the Tora, notwithstanding its innovatory character, was thoroughly imbued with the traditional reverence for the Pentateuch as God's gift to Israel through Moses. . . . The traditional flavor would have been spoiled by the slightest explicit reference to the documentary hypothesis and proposed textual emendations. Yet Mendelssohn was well aware of the problems raised by critical scholarship, and the principles that he followed . . . were designed to meet them without resorting to solutions contrary to the assumption of the unitary origin of the Tora. But the rank and file of the Jewish community . . . were much more likely to be struck by the novelty of the work than by its loyalty to accepted standards.[7]

Altmann's statement that "Mendelssohn was well aware of the problems raised by critical scholarship" is undoubtedly true. The influence, both positive and negative, of Spinoza on Mendelssohn's thought has been well documented, and Mendelssohn must have given serious consideration to Spinoza's attack on the biblical text.[8]

Mendelssohn's silence on problematical biblical passages in the *Beʾur,* as well as his outspoken defense of the unitary Mosaic authorship of the Torah in the *ʾOr La-Netivah* are therefore equally eloquent, and clearly manifest both a rejection of biblical criticism in principle and a pragmatic avoidance of discussion of problematical passages, even when the passages are discussed directly or obliquely in the classical exigetical literature—most notably in the commentary of Abraham ibn Ezra, which is otherwise cited frequently and approvingly.

What was Ibn Ezra's attitude toward the unitary Mosaic authorship of the Torah? According to Spinoza (*Theologico-Political Treatise,* ch. 8):

> Aben Ezra, a man of enlightened intelligence, and no small learning . . . [who] was the first, so far as I know, to treat of this opinion, dared not express his meaning openly, but confined himself to dark hints which I shall not scruple to elucidate, thus throwing full light on the subject. . . . In these few words he hints, and also shows, that it was not Moses who wrote the Pentateuch, but someone who lived long after him, and further, that the book which Moses wrote was something different from any now extant.[9]

Note that these are precisely the two points Mendelssohn defends: Moses as the author of the entire Torah, and the integrity and authenticity of the biblical text that we have.

Spinoza then identifies six passages in which he understands Ibn Ezra to allude to the impossibility of Mosaic authorship. Of course, Ibn Ezra could not, by Spinoza's own admission, have explicitly made such a case, and Spinoza's view is essentially a precursor of Leo Strauss's thesis of "Persecution and the Art of Writing."[10] Mendelssohn himself, as has been noted, observes a discreet silence here. (A detailed analysis follows.)

However, since Ibn Ezra wrote elliptically here, the question of his attitude toward the biblical text cannot be answered unequivocally, and there is a difference of scholarly opinion on the subject. Some accept Spinoza's reading of Ibn Ezra. For example, Nahum Sarna writes of the medieval Spanish Bible exegetes:

> There can be no doubt of their interest in critical problems of the most sensitive kind. . . . We have no evidence that among these Jews anyone openly challenged the divine origin and Mosaic authorship of the Pentateuch. . . . Thoroughly intriguing are Ibn Ezra's own views. In the first place, one wonders why he so frequently cited the "heresies" of others when the effect was to give wide circulation to the very ideas he so vehemently denounced. . . . The virulence of his attacks creates the impression that he protests too much and that he is writing with greater circumspection than real conviction. . . . Not only does he frequently not refute the objectionable opinions, but even when he buttresses invective by reasoned argument the latter is usually far less satisfying than the original "heresy." Finally, Ibn Ezra himself listed six pentateuchal passages which seem to be post-Mosaic interpolations.[11]

Uriel Simon similarly argues, in his Hebrew article on Bible Exegesis in the *Encyclopaedia Biblica,* that Ibn Ezra was a pioneer of higher criticism.[12]

Elsewhere, Simon contrasts the approaches of Radak (Rabbi David Kimhi) and Ibn Ezra to the biblical text. He suggests that this contrast demonstrates that it is precisely Ibn Ezra's conservative attitude toward the Masoretic text ("lower criticism") that enabled him to maintain, in however veiled a manner, a radical attitude on the question of the Mosaic authorship of the Pentateuch ("higher criticism").[13]

We shall return later to the relationship between a critical attitude and the question of the rationality of the text. At this point we need to note, however, that the view of Ibn Ezra as a Bible critic, maintained by such scholars as Sarna and Simon, is not held universally.

Their view is challenged, for example, by Michael Friedlaender, in his major study, *Essays on the Writings of Abraham ibn Ezra.*[14] According to Friedlaender, Ibn Ezra maintained a traditional view of the Mosaic authorship of the Pentateuch: "Ibn Ezra firmly believed that the Pentateuch, with the exception of the last few verses, was the same as written by Moses, without any alteration or addition."[15]

More recently, Amos Funkenstein has also argued against construing Ibn Ezra as a Bible critic and as believing that the Torah contains later interpolations:

> It is true that Ibn Ezra preserved many critical arguments originating in Karaite criticism and in the radical rationalist criticism of some Spanish scholars, even against the authenticity of some verses or books. . . . In general, we find that his position is totally conservative, that he does not wish to impugn the unity of the Torah or the authorship of Moses' Torah. . . . It is only for the sake of argument that he preserved some of the arguments which Bible criticism later employed.[16]

The issue of Ibn Ezra's attitude toward the Mosaic authorship of the entire Pentateuch also occupied many of the commentators on his commentary on the Torah, as far back at least as the fourteenth century.

In the nineteenth century, it is not surprising to find vigorous affirmations of Ibn Ezra as a traditionalist. Solomon Zalman Netter, author of the supercommentary on Ibn Ezra printed in many standard editions of the Rabbinic Bible *(Miqra'ot Gedolot),* argues in his commentary on Deuteronomy 1:2:

> Some say that the Sage's opinion is that Joshua wrote [the last twelve verses of the Torah] from "Moses went up" (Deut. 34:1). However, in fact Rabbi Abraham was not of this opinion. Rather, these [verses] were told to Moses prophetically and he wrote them.

Netter also argues here for the traditionalist interpretation of Ibn Ezra's view of the other problematical verses cited in this passage. Netter's traditionalist interpretation of Ibn Ezra on the last twelve verses is itself problematical, because it contradicts Ibn Ezra's explicit statement on Deuteronomy 34:1 that "in my opinion Joshua wrote from this verse to the end [of the Torah], for after Moses went up he did not write anything. He [i.e., Joshua] wrote it prophetically." It is significant that Ibn Ezra here must be applying the phrase "prophetically" *(be-derekh nevu'ah)* to Joshua, not to Moses, because Joshua could not have witnessed what happened to Moses at the end on the Mount Nevo.

It is also peculiar that Netter and so many other medieval and modern commentators sought to read Ibn Ezra as affirming the Mosaic authorship of the final verses in the Torah describing Moses' own death, when the Talmud itself (*TB*, Bava Batra 15a) records in a totally noncontroversial and nonideological manner a dispute on the question, without the slightest implication that the view attributing these verses to Joshua involves any problem. Netter's comment on Deuteronomy 1:2 is also problematical because it contradicts his own comment on Deuteronomy 34:1: "Moses certainly did not write 'Moses went up' before he went up. And once he went up, he did not come down, so that one might have said that he wrote this after he came down. The same [is true] of the other verses cited above."

Judah Leib Krinsky, author of the supercommentary *Meḥoqeqei Yehudah,* also seems to misunderstand the phrase "prophetically" *(be-derekh nevu'ah)* in Ibn Ezra's comment here as applying to Moses instead of Joshua:

> The interpretation of the twelve verses from "Moses went up" to the end is that Moses wrote them prophetically. . . . In Ibn Ezra's opinion, these [verses] were told to Moses prophetically, and he wrote them thus. . . . In his opinion, all of these verses were prophetic.

Krinsky then develops his argument further, and cites the view of Shadal:

> Some who pretend to be wise [*mitḥakmim*] and who are free-thinkers [*poqerim*] base their free opinion on the Sage's statement "if you understand the secret, etc." They tried to make the Sage fall into the same pits into which they fell. Therefore I decided to copy what the great Sage, Rabbi Shadal, who never showed favor, wrote in his commentary to Deuteronomy.

Shadal (Samuel David Luzzatto, Italy, 1800–1865) did, in fact, argue for a traditionalist reading of Ibn Ezra, and many of his arguments were those used later by Friedlaender. Shadal, however, argues interestingly and more narrowly that there is no basis for interpreting Ibn Ezra as denying the Mosaic authorship of the Torah as a whole. Ibn Ezra regarded only these verses as later additions; his language in these passages proves (contra Spinoza) that in his view the rest of the Torah is not a forgery but was written by Moses. If the Torah as a whole did not derive from the time of Moses, then these verses would not be anachronistic, in which case there would be no problem.[17]

Shadal further suggests that Spinoza's erroneous reading of Ibn Ezra may have been based on the fourteenth-century supercommentary on Ibn Ezra by Samuel ben Saᶜadiah ibn Motot. In fact, Motot (Spain, active circa 1370)[18] interpreted Ibn Ezra here as a traditionalist: "His opinion was that all this was said to Moses prophetically." Motot's contemporary, the philosopher Samuel ibn Seneh Ẓarẓa also read Ibn Ezra as a traditionalist. In his supercommentary, the *Meqor Ḥayyim* he writes that in Ibn Ezra's view, all these problematical verses were written prophetically by Moses.[19]

Both Motot and Ẓarẓa address the issue of Ibn Ezra's understanding of the meaning of the word "then" *(ʾaz)* in Genesis 12:6 ("the Canaanite was then in the land"). Ibn Ezra wrote: "It is possible that Canaan seized the land of Canaan from someone else. If it does not mean that, it has a secret meaning [*sod*], and the intelligent should keep silent."

The question is whether the term "then" means then but not before, or then but not later? Does the term refer back to an earlier time (i.e., at that time, the time of Abraham, the land was controlled by the Canaanites, but it had not previously been controlled by the Canaanites, who conquered it from others; this is the view of other commentators, such as Rashi)? Or does the term "then" refer forward, to a later time (i.e., this passage was written when the Canaanites no longer controlled the land, implying that the passage could not have been written in the time of Moses, in whose day the Canaanites were in control of the land)?

According to Motot, "then" refers back to an earlier time, and means that "at that time the Land was already in the hands of Canaan." He then says that "the secret will become clear in the portion 'These are the words' (Deut. 1)."

Ẓarẓa provides a more complete analysis of the problem:

"It has a secret meaning." According to some, the word "then" has two meanings. Then and not before, or then and not later. If we say that the word "then" means that [Canaan] was not there earlier, it has no secret meaning. If this is not the case, it has a secret meaning, and the secret is that the term "then" can also refer to "then and not now." If you understand this, you should keep silent.

In assessing the arguments, medieval and modern, regarding Ibn Ezra's attitude toward the Mosaic authorship of the entire Pentateuch, we see that the question cannot be resolved unequivocally, precisely because of Ibn Ezra's elliptic form of expression. Spinoza was not the first, as we have seen, to have raised the possibility of Ibn Ezra's having maintained something of a critical attitude, although it is also not clear whether there is a basis for Shadal's suggestion that Spinoza was familiar with Motot's views, or those of Ẓarẓa. Moreover, while Ibn Ezra's commentary on some of the passages discussed by Spinoza is certainly suggestive of such critical questioning of the text, he deals with other passages in noncontroversial ways.

At the same time, there are other anachronistic passages, not discussed by Spinoza, that raise the issue of a critical attitude. Ibn Ezra argues against the view that Joshua authored Numbers 21:1, "The Canaanite, the king of Arad, heard":

> The ancients said that this is Siḥon, and that he was called "the Canaanite" because every Amorite was a Canaanite. Many have said that this passage was written by Joshua. Their proof is that there was one king of Arad, and they found that the Judeans [*benei yehudah*] called that place Ḥormah. But [these people] haven't said anything, because that same place was first called Ẓefat, and this was the king of Arad. Actually, they are two [different] places, and there are many such cases in the Bible [*miqra*ʾ]. . . . The literal meaning [*peshat*] of the king of Arad is in eastern trans-Jordan.

Note that Ibn Ezra addresses the question here not from an ideological perspective, namely whether Joshua or Moses authored the passage, but simply from the perspective of the geographical problem involved: does a common name necessarily refer to the place in the western land of Israel later known to the Jews, or can it also refer to someplace the Israelites came across in eastern trans-Jordan prior to the conquest of the land?

Accordingly, we must be careful in our reading of Ibn Ezra not to infer too little or too much. He seems not to have objected to the radical ideological implications of a critical attitude per se, for example, on anachronisms, and contented himself with counseling discretion: "the intelligent should keep silent." Rather, his arguments are often posed in narrow, methodological terms, as we have seen here, and as we shall see in his treatment of other passages, especially Genesis 36:31.

However, just as Ibn Ezra seems not to have had any fundamental ideological problem with at least a moderate amount of Bible criticism (keeping in mind Shadal's point that these problematical passages are only anachronistic if, in general, the Torah is affirmed as having been written in the time of Moses), he also cannot have rejected all prophecies of the future as later interpolations. To do so would have been to deny the phenomenon of prophecy itself. The issue for Ibn Ezra, therefore, cannot have been whether a prophet could predict the future. What is questioned, rather, is the intelligibility of the prophecy to the prophet himself and certainly to his audience. As we shall see, Ibn Ezra rejects as impossible and as incompatible with the very rationality of revelation any revelation that is inherently unintelligible. If revelation is to be meaningful, it must be comprehensible to its recipients. Accordingly, in another important study of Ibn Ezra, Uriel Simon concludes:

> Ibn Ezra's objection to anachronisms does not arise, therefore, from the absurdity inherent in premature information about the future. Rather, only the fact that it is presented as already known and familiar undermines the reasonableness of its style and the clarity of its content.[20]

Whatever Ibn Ezra's attitude may have been on the question of the Mosaic authorship of the entire Pentateuch, in at least one passage he seems to raise the question of redaction criticism. The widely accepted rabbinic principle of "there is neither earlier nor later in the Torah"—that is, that the Torah does not always present material in its proper chronological order[21]—may be applied routinely, without ideological controversy. In his long commentary on Exodus 6:28, however, Ibn Ezra's phrasing goes beyond this standard rabbinic hermeneutic principle: "One should be astonished at the arranger of the portions [*mesader ha-parshiyot*]; why he connected this verse to the ones after it."

What does the expression "the arranger of the portions" mean? If Moses wrote the text, as tradition claims, who is this redactor who arranged the text in an astonishing manner? The rabbis often offered homiletical explanations for texts that appear to be out of context or proper chronological order, but Ibn Ezra's phrasing here seems to imply something far more radical and fundamental, namely a later process of redaction. He continues by saying: "Perhaps the one who made the pauses [i.e., who divided the text into sections and paragraphs] knew why he did this, because his knowledge was greater than our knowledge." Ibn Ezra may have been open to what is called redaction criticism, in addition to the critical questions of authorship.

The evidence on Ibn Ezra's attitude toward the text is thus ambiguous, probably deliberately so. We cannot necessarily project onto him the later critical attitude of Spinoza. Shadal may well be correct that Ibn Ezra's questioning of several problematical passages proves that, in contrast to Spinoza, his general attitude was traditional; for, if the Torah as a whole, and as we have it, cannot be attributed to Moses, why raise questions about a few anachronistic passages? On the other hand, we cannot necessarily project onto Ibn Ezra a traditionalist view, which, in modern times, has become ever more rigid in response to Spinoza's criticism. Ibn Ezra's smoke may well conceal a critical fire. The fire, however suggestive it was to Spinoza, does not justify the latter's far more radical extension of the criticism to the denial of the Mosaic authorship of the Pentateuch in general. Nor does the smoke justify the nineteenth- and twentieth-century retrieval of Ibn Ezra as an orthodox traditionalist.

In the case of Mendelssohn, however, whose knowledge of and indebtedness to Spinoza are well established,[22] the case is far clearer. In his *ʾOr La-Netivah,* his introduction to the Torah, and his Hebrew Pentateuch commentary, the *Beʾur,* Mendelssohn explicitly reaffirms the unitary Mosaic authorship of the entire Torah, including the last twelve verses of Deuteronomy.[23]

Even more astounding is the fact that Mendelssohn consistently avoids any reference to Ibn Ezra's suggestive comments on these problematic passages. When the commentary deals with these verses at all, it treats them in a traditional manner, and totally ignores the critical implications of the verses' anachronisms and of Ibn Ezra's comments, even when, regarding these same passages, Mendelssohn cites Ibn Ezra on other matters, such as grammar.

Mendelssohn, as noted, affirms the Mosaic authorship of the last twelve verses of Deuteronomy, although attributing them to Joshua had ample traditional precedent and scarcely could have been construed as suggesting anything critical about the text. The verses were given prophetically, regardless of whether Moses or Joshua was the prophet.

Mendelssohn discusses various points, including some raised by Ibn Ezra, in his commentary on Deuteronomy 1:1–2, but ignores totally the issues raised by Ibn Ezra that formed the basis of Spinoza's argument. There is similar silence in his discussions of Deuteronomy 3:11 and 31:9. In Deuteronomy 27:2 Mendelssohn sides with Ramban against Ibn Ezra's view that Moses wrote down summaries of the commandments on the twelve stones, but is silent on anything reminiscent of Spinoza's argument.

Mendelssohn's treatment of Genesis 22:14 is equally traditionalist and is silent on any critical questions. Ibn Ezra comments cryptically: "The meaning of 'on the mountain the Lord will be seen' [may be found in the commentary to] Deuteronomy [1:2]." Mendelssohn cites Rashi's explanation that "on the mountain the Lord will be seen" or "on the mountain of the Lord will be provided" means that this is the mountain on which, in later generations, God would be seen by His people worshiping in the Temple erected on that spot. In other words, "that day" or "today" *(ha-yom)* refers not to a later author writing the text, but to later generations reading the text. Mendelssohn then adds: "These are the words of Moses which Moses wrote in the Torah. He meant to signify that place and to inform the people of his generation about it."

Mendelssohn's silence on Ibn Ezra's critical implications is most obvious in his treatment of Genesis 12:6, "the Canaanite was then in the land," specifically because he cites only the noncontroversial first half of Ibn Ezra's comment. Ibn Ezra, it will be recalled, suggested that if "then" refers to an earlier time, it simply means that at the time of Abraham the Canaanites controlled the land, but that they did not control it previously, whereas if "then" refers to a later time, that is, then but not now (when this passage in the Torah was authored), "it has a secret meaning, and the intelligent should keep silent."

According to Mendelssohn:

> The term "then" indicates a particular time, sometimes to negate an earlier time, i.e., then and not before. Sometimes it negates a later time, i.e., then and not now. Here, according to Rashi's commentary, it negates the earlier time, and that is also the interpretation of Ibn Ezra at the beginning of his words, and this is also how it is translated in the Aramaic.

On Genesis 36:31 ("These are the kings who ruled in the land of Edom before any king ruled over the children of Israel") Mendelssohn touches, however lightly, on a critical reference in Ibn Ezra. Ibn Ezra comments here:

> Some say that this portion was written prophetically. Yiẓḥaqi says in his book that this portion was written in the time of Yehoshafat (cf. 2 Kings 8), and he interpreted the generations [of kings] as he wished. For his name has been called Yiẓḥaq; everyone who hears will laugh at him (cf.

> Genesis 21:6, 27:36). . . . God forbid that it be as he said, in the time of Yehoshafat; his book should be burned. . . . The true interpretation of "before any king ruled over the children of Israel" is [that it refers] to Moses the king of Israel, as it is written, "He was king of Yeshurun" (cf. Deuteronomy 33:5).

Mendelssohn cites Ibn Ezra here, but again, only partially, and adds his own explanatory comments:

> Ibn Ezra wrote: Some say that this portion was written prophetically, because they thought that "before any king ruled over the children of Israel" [refers to] Saul, which Moses could only have known prophetically. [Ibn Ezra] cited the opinion of Yiẓḥaqi, who was Isaac ben Yashush[24] the Spaniard, and argued against it. The end of [Ibn Ezra's] words is "the true interpretation of 'before any king ruled' is [that it refers] to Moses the king of Israel, as it is written 'He was king of Yeshurun.'"

Mendelssohn continues to comment on the passage, beginning with Rashbam's similar view that the king referred to here is Moses.

For our purposes, what is important is that Mendelssohn mentions Ibn Ezra's reference to Isaac ("Yiẓḥaqi") but, significantly, he omits the actual argument. Referring to Ibn Ezra's argument with Isaac is safe for Mendelssohn, because Ibn Ezra himself condemned the radical interpretation proposed by Yiẓḥaqi. Nevertheless, the argument itself is not quoted, since doing so would introduce a controversial issue into Mendelssohn's own text.

We should probably take with a grain of salt Ibn Ezra's mockery of Yiẓḥaqi ("everyone who hears will laugh at him") and recommendation that his book be burned. First of all, Ibn Ezra is arguing narrowly against the faulty chronology Yiẓḥaqi proposed. Ibn Ezra does not suggest that the anachronism of the verse raises any broader ideological issue.

In addition, we need to note that Ibn Ezra's harsh denunciation of Yiẓḥaqi is by no means unusual. In a recent study,[25] Uriel Simon argues persuasively that Ibn Ezra often used harsh language and biting humor when he was criticizing a specific view, even of people he otherwise admired and whom he praised and cited positively elsewhere, such as Ibn Janaḥ, Saʿadiah Gaʾon, and Dunash ben Labrat. He even subjected his own earlier views to such attack, "after realizing that he had formerly subscribed to an erroneous opinion."[26]

> This means that when he uses harsh language against an author or a work, Ibn Ezra means no more than to give vehement expression to

> genuine anxiety over the damage liable to be caused by a fallacious exegetical method or erroneous gloss. . . . Ibn Ezra's anxiety on this point follows directly from the fundamental principle of the Spanish scholars that philology and theology are interrelated disciplines, each protecting the other: philology worthy of the name protects against errors of doctrine, while pure belief shields against philological errors. Hebrew linguistics and scriptural exegesis are both holy labors, because the scientific endeavor has far-reaching results in the realm of doctrine—just as it can illuminate the texts it can also befog them.[27]

Misreading the text, as Yiẓḥaqi did here, is dangerous, and the error must be exposed and corrected. The error, however, is methodological not ideological.

Mendelssohn's silence in all these passages is deafening, and clearly cannot be accidental. His citation of only the first half of Ibn Ezra's interpretation of "then" in Genesis 12:6, as well as his mere reference to Isaac without citing Ibn Ezra's actual argumentation in Genesis 36:31 can only be a form of self-censorship. The controversy in Orthodox circles that his German translation of the Torah and *Be'ur* aroused, was clearly of paramount concern to Mendelssohn who, as we have seen, clearly wished to be, and to have his work, considered acceptable in traditionalist circles.

Despite Mendelssohn's subsequent reputation in those circles for having paved the way for radical innovations and what the traditionalists saw as the aberrations of the Reform movement, his own position was clearly and explicitly to affirm, preserve, and enhance Jewish tradition in a time of modernization. This is evident in his biblical work, which is overtly traditional in nature and tone, and was written for Jewish readers; and it is also explicitly visible in *Jerusalem,* his philosophical defense of Judaism in a modern context, written in German for a general (i.e., non-Jewish) audience.

In *Jerusalem,* Mendelssohn states with admirable forthrightness that if it were true that traditional Jewish loyalty is inconsistent and incompatible with the type of modernization he was advocating, he would have to remain loyal to the Torah on both a philosophical and a sociopolitical level, and would have to give up his philosophical and political stance.

Thus, Mendelssohn writes in response to "Der Forscher" (The searcher), who occasioned the writing of the *Jerusalem* by questioning whether Mendelssohn's philosophic appeal for toleration is compatible with the Torah as a divine system of law that admits of no right of dissent or deviation:

> This objection goes right to my heart and troubles me deeply. I must confess that this view of Judaism . . . is shared by many of my coreligionists. If I were convinced that it is true, I would retract my statements, despite the inevitable embarrassment I would have to face, and I would subordinate reason to the yoke of faith.[28]

Similarly, toward the end of the book, he addresses the Christian community regarding Jewish political and social rights:

> And you, my brothers and fellowmen, who are followers of the teachings of Jesus, how can you blame us for doing what the founder of your religion himself has done and sanctioned by his authority? Can you seriously believe that you cannot reciprocate our love as citizens and associate yourselves with us for civic purposes as long as we are outwardly distinguished from you by our ceremonial law, do not eat with you, or do not marry you? . . . The founder of your religion himself would not have done these things or have permitted us to do them either. . . . If we can be united with you as citizens only on the condition that we deviate from the law which we still consider binding, then we sincerely regret the necessity of declaring that we shall renounce our claim to civil [equality and] union with you.[29]

Mendelssohn's traditionalist stance and intent, therefore, both as a philosopher and certainly as a biblical exegete cannot be doubted. If Simon's view is correct that Abraham ibn Ezra, before Spinoza and in contradistinction to Radak, reaffirmed the traditional integrity of the biblical text, on the level of "lower criticism," in order not to undermine his philosophic freedom and the rational foundations of his faith,[30] it is certainly all the more true, on the level of "higher criticism," for the post-Spinoza Mendelssohn. To have engaged in biblical criticism would have been to contradict his own deeply held traditionalist belief in the divine authority and Mosaic authorship of the Torah. To have discussed the critical issues raised by Spinoza and even those raised by Ibn Ezra would have been to undermine the traditionalist religious and pedagogic purposes for which Mendelssohn engaged in what was already a sufficiently controversial undertaking. Mendelssohn, then, followed Ibn Ezra's admonition that "the intelligent should remain silent" by ignoring and remaining silent on the problematical implications of Ibn Ezra's own work.

The Rationality of Scripture

As we have seen, Uriel Simon has argued that Ibn Ezra sought to avoid undermining the rational foundations of his faith by questioning the integrity of the biblical text ("lower criticism") while remaining open to the possibility of non-Mosaic authorship of various passages ("higher criticism").

In a sense, and paradoxically, it is the rationality of revelation in Ibn Ezra's scheme that may render a conservative attitude to the text necessary, while permitting a free, if discreet, attitude to the more radical question of authorship.

We must bear in mind that, for Ibn Ezra, revelation is not only a historic event. Revelation is, in its very essence, a rational process. Moreover, it is not limited to the written biblical record. Throughout his commentary, Ibn Ezra reaffirms—against Karaite literalism—the need for, and the validity, authority, and accuracy of, the oral traditions of rabbinic Judaism. The oral Torah, for Ibn Ezra, is no less revealed than is the written Torah.[31] To question the text as we have it, is to question the integrity of its preservation and transmission over the centuries; it would also undermine the authority of the traditional canon and of the Masoretes, whom Ibn Ezra held in such high regard and whose precise and exacting standards he admired so greatly. In short, to question the written text as received and transmitted traditionally, is to undermine the authority and reliability of rabbinic and masoretic tradition.

On the other hand, despite its apparent paradoxicality, the belief in the revealed authority of the text, which for Ibn Ezra precludes "lower criticism," need not preclude "higher criticism." Later authors, beginning with Joshua, were also guided by revelation. The activities of the prophets, Ezra, and Soferim, and even the rabbis themselves, are ultimately also of revealed origin, given the Pharisaical and rabbinic notion of "oral Torah" set forth explicitly in the opening lines of Mishnah Avot—"Moses received the Torah at Sinai, and transmitted it to Joshua, Joshua to the elders, etc."—and culminating with Hillel and Shammai.

Although the text in Avot explicitly refers to Moses receiving the Torah at Sinai, the clear concern here is not the narrower issue of the unitary Mosaic authorship of the entire Pentateuch, but rather the much broader issue of the divinely revealed authority of the Torah. In this context, we must note that elsewhere the Mishnah (Sanhedrin, ch. 10, "Pereq Ḥeleq") categorizes a Jew who denies the revelation of the Torah per se (but not a Jew who denies the unitary Mosaic authorship of the Torah) as one of those excluded from a portion in the world to come. Maimonides, in the eighth of his "Thirteen Principles" based on this text, comments that such a person is one who thinks that the Torah contains

> a kernel and a shell, and that these histories and stories serve no purpose, and that Moses composed them. This is what is meant by denying that the Torah is divinely revealed. They said that this is a person who believes that the whole Torah is revealed except for one verse, which God did not say but which Moses wrote on his own.[32]

Note that the heretical position is actually the assertion of Mosaic authorship, in this case Mosaic authorship uninspired by revelation! The issue that concerned the rabbis and Maimonides here is not whether Moses authored the entire Torah but whether the entire Torah is divinely revealed.

For Ibn Ezra, then, as for at least some rabbinic traditions, additions to the Mosaic text by Joshua are certainly not a problem. Joshua, too, wrote them "prophetically," and there is ample rabbinic precedent for suggesting Joshua's authorship of various passages. The problem is, of course, more pronounced when dealing with later interpolations. But they, too, were evidently sufficiently endowed with revelatory authority, whether prophetic or other, to have passed traditional canonical muster and the exacting standards of the Masoretes (whose authority was also ultimately of revealed quality, given the rabbinic notion that the basis for the later oral Torah is ultimately divine).

It seems to me that Ibn Ezra's position on Bible criticism follows consistently from the rationality of scriptural revelation. As I have suggested, to question the text itself is to challenge the authority of oral Torah by imputing error to those who preserved and transmitted it. On the other hand, to reject even the possibility of later, non-Mosaic, authorship of some anachronistic passages in the Torah or prophets is to challenge the rationality of revelation with absurd results.

The issue boils down to what Harry Wolfson regarded as the Philonic structure of Western philosophy, in contradistinction to the medieval Latin Averroistic "double truth" theory.[33] Revelation and reason are not separate categories, in which a proposition can be true according to the one system and false or dubious in the other. To the contrary, belief in both revelation and reason implies that, properly comprehended, they must ultimately convey the same truth and meaning, and must be understood in light of each other.

A passage in Scripture which, when read literally, offends reason, must then be reread in a manner compatible with reason. This does not merely mean taking Scripture nonliterally when necessary—a problem to which we shall return. For Ibn Ezra, it may also mean occasionally questioning the traditional assumptions regarding the

Torah's unitary Mosaic authorship (while affirming it in general), for example, where affirming such a traditional view is rendered absurd by anachronisms, or where it would have been meaningless for Moses (or another prophet at a given point in history) to talk in terms or to refer to events that would have been unintelligible or incomprehensible to the people being addressed, if not to the prophet himself.

Nevertheless, even if this argument infers too much in the case of Ibn Ezra, we can, I believe, definitely recognize that affirming the integrity of the text, on whatever level, is not the same as taking it literally. In the first case, one is affirming that the text as we have it accurately reflects divine revelation, however understood. In the second case, one is dealing not with the source and integrity of the text, but with its meaning.

Saʿadiah Gaʾon, whose rationalist approach toward Scripture had a deep impact on Ibn Ezra, and whose interpretations are frequently cited in the latter's commentary, clearly established the need for a conservative attitude toward the text, which must be taken literally, as a rule, except under certain circumstances.

> I say, furthermore, that those who interpret the verses of Sacred Writ allegorically fall into four categories. They may do so either to harmonize a verse (a) with the evidence of the senses, (b) with the testimony of reason, (c) with other biblical passages, or (d) with tradition.[34]

Unnecessary allegorization, Saʿadiah argues, fosters heresy. And again, when arguing in favor of a literal reading of verses alluding to the resurrection of the dead, Saʿadiah says:

> Every statement found in the Bible is to be understood in its literal sense except for . . . one of the following four reasons. It may . . . be rejected by the observation of the senses. . . . by reason. . . . by an explicit text of a contradictory nature, in which case it would be necessary to interpret the first statement in a non-literal sense. . . . Finally, a biblical statement to the meaning of which rabbinic tradition has attached a certain reservation, is to be interpreted by us in keeping with this authentic tradition. . . . There exist, then, only these four possible reasons for a non-literal interpretation of the verses of Sacred Writ, there being no fifth.[35]

Compare this with an alternate version of this passage (which was the basis for Judah ibn Tibbon's Hebrew translation) where Saʿadiah posits the same four conditions for reading the text non-literally. In all other cases, he concludes, it is neither necessary nor permissible to search for allegorical or other non-literal meaning.[36]

A conservative attitude toward the text and toward the literal meaning of Scripture *(peshat)* follows necessarily for Saʿadiah (and Ibn Ezra, as we shall see) from the fact that these are "the books of God that have been transmitted to us." Another consideration, of course, is the fact that whereas Jewish religious life rests on the observance of the biblical precepts and would be completely undermined by freely taking these commandments allegorically, as was often the case in Christian exegesis, such freedom is unwarranted by the rationality of the revealed word as well as destructive to traditional Jewish practice.

These considerations underlie Ibn Ezra's reaffirmation of *peshat* in his interpretation of Exodus 13:9, "Let it be a sign for you on your hand and a reminder between your eyes." Rashi, reflecting the standard traditional rabbinic interpretation of this passage, understands it to be a reference to the *tefillin:* "It means that you should write these portions and tie them to your head and arm." His grandson, Rashbam, while not denying the validity of this rabbinic interpretation and practice, suggests that the literal meaning of the verse is simply that it serve as a reminder:

> According to the depth of its literal meaning [*ʿomeq peshuto*], it should always be a reminder for you, as if it were written on your hand, such as [the verse] "Place me as a seal on your heart" (Song of Songs 8:6); "between your eyes," such as a piece of jewelry or a golden chain which one is accustomed to place on the forehead for beauty.

Ibn Ezra rejects such figurative reading of the verse. Scripture may only be taken figuratively when, as in the book of Proverbs (*mishlei,* proverbs, from the word *mashal;* in this context, something figurative), the text explicitly states its figurative character *(mashal),* or when the literal sense contradicts reason:

> There are some who disagree with our holy ancestors, by saying that "a sign . . . and a reminder" [should be understood to mean something] in the manner of "They shall be a lovely chain for your head and necklaces for your throat" (Proverbs 1:9); and that "tie them as a sign upon your hands" is like "Tie them always on the tablet of your heart"; and also that "Write them on the doorposts of your house" is like "Write them on the tablet of your heart"; and that what should be a sign and a reminder [means] what should be fluent in your mouth, for the Lord brought you out of Egypt with a strong hand. This is not the correct way, for at the beginning [of the book of Proverbs] it is written "The Proverbs of Solomon." Everything mentioned [by this commentator] is meant figuratively [*ʿal derekh mashal*]. But there is no passage in the

> Torah which is, God forbid, meant figuratively; rather, it is meant literally [*ke-mashmaᶜo*]. Therefore we never take it out of its literal context [*mi-yedei peshuto*]. For its literal meaning does not contradict reason [*shiqul ha-daᶜat*], such as "Circumcise the foreskins of your heart" does, which we must correct in accordance with reason [*le-taqqeno le-fi ha-daᶜat*].

On a more fundamental and methodological level, Ibn Ezra argues in his introduction to the Torah for serious respect to be paid to the literal text, insisting that rationality is the very basis for its revealed authority. Therefore it is also rationality, in addition to proper philology and exegetical methodology, that provides the primary criterion for deviating from a literal reading of the text when it offends reason.[37]

In his survey of five different exegetical methodologies in his introduction to the Torah, Ibn Ezra compares the truth to the center of a circle. The exegetical approach of the Babylonian academies is so faulty as to resemble the circumference of a circle, which never reaches the truth at the center. (He mentions by name Isaac the Old [*Ha-Yashish*]. Saᶜadia Gaᵓon, and Samuel ben Ḥofni.)[38] Their method is faulty because they have not sufficiently mastered "the external sciences," and they accordingly fail to provide proofs *(reᵓayot)* for their conclusions.

The second deficient approach is that of the Karaites, who think they are at the center of the circle but don't even know its location, such as ᶜAnan ben David and Benjamin Nahawendi.[39] Their exegesis is faulty because of its inherent subjective individualism, even regarding the commandments. They are ignorant of proper Hebrew and grammar and, without having any recourse to authentic (i.e., rabbinic) oral tradition *(qabbalah u-masoret),* they have no way to understand many matters, regarding such biblical laws as the calendar upon which so much of Jewish observance depends, but which are not explicated in the Bible, and for which the Karaites therefore lack decisive evidence.

The third approach, which is characterized by darkness *(ḥoshekh va-ᵓafelah),* and is completely outside the circumference of the circle, is that of Christian allegorists, who indiscriminately find secret meaning *(sodot)* everywhere in Scripture. One should, however, only seek such secret meaning when the literal meaning *(peshat)* contradicts reason or experience. They are only correct in that they subject every matter, whether pertaining to a major or minor commandment, to the judgment of reason *(deᶜah, daᶜat):*

> For reason has been implanted in the [human] heart by divine wisdom. If reason cannot tolerate something, or if it destroys what is clearly [known] empirically [*ba-hargashot*], then one should seek its secret meaning, because the judgment of reason is the foundation, and the Torah was not given to those who lack reason. The angel [intermediating] between man and his God is his intellect [*sekhel*]. [However], we should interpret whatever reason does not deny literally [*ki-feshuto u-mishpato*]. We should understand its measure [*matkonet*], and believe that this is its truth, and we should not grope along the wall like the blind. [Rather,] we should take things in according with our needs. Why should we turn clear things [*nirʾim*] into hidden [*nistarim*]?

The fourth approach, which is "close to the center" of the circle, is the approach of the scholars of Greece and Rome (i.e., the Jewish scholars living in the eastern Byzantine and western Roman Christian empires, as opposed to the Babylonians Jews, who lived in the realm of Islam). Their approach is faulty because they rely excessively on rabbinic homiletics *(derash),* and not on reason or grammar. At least these scholars rely on the writings of the ancient rabbis. On the other hand, in that case, why bother to repeat what the ancients have already said? These scholars do not, moreover, recognize that one rabbinic homily can often contradict another, and that rabbinic statements (no less than scriptural passages) may also have an implicit secret meaning. Rabbinic statements may be meant allegorically. By taking these statements literally, one ends up contradicting reason. In short, there is no end to rabbinic homiletical exegesis, and one should rather abide by the rabbinic principle that "the Bible never leaves its literal meaning" *(ein miqra yoẓe mi-yedei peshuto).*

The fifth and true approach followed by Ibn Ezra avoids such false and faulty interpretations, by basing itself on philology. It seeks, first of all, to understand the proper grammar of the text. There may be occasion to resort to rabbinic homiletical exegesis, but only to add to what the rabbis said, not merely to repeat it. In any event, "the literal meaning is never replaced by the homiletical meaning, for the Torah has seventy faces."

To reiterate: reason is, for Ibn Ezra, fundamental to the very notion of revelation, and therefore provides the primary basis for proper exegetical method. All three Jewish approaches described by Ibn Ezra ultimately fail for lack of solid, scientific methodology. The Babylonian scholars (the first approach), the Karaites (the second approach, which also fails for lack of a reliable tradition), and the scholars of Greece and Rome (the fourth approach, which also fails because of excessive literalist reliance on rabbinic tradition) are all guilty of ignorance of science in general, and specifically of philology, linguistics, and grammar. They don't know how to construct proper scientific proofs (the Babylonians), they don't have any basis for avoiding the errors of subjectivity (the Karaites), they don't know when to take the text literally (the Christians), or they don't know when to take the text as well as rabbinic *derash* figuratively (the Greek and Roman scholars). In all these cases, reason is the key to understanding revelation, and reason, including fluency in "the external sciences." is the foundation of any scientific exegetical method.

The rationality of Scripture recurs as a theme in Ibn Ezra's various commentaries. Two examples will suffice: Rationality provides the basis in the first case for rejecting excessive and literalist reliance on rabbinic *derash;* and in the second case, for rejecting the Karaite's absurd subjectivity, untempered by the needed guidance of rabbinic tradition.

In his long commentary to Exodus 20:1, Ibn Ezra expounds at great length on the differences between the versions of the Decalogue in Exodus 20 (the actual revelation at Sinai) and Deuteronomy 5 (Moses' paraphrase).

> In the first [version] it is written, "God spoke all of these words, saying" (Exodus 20:1), and in the second [version] "These are the words which the Lord spoke to all of your assembly" (Deuteronomy 5:18). When we searched in the words of the Sages what they had to say about this, we found that they held that "'remember' (Exodus 20:8) and 'observe' (Deuteronomy 5:12) were said in one statement."[40] This statement is the most difficult of all the problems we have, as I shall explain. God forbid that I should say that [the Sages] did not speak correctly, for our knowledge is insignificant compared to theirs. It is only that people in our generation think that what they said is meant literally [*kemashma*ʿ*am*). This is not the case, as I shall explain at the end, after I have mentioned the problems. Finally, I shall explain the correct way [*ha-derekh ha-yesharah*][41] in order to resolve all the problems and questions in this portion. It is impossible that "remember" and "observe" could have been said simultaneously, except by miracle. But [in that case] we would still acknowledge that we should ask, why doesn't it say [both] "remember and observe" in both the first and the second [versions]? What shall we do with such verses as "remember" and "observe," if they were said simultaneously, and why didn't the Sages mention this? What is even more astonishing than two words, which mean the identically same thing, having been said simultaneously, is that many [different] verses, which do not mean the same thing, could have been said simultaneously in a miraculous manner. . . . *Reason cannot tolerate any of these things.* The most difficult of what I mentioned is that all the wonders performed by Moses bear some resemblance to other things; and the

> intelligent will understand.[42] But this would be the most wondrous of all, that God would have spoken "remember" and "observe" simultaneously, [in which case] this should have been explicitly written down in the Torah, more than all of the [miraculous] signs and proofs which were written down. If we should say that God's speech is not like human speech, then how could the Israelites have understood God's speech? For if a person would hear "remember" and "observe" simultaneously, he would not understand either one. One could not understand what the speaker spoke, even one word like "remember" [*zakhor*], if one does not hear the [letter] *zayin* before the *kaf* and the *resh*. Now we know that the perception of the eye is more noble than the perception of the ear, for we know with absolute proofs that the moment we see the lightning is the same moment as that of the thunder, but the eye sees it from a distance, whereas the air conveys the sound [of the thunder] to the ear, and [the sound] proceeds slowly and only reaches the ear after a moment has passed. . . . So the sound of the letter *zayin* [of the word *zakhor*] enters the ear before the *kaf* and the *vav* and the *resh*. Now if we say that this was a wonder, that "observe" and "remember" were said simultaneously, how could the ear hear [them]? And if we say that it is a wonder that the ear heard two words simultaneously, when it is not habituated to hearing two letters [simultaneously], why did the Sages not mention this? . . . And what should we [then] do with the remaining problems of the differences between the verses [in the first and second versions], which do not mean the same thing? . . . Now I shall explain for you the aforementioned questions. Know that God said all the Decalogue, as written in this portion; as it says, "God spoke all of these words, saying," beginning with "I am" (Exodus 20:2) and ending with "whatever belongs to your fellow" (Exodus 20:13). Moses, when he mentioned the Decalogue in the second [version], said, "These are the words which the Lord spoke to all of your assembly" (Deuteronomy 5:18), one right after the other.

The point is clear. Consistent with his criticism of the unscientific approach of the Jewish scholars of Greece and Rome (the fourth approach in the introduction), Ibn Ezra rejects on rational grounds a literal reading of the rabbinic *derash* that both versions of the Decalogue were spoken simultaneously. The issue is not whether God could have revealed two different sounds and, more important, two different meanings simultaneously. The issue is whether the human ear is capable of simultaneously and intelligibly perceiving two different sounds, and whether the human mind is capable of simultaneously and intelligibly conceiving two different ideas. As a rational process, revelation must be subject to rational limitations, but those limitations reflect the human recipient, and not the divine giver, of the message.[43]

Similarly, it is on rational grounds that Ibn Ezra rejects as absurd the Karaite literalist reading of the *lex talionis* in Exodus 21:24. Fundamental to the Rabbanite critique of Karaism in general, as well as to the Karaites' reading of this particular passage, was the notion mentioned by Ibn Ezra in his introduction that since there are many matters for which the Torah gives no explicit or specific instructions, without recourse to reliable tradition one has no assurance of correct understanding or accurate interpretation, and the problem of subjectivity and individualism, and their destructive implications for unity in communal life and uniformity in observance, becomes paramount.

In the case of the *lex talionis,* the challenge for the Rabbanite position was to demonstrate that the principle of compensation is not merely a later rabbinic *derash* superimposed upon the original *peshat,* but that it was the original *peshat* when the *peshat* is correctly understood, in accordance with the dictates of reason.

This passage, then, is a primary case cited by the Rabbanites to support their claim that, without recourse to reliable tradition, the unguided individual can arrive, in his subjective reading of the text, at all kinds of incorrect interpretations. To borrow a phrase from the Protestant rejection of the "magisterium" of the Roman Catholic Church, which in some ways parallels the Karaites' rejection of the authority of rabbinic "Oral Torah," "sola Scriptura" ends up being "nulla Scriptura."

The Rabbanite argument could be grounded in a comparison with other biblical texts in which the expression "X for X" was explicitly linked to compensation, as in Leviticus 24:18, or as in Judges 15:11, where the expression "As they have done to me, so have I done to them" clearly implies not an identical action but giving the offender his just deserts.

Rashi, in his comment on this passage, merely referred the reader to the talmudic understanding of the *lex talionis:*

> He blinded the eye of his fellow, and pays him the worth of his eye, i.e., however much his value is reduced if he were sold [as a slave] in the market. And so for the other cases. Actual cutting off of the limb is not meant here, as our rabbis explained in the Talmud.[44]

Ramban cites Leviticus 24:18 for support of the Rabbanite view:

> We know from rabbinic tradition that this is compensation, as we find this expression in the context of payment: "One who kills a beast must pay for it, life for life" (Leviticus 24:18). . . . The general principle is that in every place the tradition is true.

Ibn Ezra employs such standard Rabbanite argumentation, but adds to it the critical point that this position is the only one possible in rational terms. The Karaite position is absurd, he argues, following Saʿadiah Gaʾon: "Reason cannot tolerate this." Therefore, unless one wishes to impute irrationality to the revealed text, one must conclude that compensation is the correct meaning of the *peshat* itself.

In his long commentary here, Ibn Ezra cites a dispute between Saʿadiah and a Karaite, Ben Zuta:

> Rabbi Saʿadiah said: We cannot interpret this verse literally [*kemashmaʿo*]. For if a person struck the eye of his fellow, and a third of his vision is lost, how can he be struck with the same injury without any greater or lesser [injury]? Perhaps he will become completely blind, or the burn or the wound or the bruise would be more severe. If they were in a dangerous location, perhaps he will die. *Reason cannot tolerate this* [*ʾein ha-daʿat sovelet*]. Ben Zuta said to him: But is it not written elsewhere, "Whenever someone makes a blemish in a person, so should be done to him" (Leviticus 24:20)? Saʿadiah replied. . . . This means, so should he be given a punishment. But Ben Zuta replied, "As he did, so should be done to him" (Leviticus 24:19). The Gaʾon replied: Samson said, "As they did to me, so have I done to them" (Judges 15:11), but Samson did not take the [Philistines'] wives and give them to other men; he only gave them what they deserved. Ben Zuta replied: But if the one who struck the other is poor, what should his punishment be [i.e., how can he pay compensation]? The Gaʾon replied: If a blind person blinds a person who sees, what should be done to him? The poor man may perhaps become rich and [then] pay, but the blind man will never be able to pay [with his sight]. The general principle [*kelal*] is: we cannot properly interpret the commandments of the Torah if we do not rely on the words of the rabbis. . . . For as we have received the Torah from our ancestors, so have we received the oral Torah, and there is no difference between them.

These arguments are later summarized by Ibn Ezra, in his commentary to Leviticus 24:19 (referred to in his argument here), where he observes: "The Gaʾon brought proofs based on reason" [*shiqqul ha-daʿat*].

It should be noted here that Ibn Ezra's contemporary and friend, Judah Ha-Levi, whose views he cites in his commentaries, similarly cited Leviticus 24:18–20 to prove that Exodus 21:24 must mean compensation, not physical retaliation; that this proves the need for tradition [*al-taqdir; qabbalah*]; and that "reason contradicts"[45] reading the text literally as the Karaites do. Ha-Levi's rationalist claim here need not surprise us. Ha-Levi was certainly a sharp critic of the Aristotelian rationalism of the day (actually, in his view it was pseudorationalism, and he harshly criticized some of its basic features such as the theory of emanation, not on religious grounds but as bad philosophy), and he certainly clearly denied the rationalist explanation of the phenomenon of prophetic revelation as a function of reason. Nevertheless, although revelation itself is not a function of reason but of a special prophetic faculty transcending reason, there is nothing in revelation that can contradict reason.[46]

Philosophic exegetes such as Saʿadiah Gaʾon and Ibn Ezra (and, in his own way, to some extent also Judah Ha-Levi) differ from the nonphilosophic exegetes in their insistence that it is the very rationality of Scripture that precludes taking the text literally here: "Reason cannot tolerate this." For Ha-Levi, as we have seen, revelation itself is nonrational, but it can never contradict reason. For rationalists like Saʿadiah and Ibn Ezra, revelation is itself fundamentally a rational process. In either case, reason is so fundamental to the truth of revealed Scripture that any text that, when taken at face value, contradicts reason cannot in fact truly mean what it appears to say, and must then be taken figuratively. It is reason, then, that ensures the integrity of proper exegetical method, safeguarding against the errors of Rabbanite and Karaite Jews, as well as Christians, who either took the text too literally or not literally enough.

Astrology as a Rationalist and Naturalist Cosmology

One of the most curious features of Ibn Ezra's thought in general, and of his Bible commentaries in particular, is his resorting to astrological explanations of various scriptural phenomena, such as the *terafim* (Genesis 31:19, 1 Samuel 19:13). Such astrological interest, at first glance, strikes us as peculiar for a person committed to a rationalist and scientific approach to life, and for whom revelation must be understood fundamentally in rational terms.

Upon reflection, however, one can understand Ibn Ezra's interest in astrological interpretation of Scripture as consistent with such a rationalist and scientific approach. Recent studies by Tzvi Langermann and Gad Freudenthal[47] have attempted to understand how astrology represented, for such diverse medieval thinkers as Ibn Ezra and Ralbag (Gersonides), a naturalist cosmology.

Ibn Ezra's interest in astrology was not limited to the purely "theoretical" level but extended to "practical" astrology as well. He may have translated into Hebrew Arabic manuals of practical astrology. Ralbag, on the other hand, while not precluding the possibility of practical astrology, did not relate to it directly.

In the case of Ibn Ezra, astrology constitutes a consistent element within a larger Neoplatonic cosmological structure, which he outlines, inter alia, in his commentary to Exodus 3:15 and 6:3. Below God, the absolute One, are three realms. The highest of these is the supreme realm *(ʿolam ʿelyon),* the realm of the angels that resembles the human rational soul *(neshamah).* Below this is the intermediate realm *(ʿolam ʾemẓaʿi),* the incorruptible stars and planets. The third and lowest realm is the terrestrial, sublunar realm, consisting of minerals, plants, animals, and humans. Astrology, then, involves understanding the influences of the higher realms on the lower, particularly on human affairs. However, and this is critical for Ibn Ezra as a faithful Jew, it is absolutely out of the question to worship the stars, which are "servants" *(meshartim)* possessing no independent will or conscious purpose, and whose activity is purely automatic and necessary.[48]

Astrology, for Ibn Ezra, is therefore not magic or theurgy, and he argues against a magical or theurgic interpretation of the *saraf* in Numbers 21:8. Astrology is, rather, a way of understanding how various components of natural reality influence each other, and thus represents a scientific or rational cosmology. Accordingly, Ibn Ezra's astrological interpretations are an attempt to provide appropriate scientific explanations of peculiar phenomena alluded to in Scripture.

Astral influence, however, is not merely a function of the arrangement or constellation *(maʿarekhet)* of the higher power *(koʾaḥ ʿelyon).* The influence of the higher power is affected by the receiver *(meqabbel)* below, in light of what Ibn Ezra calls its *toledet,* its constituent makeup or physical constitution. As Ibn Ezra explains in his introduction to Kohelet (Ecclesiastes), in the scheme of emanation, one agent can produce one effect, but these effects can differ because of the differences among the receivers. The differences among the receivers, in turn, also reflect differences in the constellation of the astral agents influencing them.[49]

Despite the obvious deterministic implications of such an astrological scheme, Ibn Ezra does affirm an element of free will. Free will can be limited, as when Pharaoh's heart was "hardened," in the sense that "individuals receive from the universals according to their constitution [*toledet*], and because of the power of the universals they can change their constitution a bit."[50] In general, the effects of the stars cannot be changed. But it is precisely their predetermined predictability that provides an element of free will, since the person who knows of a certain effect can take steps to avoid it: for example, if you know that the train is scheduled to come at a certain hour, you have the ability to clear the track. As Tzvi Langermann has put it:

> It is quite clear to me that the salvation from astral decrees which is available to man refers, in Ibn Ezra's view, to man's ability to foresee impending disaster, usually by the science of astrology, and to take the appropriate precautionary measures. . . . To this extent, only, can man utilize his potential access to a superior power (viz. his intellect).[51]

Within this general scheme, however, there is an important exceptional feature. Picking up on the talmudic phrase that "Israel has no constellar sign" *(ein mazal le-yisra'el),*[52] Ibn Ezra states: "It is well established that every nation has a known star and constellation, and that there is a constellation for every city. But God gave Israel a great superiority by his, rather than a star's, being their guide, for Israel is God's portion."[53]

Tzvi Langermann explains this as follows:

> The Deity has delegated to the stars the governance of the sublunar world. Israel, however, has a special status, which is manifest most decisively in its possession of the Torah. As long as a Jew is engaged in the study and observance of the Torah, he is linked to a spiritual realm which is itself superior to the stars. In this way, a Jew may liberate himself from the decrees of the stars.[54]

Israel is thus ruled directly by God, and not by any astral intermediaries, and the Torah provides a way for the Jew to escape general astral influence. Israel's unique status is not, however, a function of any special physical or biological faculty, as suggested by Judah Ha-Levi's theory of a Jewish genetic faculty for divine communication, the *'amr 'ilahi ('inyan 'elohi).* Such a physical faculty would be, for Ibn Ezra, a necessary component of one's physical constitution *(toledet),* and would then necessarily be subject to astral influence. It is only by living according to the Torah's teachings that Israel is exempted or saved from astral influence; without the Torah, there is no difference between Jew and non-Jew.

Ibn Ezra and Ha-Levi thus present us with opposite interpretations of Jewish distinctiveness. For Ha-Levi, it is the genetic distinctiveness of the people of Israel that makes possible the revelation of the Torah to them. For Ibn Ezra, it is the divinely revealed Torah that makes possible the existence of the people of Israel as a special group, governed directly by God's law rather than indirectly through a system of astral influences.

In both cases, the interpretations of Jewish distinctiveness are attempts at a scientific explanation of an observed historic anomaly, Jewish survival and distinctiveness. In the case of Ha-Levi, that historic anomaly is explained in terms of a unique physiological or biological faculty, transmitted genetically, and as such, the phenomenon of a distinctive Jewish faculty is no more remarkable than is the phenomenon of a distinctively human faculty—reason—among all the animal kingdom.[55]

For Ibn Ezra, the explanation is equally scientific, and by no means involves any magical or miraculous considerations. The Torah, even more than the science of astrology, provides its adherents with insights into the natural structure of reality, thus enabling the person who follows it to take necessary precautions and to avoid harm. Indeed, the power of the Torah is superior to that of astrology, and thus provides a mechanism for transcending astral influence.

In his commentary to Exodus 33:21, in which he cautions against worshiping the stars as ineffectual, Ibn Ezra says:

> The servants [i.e., the stars] cannot change their path, and the subservience of each of them is the rule given it by God. . . . Worshiping the works of the heavens cannot be beneficial for [a person], for whatever was decreed for him according to the constellation of the stars at his birth will happen to him, unless a power superior to the power of the stars protects him, and he cleaves to it, so that he will then be saved from the decrees.

Ibn Ezra then continues to tell the story, which he calls an "important parable" *(mashal ḥashuv)* of people being saved from astral decrees, when a prophet warned them of an impending flood. The flood was astrologically predictable. The people, however, because they followed the prophet out of the city to pray to God, were saved from the flood.

This view of astrology, which affirms a prophetic power superior to that of the stars and thus enables at least certain people to escape astral influences, may also be found in the *Letters of the Pure Brethren (Rasaʾil ʾIkhwan al-Ṣafaʾ),* as is the story of the people of a city being saved from a flood.[56] There is an important difference, however: in Ibn Ezra's version, the people are warned by a prophet, whereas in the version of the Pure Brethren, the king of the city was warned by his astrologer *(munajjim).*

Nevertheless, the structure is similar: God, whose power transcends that of the stars, can enable people to escape the otherwise inevitable influences of the stars by making available advance knowledge of the inevitable.

As described in these *Letters:*

> It is possible to take precautions and safeguards against such misfortunes . . . For the astral signs and the indications of divination serve solely to inform us in advance of the events which the Lord of the stars . . . will accomplish. Help is to be sought in the Lord of the stars, the Power beyond the spheres, beyond the stars. . . . What is known to be inevitable must inevitably take place. But God may avert from its victims an evil which is about to occur or transform it to a good or a benefit. . . . Then the usefulness is established of knowledge of the stars and of foreknowledge of events and the means by which precautions may be taken against them and their evil effects may be averted, or by which it may be sought to alter their outcome to yield good and beneficial effects.[57]

In some respects (although obviously without the astrological component), Ibn Ezra's theory bears at least a formal resemblance to Rambam's theory of providence in the *Guide of the Perplexed* 3:17 and especially 3:51. For Rambam, providence functions intellectually, by attaching in the sublunar world only to species, except for human individuals to whom it attaches in proportion to their intellectual development. The similarity with Ibn Ezra consists, then, of humans being able, by virtue of knowledge, to escape what happens to animals (which, for Ibn Ezra, is astrally determined, whereas for Rambam it is by chance), and thereby to be saved from harm.[58]

Given Ibn Ezra's Neoplatonic cosmology in which higher powers exert influence on lower realms, his astrological interest can be seen as a rational or scientific interpretation of reality. In his view, direct divine intervention, superseding the inferior influences of the stars, is understood not magically or theurgically, but naturalistically, in terms of a knowledgeable person's ability to take advantage of predictable phenomena by employing the necessary measures to avoid evil effects. The Torah, which in any event should be interpreted, wherever appropriate, in light of science, certainly needs to be elucidated wherever it touches on astrology, because the Torah provides a divine guidance for the people of Israel. The Jews are thus assured of direct divine protection, through advance knowledge, from the otherwise inevitable effects of the stars. A scientific and rational Bible exegesis, accordingly, needs to involve astrological considerations: the Jews need to know the effects of the stars, if only to escape those effects through Torah.

Exegesis and *Weltanschauung*

Ibn Ezra brings to the biblical text a hidden, or not so hidden, rationalist agenda as an exegete. One of the fascinating benefits of studying and teaching exegesis is developing an appreciation of the correlation between the commentators' exegetical approaches and their underlying ideological premises.

Good literature often admits of diverse levels of meaning, and this is certainly the case with biblical literature. A diversity of exegetical approaches to a given passage may bring out differing dimensions of meaning in the text itself, as in the oft-cited statement of the rabbis, "the Torah has seventy faces," and "the words of Torah are like a hammer breaking a rock, dividing into several meanings."[59]

On the other hand, diverse exegetical approaches may teach us as much or more about the interests and underlying ideological premises of the exegetes than they do about the text. When teaching Jewish Bible exegesis, I often ask my students to attempt the following exercise. Study a favorite biblical passage, and list the questions that we today ask about this passage; then study the classical Jewish exegesis of this passage, and compare the questions that concerned the rabbis and medieval commentators with the questions that concern us. When we compare their questions with ours, what do the differences teach us about the text in question, and what do the differences teach us about their and our respective interests, concerns, and commitments?

In the case of philosophic exegesis, it seems to me that this question becomes all the more significant. As I stated at the outset, philosophic Bible exegesis is, at the same time, a way of understanding or analyzing Scripture philosophically and a way of reconciling the differing approaches of "faith and reason."

Therefore, when philosophical exegetes provide diverse interpretations of a given scriptural passage, they may simply be reflecting different insights into the meaning of the text. Or (and this may often be the case, especially in passages that somehow relate to or touch on issues of philosophic significance), their differing interpretations may both reflect, and be necessitated by, radically different ideological or philosophical positions. The exegesis can, then, provide us with interesting and valuable insight into the consistent philosophical scheme (if not system) of the commentator.

Approached in this way, a philosopher's Bible exegesis can be seen as a consistent and necessary extension of his or her philosophic structure. Exegesis can thus shed further light on the person's philosophy, and proves to be a philosophic literary genre. By its very nature, exegesis cannot be a systematic method of philosophizing; it is shaped by the text it follows. The text provides the occasion and subject of the philosophizing and for working out a consistent philosophic stance.

I should like to provide one specific example of how philosophic

Bible exegesis can, at the same time, shed interesting light on the meaning of the text while furnishing the occasion for a philosopher to restate his or her ideological priorities, by contrasting the treatment of the opening line of the Decalogue, "I am the Lord your God who brought you out of the land of Egypt" (Exodus 20:2 and Deuteronomy 5:6), in the commentaries of Ibn Ezra and Mendelssohn.

Zev Harvey has discussed the different approaches of Ibn Ezra and Judah Ha-Levi to this passage.[60] I should like to add to Harvey's excellent treatment of the subject, by contrasting Ibn Ezra's interpretation with that of Mendelssohn (who was, in so many ways, deeply influenced by Ha-Levi's philosophy),[61] and by presenting those interpretations as consistent extensions and necessary components of a philosophic *Weltanschauung*.

What are the cognitive status and philosophic implications of "I am the Lord your God . . ."?

For Judah Ha-Levi, historical truth is superior to and more certain than metaphysical speculation. The personal "God of Abraham," who is the object of human love, is known historically by his public (and therefore undeniable) and miraculous involvement in the life of the people of Israel, whereas the impersonal "God of Aristotle," which at best is the object of rational speculative knowledge, has no relation to human life and existential concerns. Revelation is, for Ha-Levi, an indisputable historic event, and as such cannot possibly be reduced to some kind of impersonal process of emanation. Indeed, there is no clearer or more bitingly sharp critique of the theory of emanation (on rational, not religious, grounds) in the Jewish philosophy of this period than Ha-Levi's in the *Kuzari*. The theory of emanation is wrong not because it conflicts with revealed religion but because it is bad philosophy, and has no scientific validity.[62]

In Ha-Levi's interpretation (as cited by Ibn Ezra), God identifies Himself to the people in terms of the Exodus, a certain and undeniable fact of their national historical experience. In the same way, at the beginning of the dialogue of the King of the Khazars and the Jew (*Kuzari* 1:10–25), Ha-Levi has the king question why the Jew defines his belief in historical terms of God as the redeemer of the people, rather than in natural terms as the creator and ruler of the world. Ha-Levi's Jew explains that a religion that understands God in such natural terms is based on dubious rational speculation, whereas when God is identified in historical terms (such as in the opening of the Decalogue), the claim is undeniable and certain, because it is based on empirical fact or on "tradition [*tawatur; qabba-*

lah] which is like empirical fact" in terms of reliability and certainty.[63]

Ibn Ezra, on the other hand, regarded the historical reference here as essentially a concession to the primitive level of understanding of the Israelites who had just recently been brought out of Egyptian bondage. These common people had no way to know God scientifically, through the study of nature. The Torah therefore had to refer to their immediate historic experience, since the Torah was addressed to the entire nation: "In my opinion, the Torah was given to all, and not just to one person alone."[64] A more certain and a truer conception of God (for which the people were not yet ready) would have to be expressed in terms of the Neoplatonic structure of natural reality, and for Ibn Ezra, as we know, this structure of emanation entails astrological components. He therefore brings astrological considerations into his discussion of our passage.

The influences of the stars were such that Israel should have continued as slaves. However, Israel has, in the Torah, a power superior to that of the stars, and a direct relation to God, who, out of His love for and convenantal commitments to the Israelites' patriarchal ancestors, miraculously superseded the astral decrees. For Ibn Ezra, "I am the Lord your God . . ." means that God can be known only by His actions, that is, His influences in the world, which only Israel acknowledges. In other words, only Israel understands that the stars are mere servants *(meshartim)*, and thus only Israel has a true understanding of astrology, in which the stars have no independent power or will of their own. "I am the Lord" is a rational truth that only Israel affirms; "who brought you out of Egypt . . ." is but a concession to the primitive level of the Israelites who could not possibly be expected to understand the true scientific (including astrological) meaning of "I am the Lord your God."

The differences between Ha-Levi and Ibn Ezra on the meaning of "I am the Lord your God who brought you out of the land of Egypt" are thus not merely exegetical. They reflect fundamentally opposing philosophical views of God and the world, according to which revelation must consistently be seen either as a historical process transcending mere reason or as a natural, rational process consistent with a Neoplatonic theory of emanation and astral influence.

Mendelssohn approaches our passage in the consistent light of his own philosophic *Weltanschauung*. He shares with Ha-Levi a fundamental respect for historic truth as the basis for revelation. Rational and scientific truth is inherently universal and does not provide any basis for Jewish distinctiveness. Indeed, "natural religion" consists entirely and exclusively of rationally demonstrable truths, and is therefore the universal basis of all true religions, including, but not limited to, Jewish religion. A particular revelation is affirmed as a historical fact, not as a rational truth. Revelation itself, being historically conditioned and limited to a particular people at a particular time and place, cannot convey the truth, which must be universally accessible to all humans through reason. What is conveyed in revelation is law, not truth, and "revealed religion" (in the sense of the truths of natural religion) is a contradiction in terms.

That being the case for Mendelssohn, "I am the Lord your God . . ." cannot be construed as a commandment at all, but rather as the historical preamble or preface to the subsequent commandments. It reiterates the historical truth upon which the legal injunctions are founded: because I am the God who brought you out of Egypt (a historic fact of the people's experience), therefore you should have no other gods in My presence, you should make no images, and so forth. It is, in short, the foundation of the other commandments, not one of them.

Ibn Ezra had interpreted "I am the Lord your God" as a rational truth and, therefore, like Rambam after him, had posited it as the most fundamental of all the commandments. There are, Ibn Ezra argues, commandments of the mouth and hands (i.e., speech and actions), but most fundamental of all is the commandment of the heart, that is, to know the truth about God, which is at once the *arche* and *telos* of all the other commandments. Mendelssohn, while obviously agreeing that belief in God is a rational truth fundamental to all other religious affirmation and behavior, could not possibly construe it as a commandment. To do so would have been to confuse rational truth, which must be universal, with the content of a particular revelation, which can only govern behavior, not convictions.

According to Mendelssohn's interpretation, in purely syntactical terms, this verse, unlike the subsequent verses of the Decalogue, contains no imperative verb, but is merely a descriptive historical statement. Moreover, as Mendelssohn later developed his political philosophy and philosophy of Judaism in *Jerusalem,* belief admits of no command or coercion, whether human or divine. One can only coerce a person's external behavior. The inner convictions of the heart are subject and responsive only to persuasion, not to coercion. To command belief in God, even in divine revelation, is, therefore, again, a contradiction in terms. One of Mendelssohn's explicit aims in *Jerusalem* was to provide a theoretical philosophic framework separating religious law from coercive political power. To suggest that human convictions are subject to command, even if only divine command, is to misconstrue the very nature of both rational truth and revelation, and is, furthermore, to open a dangerous breach in the absolute barrier between religion, which must be free, and the legitimate but coercive political power of the state. It thus involves not only theoretical error but an immediate and practical danger to enlightened society.

Conclusion

The interfacing of Scripture and philosophy in Bible exegesis enhances our understanding and appreciation of both. It enables us to see a pre-or nonphilosophic body of literature in light of philosophic insights and provides an occasion for and challenge to further philosophizing.

Despite all the difficulties in teaching Jewish philosophical Bible exegesis because of language, literary references, and modes of thought and expression with which students may not be familiar, it remains an important, and as yet insufficiently explored, philosophic literary genre.

Notes

Unless otherwise identified, all translations from the Hebrew are by the author.

1. Cf. Daniel J. Lasker, *Jewish Philosophical Polemics against Christianity in the Middle Ages* (New York: Ktav, 1977), p. 34, and "Averroistic Trends in Jewish-Christian Polemics in the Late Middle Ages," *Speculum* 55, no. 2 (1980): 294–304. Also cf. Lasker's Hebrew introduction to his edition of Ḥasdai Crescas, *Bittul Iqqarei Ha-Noẓerim* (Ramat Gan and Beer Sheva: Bar Ilan, 1990), p. 16, and the foreword to his English version, *The Refutation of the Christian Principles by Hasdai Crescas* (Albany: SUNY Press, 1992), pp. 5–6.

2. Harry Austryn Wolfson, *Philo: Foundations of Religious Philosophy in Judaism, Christianity and Islam* (Cambridge, Mass.: Harvard University Press, 1947), 1:103. The title of the Hebrew translation of Wolfson's monumental study was revised to read: *Philo: Foundations of Jewish Religious Philosophy* (Jerusalem: Mosad Harav Kook, 1970). This is, of course, a clear distortion of Wolfson's classic view of Philo as the archetypal religious philosopher for Judaism, Christianity, and Islam, and not merely the first "Jewish philosopher."

3. Ibid. (1947), 2:447.

4. The edition of the *ʾOr La-Netivah* and the *Beʾur* (Berlin, 1783) cited here is that of Prague, 1836. On Mendelssohn's exegetical activity, see Alexander Altmann, *Moses Mendelssohn: A Biographical Study* (Tuscaloosa: University of Alabama Press, 1973), ch. 5. Mendelssohn discusses his project in *ʾOr La-Netivah*, pp. 12b–14b, where he explains that he wrote the commentary on the first portion *(parashah)* of Genesis, whereas the rest of the commentary to Genesis was written by Dubno, with parenthetical notes by Mendelssohn. The commentary to Exodus was written by Mendelssohn, with parenthetical notes by Dubno. Hertz Weisel wrote the commentary to Leviticus, with parenthetical notes by Mendelssohn. The commentaries to Numbers and Deuteronomy were written by Mendelssohn, with the assistance of others who wished to remain anonymous.

5. Cf. my discussion of these views in "The Superiority of Oral over Written Communication: Judah Ha-Levi's *Kuzari* and Modern Jewish Thought," in *From Ancient Israel to Modern Judaism: Essays in Honor of Marvin Fox,* ed. J. Neusner, E. Frerichs, and N. Sarna, Brown Judaic Studies no. 174 (Atlanta: Scholars' Press, 1989), 3:127–56.

6. Cf. Altmann, *Moses Mendelssohn,* pp. 368–69. Mendelssohn's dedication of this work to his children for their education is reminiscent of what the author of the medieval *Sefer Ha-Ḥinukh* wrote. The latter expressed the hope, regarding his explanation of the 613 commandments, following the order of their presentation in the Torah, that "the youth may be aroused by them, and pay attention to them on Sabbaths and festivals, and turn away from going crazy in the city streets" (*Sefer Ha-Hinukh,* C. D. Chavel ed. [Jerusalem: Mosad Harav Kook, 1972], introduction, p. 29). In his discussion of commandment no. 397, the red heifer, the author states: "Although my heart urged me to write allusions to the purposes of the commandments . . . with the apology that the task is thereby to educate my son and his youthful friends, may God protect them" (pp. 503–4).

7. Altmann, *Moses Mendelssohn,* pp. 374–76.

8. On the question of Spinoza's influence on Mendelssohn, in addition to various references in Altmann's *Mendelssohn,* see Julius Guttmann, "Mendelssohn's *Jerusalem* und Spinoza's Theologisch-Politisch Traktat," *Achtundvierzigster Bericht der Hochschule für die Wissenschaft des Judentums* (Berlin, 1931) pp. 36–37; "Yerushalayim shel Mendelssohn veha-masekhet ha-teologit ha-medinit le-Spinoza," in *Dat u-Mada,* by Julius Guttmann (Jerusalem: Magnes, 1955), pp. 192–217; "Mendelssohn's *Jerusalem* and Spinoza's *Theologico-Political Treatise,*" in *Studies in Jewish Thought: An Anthology of German-Jewish Scholarship,* ed. Alfred Jospe (Detroit: Wayne State University Press, 1981), pp. 361–86.

9. Cf. R. Elwes, *The Chief Works of Benedict de Spinoza* (New York: Dover, 1951), 1:120–21.

10. Cf. Leo Strauss, *Persecution and the Art of Writing* (Glencoe, Ill.: Free Press, 1952).

11. Nahum Sarna, "Hebrew Bible Studies in Medieval Spain," in *The Sephardi Heritage,* (London: Valentine, Mitchel, n.d.), pp. 349–50. Cf. the article on Ibn Ezra by Tovia Preschel, in *Encyclopaedia Judaica* (1972) 8:1167: "Very characteristic of Ibn Ezra's thought are his mostly veiled suggestions which tend to cast doubt on the belief that the Pentateuch as we have it was written by Moses, and which have given him the title of the father of biblical criticism. Often he does not spell out these interpretations, contenting himself with a mere allusion."

12. Uriel Simon, "Tanakh: Parshanut," in *Encyclopaedia Biblica* (Jerusalem: Mosad Bialik, 1982) 8:677–80.

> Text criticism occupied Ibn Ezra only a little. He . . . needed utter certainty regarding the trustworthiness of the text and the reliability of the method as a counterbalance to his excessively free interpretation and his critical approach to the question of the identity of the authors of the books of the Bible. The problem of anachronisms troubled him greatly, and it was only with great difficulty that he was prepared to assume that prophecy is able to call a person or a place by a later name. . . . What motivated Ibn Ezra in determining the temporal background of things was exegetical-literary: the question which bothered him most was whether it is reasonable for Moses and Isaiah to have written such things, and not (as modern scholarship asks today) whether such things would have been meaningful to people in their day.

In another study, "Ibn Ezra between Medievalism and Modernism: The Case of Isaiah XL–LXVI," *Vetus Testamentum* 36 (n.d.): 257–71, Simon argues that Ibn Ezra

> was the first to attribute the second part of the book of Isaiah to an anonymous prophet who began to prophesy in Babylon on the eve of the Persian conquest. The veiled, enigmatic language in which Ibn Ezra hints at this is evidence of the magnitude of the innovation which this position represented. . . . While medieval philological exegesis was guided by the principle that "The Tora speaks the language of men," modern philological-historical interpretation is guided by the fundamental assumption that Sacred Scripture speaks in the language and ideas of men of a specific time. . . . as purposeful speech every biblical text must have been intelligible to its audience and tuned to its needs, problems, and longings. It is thus inconceivable that prophecy should have been either incomprehensible to its original audience or meaningless for it. (pp. 257–58)

13. Uriel Simon, "Ibn Ezra ve-Radaq—Shetei gishot li-she'elat mehemanut nusaḥ ha-Miqra'," *Bar Ilan Annual* 6 (1968): 191–237.

> A critical approach to the reliability of the text [i.e., "lower criticism"], like that of Radak, goes hand in hand with an absence of literary-historic criticism [i.e., "higher criticism"], and that "higher criticism," in the way taken by Ibn Ezra, is likely to be bound to the negation of "lower criticism." (p. 191)

> Ibn Ezra's freedom of thought required a counterbalance in the form of complete certitude in the reliability of the text and the authority of the method. . . . While Radak's innocent faith permitted him to question the reliability of the text, Ibn Ezra refrained from this, out of his concern that the rational foundations of his faith not be undermined. (pp. 235–36)

14. Michael Friedlaender, *Essays on the Writings of Abraham ibn Ezra* (London, 1877), pp. 60–67.

> Who wrote these books? This question he generally answers in accordance with tradition. . . . He is strongly opposed to the theory of later interpolations. . . . This censure would be very strange, and even most unwise, if he himself had been guilty of the same offense; and yet imputations of this kind are occasionally levelled against him in some of the super-commentaries, also in the works of Spinoza, whose charges were repeated *bona fide* by many historians and literati. Not that Ibn Ezra is accused of having *uttered* anything of the kind; he is simply charged with holding such an opinion. . . . It is surprising, indeed, how a charge of this nature could be made against Ibn Ezra without better evidence: "he did not state his heretical opinion openly, because he was afraid." But he utters, without the least fear, a great many things which must have displeased his contemporaries—the orthodox as well as the rationalists, the Rabbanites as well as the Karaites! . . . The phrase *yesh lo sod* [it has a secret meaning] has in no part of Ibn Ezra's writings the alleged sense; it never refers to critical researches about the correctness of the text or about the author of the book; it always indicates some philosophical theory which Ibn Ezra believes to be hidden in the Biblical text. . . . Ibn Ezra firmly believed that the Pentateuch, with the exception of the last few verses, was the same as written by Moses, without any alteration or addition.

15. Ibid., p. 67. As we shall see, Friedlaender borrows many of the arguments advanced before him by Shadal in his commentary to the Torah. Although he does mention Shadal on p. 61 n. 4, he does not cite Shadal's commentary here nor does he give him credit for many of his arguments.

16. Amos Funkenstein, *Signonot be-farshanut ha-Miqra' bi-yemei ha-beinayim* (Tel Aviv: Ministry of Defense, 1990), p. 33.

17. Shadal, *Commentary on the Pentateuch,* Deuteronomy 1:2, ed. Pinhas Schlesinger (Tel Aviv: Dvir, 1965), pp. 507–509 (Hebrew).

As is well known, this is one of the passages about which some of those who pretend to be wise *(mithakmim)* say that Moses did not write them, but that they were added to the Torah some generations later. Since they did not understand its subject, they said that it was added. We must still ask what was the intention of the one who added it; what did he think he was adding? After the Israelites came into the Land, why should we care about knowing how many days it took a person to walk from Ḥorev to Kadesh Barneʿa by the way of Mount Seʿir? Since in this generation Spinoza's books have already been distributed throughout the world and have been translated into German and French, and since praises of that man have already been written in the Holy Tongue and the readers of his books have increased even among the Jews and among the common people, I must inform that Spinoza wrote deceit and falsehood at the beginning of the eighth chapter of his book *Tractatus Theologico-Politicus,* where he said that Ibn Ezra hinted that Moses did not write the book of the Torah. It is true that Ibn Ezra hinted in a secret manner *(ramaz be-derekh sod)* [here and in Genesis 12:6 and 22:14] that there are some passages that were added to the Torah after the death of Moses. But nothing in his words and in all his hints supports thinking that he did not believe that Moses wrote his book. When [Ibn Ezra] said here, "If you understand the secret of the twelve etc., . . . you will know the truth," means that (in his view) specifically only these passages were added, not that the book as a whole was forged. If he [thought] in his heart that Moses did not write the whole book, Ibn Ezra did not lack stratagems *(tahbulot)* for giving us hint of his true thought, without hinting at some other secret which was not his true thought, and which (if the masses in his day understood him) would also have been a great abomination, no less than the different thought that Spinoza attributed to him. He said about "the Canaanite was then in the land" (Genesis 12:6): "It is possible that Canaan seized the land of Canaan from someone else. If this does not mean that, it has a secret meaning, and the intelligent should keep silent." It is dubious whether this verse was written by Moses. What is the need for all of this, if the whole Torah was not written by Moses? Everyone knows that when Ibn Ezra wrote "if you understand the secret of the twelve" he meant the last twelve verses of the Torah, which include the story of the death of Moses, and which could not reasonably have been written by [Moses] himself. Spinoza also knew this, but made himself as one who does not know, by saying that Ibn Ezra meant [not the last twelve verses of the Torah but the twelve stones], when he wrote on Deuteronomy 27:8 ("Write all the words of this Torah on the stones"), stones which according to the rabbis were twelve (Sotah 32b). [Spinoza] understood this to mean that the book of the Torah which Moses wrote was a very small book, which could have been written on twelve stones. But [if, as Spinoza suggests, Ibn Ezra meant here the twelve stones rather than the last twelve verses], where do we find Ibn Ezra ever relying so much on *haggadah* (rabbinic lore), that he might mention "the twelve" without the word "stones," if he meant the stones which, according to the *haggadah,* were twelve? Spinoza himself saw how unlikely this was to have been Ibn Ezra's intention, and therefore he added a second interpretation, which is that perhaps [Ibn Ezra's] intention was to the twelve curses (Deuteronomy 27:15). Finally, [Spinoza] cited the correct interpretation, which is that [the twelve] means [the last verses beginning with] "Moses went up," as the author of the *Meqor Ḥayyim* and Motot understood. All of this was a stratagem of Spinoza, to attract Ibn Ezra to his fortress and to make the ignorant think that Ibn Ezra also believed that Moses only wrote a very small book of the Torah, which could have been written on twelve stones. If Ibn Ezra thought that Moses only wrote a small book, [capable of being] written on twelve stones, he should have hinted at this secret in the portion dealing with the commandment to write on the stones. But he wrote to the contrary (Deuteronomy 27:1), as follows: "[Saʿadiah] Gaʾon said that they wrote on [the stones] some of the book of the commandments, as have been written in the *Halakhot Gedolot* Code, in the manner of the *azharot,* and he [i.e., Saʿadiah] was correct." He did not hint here at any secret. Ultimately, only God knows what is in a person's heart, but in everything that Ibn Ezra wrote, there is no hint that he did not believe that Moses wrote our book of the Torah. . . . Spinoza also erred regarding Ibn Ezra's words on this verse by attributing to Ibn Ezra something he never thought, and I shall not judge whether this was by mistake or by deceit, but I also have seen that the sage Motot erred in this, and perhaps Spinoza learned it from him.

On the *Halakhot Gedolot,* an early systematic and comprehensive summary of talmudic laws from the Geonic period, cf. *Encyclopaedia Judaica* (1972) 7:1167–70. On *azharot*—liturgical poems for Shavuᶜot, the Festival of Weeks, enumerating the 613 commandments—see *Encyclopaedia Judaica* 3:1007–8. Saᶜadiah Ga'on composed and included two such poems in his pioneering edition of the *Siddur* (Prayer Book). According to Shadal here, Ibn Ezra agrees with Saᶜadiah that what was written on the twelve stones was a summary of the commandments, not the whole Torah.

18. On Motot, see *Encyclopaedia Judaica* (1972) 8:1189–90.

19. On Ẓarẓa, see *Encyclopaedia Judaica* (1972) 16:939, and Dov Schwartz, "Mishnato ha-pilosofit-datit shel Rabbi Samuel ibn Ẓarẓa" (Ph.D., diss. Bar Ilan University, 1989), esp. pp. 165–67. Also cf. the discussions of Ẓarẓa in Raphael Jospe, *Torah and Sophia: The Life and Thought of Shem Tov ibn Falaquera* (Cincinnati: HUC—JIR, 1988), Appendix E; and "Ha-even veha-seneh," *Cathedra* 48 (June 1988): 3–8; and "The Rock and the Bush," *Judaism* 38, no. 2, issue 150 (spring 1989): 197–202. Also cf. Raphael Jospe and Dov Schwartz, "Shem Tov ibn Falaquera's Lost Bible Commentary, in *Hebrew Union College Annual* 64 (1993): 167–200. According to Ẓarẓa on Deuteronomy 1:7:

"If you understand the secret of the twelve, etc." . . . Some say that according to the opinion of the Sage, Joshua wrote from "Moses went up" on, as the Sage said in [his commentary on] the portion *Zot ha-berakhah* (Deut. 33:1) on the verse "Moses went up." However, in truth the Sage did not think this. Rather, all of these [verses] were told to Moses prophetically, and he wrote them down accordingly. Also, regarding what the Sage said about "Moses wrote" (Deuteronomy 31:9) . . . , his view was that this was also [said] prophetically. Also "on the mountain the Lord will be seen," for the Temple did not yet exist, so [God] said that His presence would be there. Also "his bed is an iron bed" (Deuteronomy 3:11) means what he said in this portion, that "his bed is an iron bed; is it not in Rabbat of the children of Amon?" for in truth they did not take it to Rabbat of the children of Amon until the time of Yo'av ben Ẓeruyah. Rather, [Moses] must have written all of this prophetically. And as for what he said about "the Canaanite was then in the land" (Genesis 12:6), I have already written in the portion *Lekh lekha* (Genesis 12:1) on this verse.

20. Cf. Simon, "Ibn Ezra between Medievalism and Modernism", p. 266.

21. Cf., for example, Talmud Pesaḥim 6b, and Rashi's explanation that "the Torah is not meticulous regarding the order of earlier and later, and it brings later portions before those which were said at first." Also, cf. Rashi and Ramban on Numbers 9:1, as well as the treatment of Genesis 11:26–32 by various commentators, including Ibn Ezra, and his reference there to the chronological problems in Numbers 1:1 and Exodus 40:17.

22. Cf. Guttmann, "Yerushalayim shel Mendelssohn veha-masekhet ha-te'ologit ha-medinit le-Spinoza," cited above, n. 8.

23. See the previous discussion of Mendelssohn's explicit traditionalist aims. According to Altmann, this traditionalism even led Mendelssohn to publish the German translation of the Bible—a translation intended to teach "a pure a refined German"—in Hebrew characters.

24. Cf. "Ibn Yashush, Isaac Ibrahim," in *Encyclopaedia Judaica* (1972) 8:1211. Ibn Yashush (Toledo, ca. 982–1057) was a Hebrew grammarian and Bible commentator, and court physician to the ruler of Denia: "Ibn Yashush wrote a Bible com-

mentary named Yizhaki, in which the method of investigation came very close to that of modern Bible criticism." Cf. the reference to Ibn Yashush in my article "Early Philosophical Commentaries on the *Sefer Yezirah:* Some Comments," *Revue des etudes juives* 149, no. 4 (October–December 1990): 388. Judah Leib Krinsky, in his supercommentary on Ibn Ezra, *Meḥoqeqei Yehudah,* 1:47 n. 8 (reprinted Jerusalem, 1961), notes that Ibn Ezra elsewhere cites Isaac positively as "a great Spanish commentator." Cf. n. 28. Uriel Simon rejects this identification of Ibn Ezra's "Yizḥaqi" whose lost commentary seems to have been written in Hebrew, with the linguist Isaac ibn Yashush, in whose time commentaries and grammar were often written in Arabic. Cf. Simon, "Parshanut Ha-Miqra ʿal Derekh Ha-Peshat—Ha-Askolah Ha-Sefaradit," in *Moreshet Sefarad,* ed. Haim Beinart (Jerusalem: Magnes Press, 1992), p. 97.

25. Uriel Simon, "Ibn Ezra's Harsh Language and Biting Humor: Real Denunciation of Hispanic Mannerism," in *Abraham ibn Ezra and His Age: Proceedings of the International Symposium,* ed. Fernando Diaz Esteban (Madrid: Asociación Española de Orientalistes, 1990), pp. 325–34.

26. Ibid., p. 332.

27. Ibid., p. 329.

28. Mendelssohn, *Jerusalem oder über religiöse Macht und Judentum* (Berlin: Welt-Verlag, 1919), p. 64. Translation by Alfred Jospe, *Jerusalem and Other Jewish Writings* (New York: Schocken, 1969), p. 57. Cf. the translation by Allan Arkush, with commentary by Alexander Altmann (Hanover: University Press of New England, 1983), p. 85.

29. Mendelssohn, *Jerusalem,* pp. 121–22, Jospe translation, p. 106; cf. the Arkush translation, p. 135.

30. Cf. "Ibn Ezra and Radaq," p. 236.

31. Cf. Ibn Ezra's commentary to Exodus 21:24, cited later.

32. Cf. *Mishnah ʿim Perush Ha-Rambam,* Arabic original with Hebrew translation by Yosef Kafiḥ (Jerusalem: Mosad Harav Kook, 1964), vol. "Neziqin," pp. 214–15.

33. On the "double-truth theory" see my "Faith and Reason: The Controversy over Philosophy in Judaism," in *Great Schisms in Jewish History,* ed. R. Jospe and S. Wagner (New York: Ktav, 1980), esp. p. 88; and "Faith and Reason: The Controversy Over Philosophy in Jewish History," in *La Storia della Filosofia Ebraica,* ed. Irene Kajon (Milan: Archivio di Filosofia, 1993), pp. 99–135, esp. pp. 114–15. Also cf. Daniel J. Lasker, *Jewish Philosophical Polemics against Christianity in the Middle Ages* (New York: Ktav and A.D.L., 1977), p. 185, and "Averroist Trends in Jewish-Christian Polemics in the Late Middle Ages" in *Speculum* 55:2 (1980): 294–304. Also cf. Lasker's Hebrew introduction to his edition of Ḥasdai Crescas, *Bittul ʿIqqarei Ha-Noẓerim* (Ramat Gan: Bar Ilan University Press, 1990), p. 16, and Foreword to his English Version, *The Refutation* of the Christian Principles by Hasdai Crescas (Albany: SUNY Press, 1992), pp. 5–6. Also cf. Julius Guttmann, *Philosophies of Judaism* (New York: Holt, Rinehart Winston, 1964), p. 200; Georges Vajda, *Isaac Albalag* (Paris: 1960); and A. Hyman and J. Walsh, *Philosophy in the Middle Ages* (New York: Hackett, 1967), pp. 450–51.

34. Saʿadiah Gaʾon, *Kitab al-ʾAmanat wʾal-Iʿtiqadat* 5:8; translation by Samuel Rosenblatt, *The Book of Beliefs and Opinions* (New Haven: Yale University Press, 1948), pp. 231–32.

35. Ibid., 7:2; Rosenblatt translation, pp. 265–67.

36. Ibid., Rosenblatt translation, pp. 415–16. Cf. the discussion of literal versus

figurative interpretation in my article "Faith and Reason," esp. pp. 84–87 and 100–102.

37. For a discussion of Saʿadiah's attempt to explain nonrational and irrational passages in Scripture, see the Rosenblatt translation, *The Book of Beliefs and Opinions,* esp. 2:10, 5:8, 7:2 and the discussion cited in my "Faith and Reason," n. 33. Clearly, however, the rationalists, such as Rambam, as opposed to the mystics, were embarrassed by such passages, and tended to regard them as historically necessary concessions to the primitive level of understanding of the people who received the revelation. Their use of the rabbinic expression ("the Torah speaks in human language"; e.g., *TB,* Berakhot 31b, Bava Meẓiʿa 31b, Sanhedrin 56a, etc.) clearly reflects such a view of revelation. Cf. Rambam, *Guide of the Perplexed* 1:26, English translation by Shlomo Pines (Chicago: University of Chicago, 1963), pp. 56–57. The limitations on revelation that Ibn Ezra establishes clearly, are, of course, imposed not by any limitations on God as the speaker, but by the limited human capacity to understand. Cf. Ibn Ezra's introduction to the Torah, cited subsequently.

38. Samuel ben Ḥofni (d. 1031) was one of Saʿadiah's successors as Gaʾon of the Academy in Sura. See "Samuel ben Ḥofni," in *Encyclopaedia Judaica* (1972) 14:807–9. Tempting as it might be to identify Isaac the Old (Ha-Yashish) with Isaac ibn Yashush, the identification would appear to be dubious. Ibn Yashush was, after all, a Spaniard, not a Babylonian Gaʾon, and Ibn Ezra's criticism here is aimed at the Babylonian school of exegesis. Asher Weiser, in his edition of Ibn Ezra's commentary (*Torah Ḥayyim* [Jerusalem: Mosad Harav Kook, 1986], 1:5 n. 13), notes that some propose identifying this Isaac with Ibn Yashush, while others propose Isaac Israeli. Simon, "Parshanut Ha-Miqraʾ," rejects the identification of Ibn Ezra's Isaac with Ibn Yashush. Isaac Israeli, who was born in Egypt and lived in Kairouan in the Maghreb, is equally improbable here.

39. For a survey of Karaism and the rabbinic opposition to it, see Daniel J. Lasker, "Rabbanism and Karaism: The Contest for Supremacy" in Jospe and Wagner, *Great Schisms in Jewish History,* pp. 47–72.

40. Cf. *TB,* Rosh Ha-Shanah 27a et al., and Rashi and Ramban on Exodus 20:8.

41. *Ha-derekh ha-yesharah,* "the correct way," means, for Ibn Ezra, the literal meaning, understood by proper scientific methodology, and meeting the test of rationality. Cf. Simon, "Bible Exegesis," in *Encyclopaedia Biblica* 8:672.

42. Asher Weiser (*Torat Ḥayyim,* 3:256 n. 7) suggests that here Ibn Ezra means that the intelligent will understand how to distinguish the miraculous from the natural.

43. As we have seen, it is precisely this question—the intelligibility of revelation to its recipients—that guided Ibn Ezra on the problem of anachronisms in Scripture. See Simon, "Ibn Ezra between Medievalism and Modernism," p. 266: "Ibn Ezra's objection to anachronisms does not arise, therefore, from the absurdity inherent in premature information about the future. [To object to this would, after all, be to deny the principle of prophecy altogether.] Rather, only the fact that it is presented as already known and familiar undermines the reasonableness of its style and the clarity of its content."

44. Cf. *TB,* Bava Qama, ch. 8.

45. Ha-Levi, *Kuzari* 3:46–47. (Arabic text with Hebrew translation of Ibn Tibbon, ed. Hartwig Hirschfeld [Leipzig, 1887; reprinted Jerusalem, 1970], pp. 196–97.) On Ha-Levi's nonrationalist approach to revelation, cf. Jospe, "Faith and Reason," pp. 87–88, and "Jewish Particularity from Ha-Levi to Kaplan: Implications for Defining Jewish Philosophy," in *Go and Study: Essays and Studies in Honor of Alfred Jospe,* ed. R. Jospe and S. Fishman (New York: Ktav, 1989),

pp. 307–25, reprinted in *Forum* nos. 46–47 (winter 1982): 77–90. On Ha-Levi's own rationalism and even an Aristotelian interpretation of the *Sefer Yeẓirah,* see Jospe, "Early Philosophic Commentaries," pp. 394–402.

46. Cf. *Kuzari* 1:67, 89.

47. Y. Tzvi Langermann, "Some Astrological Themes in the Thought of Abraham ibn Ezra," in ed. Isadore Twersky and Jay Harris, *Rabbi Abraham ibn Ezra: Studies in the Writings of a Twelfth-Century Jewish Polymath* (Cambridge, MA: Harvard University Press, 1993), pp. 28–85; my thanks to Dr. Langermann for his helpful advice and for sharing his work with me. Cf. Raphael Jospe, "Ha-Torah veha-Astrologiah ʾezel Rabbi Avraham ibn ʿEzra," in *Daʿat* 32–33 (1994): 31–52, and idem. "The Torah and Astrology According to Abraham ibn Ezra," in *Proceedings of the Eleventh World Congress of Jewish Studies,* Division C, vol. 2 (Jerusalem, 1994), pp. 17–24.

Also cf. Gad Freudenthal, "Levi ben Gershom as a Scientist: Physics, Astrology and Eschatology," in *Proceedings of the Tenth World Congress of Jewish Studies* (Jerusalem: World Union of Jewish Studies, 1990), Division C, I:65–72. Cf. Ronald Kiener, "The Status of Astrology in the Early Kabbalah: From the *Sefer Yesirah* to the *Zohar,*" in *Beginnings of Jewish Mysticism in Medieval Europe,* ed. Joseph Dan, pp. 1–42, (*Jerusalem Studies in Jewish Thought* 6 (1987). Also cf. the pertinent sections of Yosef Cohen, "Mishnato ha-pilosofit-datit shel Rabbi Abraham ibn Ezra" (Ph.D., diss. Bar Ilan University, 1983); Raphael Levy, *The Astrological Works of Abraham ibn Ezra* (Baltimore: Johns Hopkins University Press, 1927); Raphael Levy and Francisco Cantera, *The Beginning of Wisdom: An Astrological Treatise by Abraham ibn Ezra* (Baltimore: Johns Hopkins University Press, 1939).

48. See Ibn Ezra on Exodus 33:21. A different tripartite cosmology may be found in Ibn Ezra's discussion of the portable sanctuary *(mishkan)* in his short commentary to Exodus 25:7. The "macrocosm" *(ʿolam gadol)* is parallel to "this world"; the "intermediate realm" *(ʿolam ʾemẓaʿi)* is parallel to the sanctuary; the "microcosm" *(ʿolam qatan)* is parallel to the human being. Israel is only protected from defeat as long as they observe the Jews' rituals of the sanctuary.

49. See Ibn Ezra on Deuteronomy 5:26.

50. Ibid.

51. See Tzvi Langermann, "Some Astrological Themes," p. 51.

52. "Ein mazal le-yisraʾel," TB, Shabbat 156a, Nedarim 32a, et al.

53. See Ibn Ezra on Deuteronomy 4:19.

54. See Tzvi Langermann, "Some Astrological Themes," p. 49.

55. Judah Ha-Levi makes this explicit comparison in *Kuzari* 1:103.

56. Cf. the English translation, in Lenn E. Goodman, *The Case of the Animals versus Man before the King of the Jinn* (Boston: Twayne, 1978), p. 181. The story may also be found in Kalonymus ben Kalonymus' Hebrew version of *ʾIggeret Baʿalei Ḥayyim,* part 5, ch. 5, ed. A. M. Haberman, (Jerusalem: Sifriyat Meqorot, 1959). The Brethren of Purity (or: Sincere Brethren) were a semisecret society of philosophers in Basra in the tenth–eleventh centuries. Their "Letters" (alternately numbered 51 or 52) comprise a scientific encyclopedia, and reflect a Neoplatonic orientation. Cf. Ian Richard Netton, *Muslim Neoplatonists: An Introduction to the Thought of the Brethren of Purity* (London: George Allen and Unwin, 1982).

57. Goodman, *Case of the Animals,* pp. 177–79.

58. Rambam, *Guide of the Perplexed* 3:17, 3:51. Cf. Z. Diesendruck, "Samuel and Moses ibn Tibbon on Maimonides' Theory of Providence," *Hebrew Union College Annual* 2 (1936): 341–66.

59. TB, Shabbat 88b, and Rashi on Genesis 33:20. The image of the hammer smashing the rock is taken from Jeremiah 23:29.

60. Zev Warren Harvey, "Ha-Dibber ha-rishon ve-ʾElohei ha-historiyah: Rabbi Yehudah Ha-Levi ve-Rabbi Ḥasdai Crescas mul Rabbi Avraham ibn Ezra ve-Rambam," *Tarbiẓ* 57, no. 2 (1988): 203–16. In his postscript, Harvey briefly cites Mendelssohn, and comments (p. 216 n. 31) that "Mendelssohn's relationship to Ha-Levi does not always receive appropriate attention."

61. For a treatment of Ha-Levi's influence on modern Jewish thinkers, especially Mendelssohn, see my articles "Jewish Particularity from Ha-Levi to Kaplan" and "The Superiority of Oral over Written Communication."

62. For an interpretation of Ha-Levi in a surprisingly rationalist light, see my "Early Philosophical Commentaries on the *Sefer Yeẓirah.*"

63. See *Kuzari,* 1:25. For a discussion of various terms for "tradition" in Saʿadiah Gaʾon, cf. Raphael Jospe, "Saʿadiah Gaʾon and Moses Mendelssohn: Pioneers of Jewish Philosophy" (forthcoming).

64. See Ibn Ezra on Deuteronomy 32:39.

Toward a Comprehensive View of Jewish Philosophy: The Middle Ages and the Modern Era

ANDREY V. SMIRNOV

IT is both a most intricate and exciting endeavor for the historian of philosophy to try to penetrate the central ideas and grasp the particular ways of raising problems that are specific to the philosophic tradition he studies, and to formulate, on this basis, a view of this tradition presented as an integral entity.

The very fact that the Jewish philosophic tradition emerged and developed in a close relationship with the Greek and Arab philosophic traditions in the Middle Ages, as well as with the European tradition in modern times, renders particularly relevant the task of revealing the internal foundation on which the unity of Jewish philosophic thought rests. Is Jewish philosophy merely an assimilation of foreign ideas and their adaptation to a Jewish outlook, or is it an autonomous and self-sufficient historical-philosophical phenomenon? Because an article of this length cannot provide an exhaustive answer to the question, I shall try to highlight only the principles that underlie the approach to dealing with it.

1

Genuine history of philosophy is impossible either as doxography or as an autonomous science; genuine history of philosophy is possible only as a self-consciousness of philosophy, as an awareness of its own "I." In its history, philosophy perceives itself, and also perceives its fundamental problems and ways of solving them. It becomes aware of itself as an indivisible organic entity with nothing obsolescent or irrelevant in it, where the ideas of any philosopher who belongs to a given tradition are ever alive and relevant, since it is only when combined, that these ideas make up the "I" of the tradition.

A philosopher's ideas can engage in a dialogue with notions and ideas of our own and can be understood only if we are able to single out and correctly formulate the ultimate premises from which this thought proceeded. Only this can ensure that the ideas of the past are understood. At the same time, a dialogue is possible only if there exists some common problem that all the parties in such a dialogue seek to solve. If the history of philosophy is conceived as such a dialogue of philosophers, and is viewed as the "I" of philosophy itself, we shall develop an understanding of philosophy as a consistent and integrated process of the advance of thought; its unity is maintained by the unity of the fundamental philosophic task to be fulfilled, while its homogeneity is ensured by the intrinsic continuity in the development of ideas geared toward the fulfillment of the task.

Therefore, if we want to understand any philosophic tradition as integral and homogeneous, we should try to identify the fundamental philosophic problem that had given rise to the tradition, and whose development constituted the effort to solve the problem; we should follow the uninterrupted and interrelated succession of attempts at solving the problem that formed the tradition. How can such an approach be applied to the history of Jewish philosophy?

2

Philosophy is the quintessence of the spirit of a people. The unique and particular features, the aspirations of a people, that both reflect and determine its historical destiny, are conceptualized in philosophy. Therefore, the fundamental philosophic task of the tradition that a people develops is to express conceptually the universal and continuing aspiration of the people's spirit.

In this context, a fundamental trait of the Jewish people's spirit that we should concentrate upon is, in my opinion, the historical and ethical character of experiencing being. Apparently Jews were the first to have formed the notion of the uniqueness of a historical process where the past (revelation) and the future (God's Kingdom on Earth) are of special significance and value. However, it is not only past and future that are characterized by ethical undertones, but the present as well: the course of being, the vicissitudes of the Jews' historical destiny, depend on how they abide by the Law and how faithful they are to it. Human ethics are of no less significance in determining the course of being than is divine omnipotence. The God of the Jews is a living God who directly reacts to the deeds and actions of His people.

This is the most important feature of the Jewish people's spirit, which is essential for understanding its philosophy. Philosophy is the endeavor to understand and interpret, to encompass in integrated knowledge, the universe of being. A distinctive feature of Jewish philosophy is the injection of ethics into being: the category of being does not exist without the categories of will, power, force, and freedom, and it may be interpreted only through the latter (but not vice versa). Philosophy is not feasible without the notion of continuity of being; however, the ontological continuum for Jewish philosophy is first and foremost, and predominantly, an ethical continuum. The aspiration to understand the continuum of being as ethical continuum is, in my opinion, the fundamental task of the Jewish philosophical tradition; it constitutes its foundation and its unity.

3

To be fulfilled, this general philosophic task must be rendered concrete; in other words, some general pattern of solving it must be formed. In the history of the Jewish philosophic tradition we are able to discern two major periods with two different ways of dealing with the fundamental philosophic task corresponding to them; these are the Middle Ages and the contemporary period.

In the medieval approach to solving the fundamental problem of Jewish philosophy, the ontological continuum is perceived as emerging from divine essence, thanks to the act of God's will; it includes the world and man. Man is microcosmic; he combines the divine and earthly worlds. Man's free will constitutes the last inalienable element of this approach. The free and omnipotent will of God and the free will of man are two opposite categories that must be harmonized; the tension between them constitutes the main contradiction of Jewish medieval philosophy and the principal motivating force in its development. The free will of God creates the continuum of being and, consequently, includes man with his free will. However, to remain free, man's will must be autonomous; while such autonomy (which should be understood in the ontological sense as well) hinders continualization of being. Such is the central and basic problem, and the attempts at solving it produced a wide range of medieval Jewish philosophic doctrines.

The limitations of an article rule out any detailed analysis of all the nuances in the attempts to solve this problem in medieval philosophic doctrines; therefore I shall dwell only upon the key questions. An unavoidable consequence of being concise is a high degree of sketchiness, but I adopt this manner quite deliberately.

God constitutes the prime foundation of the continuum of being of all the philosophic systems elaborated by medieval Jewish thinkers. Apparently, Philo of Alexandria was the first philosopher to have suggested that the prime foundation of being must be ontologically absolutely transcendental to being: it is the transcendence of God that makes it a genuine prime foundation, absolutely established and firm. However, the prime foundation must also be immanent to being. Since immediate ontological immanence is impossible, the gap between God and the world is filled by the act of creation. The category of creation is thus introduced into philosophy and rationalized. The immanence of God as the prime foundation of being in the world also introduces the notion of ethics, for creation, undoubtedly, should be perceived as an ethical act of divine will, while the transcendence of God to the world is described in terms of ontology. Thus two opposite relations of the prime foundation of being to being—that is, transcendence and immanence—may be conceived without a contradiction.

It is clear, however, that transcendence and immanence are not two relations that differ from one another, but two facets of the same relation between God and the world. In other words, the descriptions of God's relation to the world in the language of ontology and in the language of ethics must ultimately be identical. Philo succeeded in establishing such identity only in the notion of Logos: Logos expresses the unity of the creative activity of divine forces, divine omnipotence, and divine goodness. Beginning with Saᶜadiah ben Joseph, medieval Jewish philosophers attempt to solve this problem in terms of the category of divine essence. Until Hasdai Crescas, ontological language (the problem of the unity of divine essence, in negative and positive theology) is used to express the transcendence of God to the world, while the language of ethics (creative divine will, goodness of divine essence) serves to express God's immanence. But since God is as much transcendental as He is immanent to the world, the problem of the identity of divine will and divine essence inevitably emerges.

An important aspect of this problem is that the divine will must be applied to some object (matter) that is external to the divine will and essentially different from it. At the same time, this object of divine will cannot have any other source but the divine essence. Thus, a single divine essence must give rise to two essences opposed to each other: divine will, and matter. While Philo still viewed matter as the ultimate principle of the world alongside the divine cause, Saᶜadiah refused to recognize them as things of the same order. Ibn Gabirol made a deliberate attempt to solve this problem: he tried to trace both divine will and matter to the category of a single, infinite, absolutely transcendental, divine essence. However, the solution he proposed generated perhaps just as many contradictions as it solved. After Ibn Gabirol, Jewish philosophy abandoned all attempts to establish the identity of ontological and ethical descriptions of God's relation to the world: even such thinkers, standing poles apart, as Ha-Levi and Maimonides agreed that this is something utterly impossible.

Another central problem for all medieval Jewish philosophers was matching the idea of the free will of man with the idea of divine omnipotence, omniscience, and goodness. The free will of God and the free will of man must be integrated in a way that does not contradict the notion of divine justice. The complexity, if not impossibility, of solving this problem is exemplified by the fact that many medieval Jewish philosophers abandoned the soil of philosophy and opted for the language of theology. In those cases when attempts were made to deal with the problem by purely philosophic means, there was always the dilemma of choosing one of two ways: either recognizing the self-sufficing character of human will stemming from the immediate ethical sense that distinguishes between evil and good and forms from this knowledge the notion of God's goodness, thereby confining the absolute freedom of His will to the limits of moral law (Joseph al-Basir); or preserving the absolute freedom of divine will, and recognizing the freedom of human will merely as a psychological phenomenon, ontologically accepting the determined nature of human actions (Crescas).

As medieval Jewish philosophy developed, it became progressively clear that the identity of ontological and ethical languages in the description of God's transcendence and immanence cannot be established. This resulted in the emergence of Crescas's philosophy, which, in my view, occupies a special place in the history of medieval Jewish philosophy. Crescas abandons the principle of the identity of ontological and ethical languages in favor of the latter: he believes that the issues of God's transcendence and immanence to the world, freedom of divine will and human will, may be described exclusively in ethical categories, while the problems that were traditionally formulated in the language of ontology were of no decisive significance. Divine essence is the prime foundation of being, as an absolute fullness of goodness and joy. God's immanence to the world is perceived as an incessant emanation of goodness (i.e., of being) from divine essence. This emanation is not a necessary process, but a consequence of divine will, which is perceived as the will for goodness. The free will of man is the will for felicity and joy, which Crescas declares to be primary sensations that do not depend on anything.

Crescas does succeed in solving the problem that proved a stumbling block for all medieval Jewish philosophers: God's immanence and transcendence to the world are described in the category of ethics. However, an inevitable consequence in the case of Crescas was his view of the application of divine will.

4

The specificities of medieval Jewish philosophy that I have tried to emphasize stand out even more graphically when compared with medieval Arabic philosophy. References to the closeness of the two traditions have grown commonplace; however, this closeness has never crossed a certain border.

An inevitable logical consequence of the development of Muʿtazilite doctrine in Arab philosophy was Ashʿarism that refused to recognize freedom of human will and the good character of the divine will. On this point, Jewish philosophy did not follow the logically necessary (for the Mutakallimūn) conclusions drawn by Ashʿarites, and set itself in opposition to the Kalam whose ideas it had successfully assimilated up to the point where they ran counter to its basic propositions. While Jewish philosophers throughout the Middle Ages tried to preserve the idea of creation as a free act of divine will, practically all Arab philosophers were doing exactly the opposite, interpreting creation as a necessary and ontologically determined process. When creation was perceived as an act (as was the case in Ismaʿilite philosophy), the category of divine essence was removed from the framework of the philosophic system. It is not by chance that medieval Jewish philosophy did not assimilate the ontological ideas of Arab mysticism; of all medieval Arab philosophic schools, Sufism is the least compatible with the notion of free divine and human will.

5

Medieval Jewish philosophy never solved its central problem of harmonizing free, creative, divine will with the free will of man responsible for his actions. The principal cause of this failure was the bias toward interpreting divine will as an ontological as well as ethical category, as the foundation of moral law and, at the same time, as the primary source of being. It is obvious that, for the sake of further development of Jewish philosophy, the category of divine essence has to be redefined in principle.

The present stage of Jewish philosophy, which began in the eighteenth century, is far from over. A new approach to solving the fundamental problem of Jewish philosophy took shape during this period and its potential by no means has been exhausted.

The fact that the problem of harmonizing two autonomous wills, divine and human, has been eliminated, while the problem of ethics focuses exclusively on man, makes for a type of solution that differs in principle from the medieval approach. Moses Mendelssohn perceived creative divine reason as identical to supreme moral perfection; but such an approach is possible only after the content of the main categories of philosophy is revised. The ontological continuum is now conceived as being self-sufficient, and as having its foundation in itself; the divine essence is no longer its prime foundation. Freed from its ontological function, it may be perceived as the expression of the ethical ideal, and play an exclusively regulatory role. The free will of man is not confronted by the free will of God the creator; man with his ethical norms finds himself face to face with the world.

The conception of the world as ethically necessary and justifiable, with man at its center, is the leitmotif of the quest unfolding at this new stage of Jewish philosophy. Hermann Cohen is one of its most vivid representatives; his philosophy views man's ethical consciousness as autonomous and independent. The possibility of conceiving being in the category of ethics is ensured by the correlation of these two realms; a necessary link exists between logical cognition of nature and ethical knowledge. Without the supreme principle of unity, such a link would be impossible; this unity rests on the idea of God. The future is of special value; it is in the future that ethical postulates and inferences are to be translated into reality. Therefore, ethical consciousness aspires toward infinity. The unchangeability of nature as the object of the realization of ethical norms, should correspond to this aspiration. In the future New Kingdom of justice, the ethical merges with the ontological; being does not contradict morality.

The aspiration to inject ethics into being as a triumph of the human ideal, as set forth by Cohen, at the same time expresses the continuing aspiration of Jewish philosophy. The new historical stage opens up new prospects. I feel that Jewish philosophy contains in itself, in its past and present, sufficient potential for fruitful development. Should this statement also be understood as a question addressed to the future? Life itself will provide an answer.

Nineteenth-Century Jewish Thought as *Shevirat Ha-Kelim* ("Shattering of the Vessels")

GERSHON GREENBERG

Theoretical Considerations

IN discussing nineteenth-century Jewish thought/philosophy—which is generally associated with developments between Mendelssohn and the late Hermann Cohen/Franz Rosenzweig, rather than exactly with the years 1800–1900—let us first look at those historians who have already discussed it: Bernfeld (1897), Wiener (1933), Guttmann (1933), Schoeps (1934–35), Lewkowitz (1935), Agus (1941), Heinemann (1942), Rotenstreich (1945 and 1968), Arthur Cohen (1962), Fleishmann (1964), Schwarcz (1966), Fackenheim (1973), and Schweid (1978).[1] Even though these historians revolve around a common cultural center of gravity, namely German-Jewish thinking, they differ markedly in their approaches.

1. Their concerns fall into different subdisciplines: (a) history of Jewish philosophers, individually considered (Guttmann, Agus); (b) intellectual-social history (Bernfeld, Wiener, Schweid); (c) Jewish thought and non-Jewish philosophy, historically considered (Lewkowitz, Fackenheim); (d) critical history of Jewish ideas (Schoeps, Cohen); (e) religious-philosophical problems, historically considered: (Rotenstreich [comprehensive], Heinemann *[mitzvot]*, Fleishmann [Christianity], Schwarcz [revelation]). Although some of our historians make it clear that they are covering one aspect of the whole (Fleishmann, Schwarcz, Fackenheim), most imply that their approach is *the* approach (Bernfeld, Schoeps, Schweid, Agus, Rotenstreich). Lewkowitz, for example, stated: "With the beginning of the nineteenth century, the ghetto walls fell. . . . Not only individual thinkers, but the Jewish collective entity faced the task of bringing its Jewish-religious consciousness into inner harmony with life within European states and European culture."[2]

2. There is no consensus when it comes to the pivotal term for their subject. Some use "thought" (Rotenstreich, Schweid, Fleishmann), some "philosophy" (Schoeps, Guttmann, Agus, Fackenheim), and others something else: "knowledge of God" (Bernfeld), "religion" (Wiener), "intellectual streams" (Lewkowitz), "theology" (Schoeps). Thus, the same nineteenth-century individuals are often placed under several different categories. Schoeps makes a point of saying that there is much nineteenth-century apologetic, polemic, popularistic, and textbook material that "sails" under the "pirate flag" of "Jewish philosophy."[3]

3. Taken together, our historians agree on including for their consideration only four figures (Ranak, Steinheim, Samuel Hirsch, Formstecher). Sometimes a significant thinker is covered only by one or two writers—for example, Francolm (1846) by Wiener,[4] Krochman (1863) by Schweid,[5] P. L. Hurwitz (1831) by Schoeps,[6] Benamozegh (1877) by Fleishmann,[7] Lazarus (1898/1911) by Guttmann and Rotenstreich[8] (but not by Schoeps, who described the *Die Ethik* as unbearable moralizing).[9] Or a significant thinker is completely omitted—notably Marcus Beer Friedenthal (1816–1846), or David Einhorn (1854). American figures, from Gershom Mendes Seixas through Meir Rabinowitch and Emil Hirsch, are omitted en masse. Some historians routinely include nationalist thinkers (Bernfeld, Rotenstreich, Schweid); others routinely exclude them (Wiener, Schoeps).

4. Some historians of Jewish thought in the nineteenth century presume that a linear development took place. Schoeps speaks of a "development of systematic philosophy of Judaism in the nineteenth century" and also of a linear progression from "religious philosophy in the early post-Mendelssohn period" to the "speculative epoch of Jewish religious philosophy." Guttmann proceeds from "post-Kantian idealism in Jewish religious philosophy" to "the renewal of Jewish religious philosophy at the end of the nineteenth century." Others speak of parallel, self-enclosed developments: Heinemann, Rotenstreich, Schweid.

What could this "free-for-all," disintegrated situation—which does not exist in the history of modern philosophy or the history of medieval philosophy—be telling us? Could it be that once the common sources of Judaism that had provided enclosures within which Jewish thinkers differed with one another, namely Torah revelation and community, disappeared with the Emancipation, there was indeed a free-for-all in Jewish thought and that the historians are only reflecting it?

Caesar Seligmann observed that throughout Judaism's religious development, the historical path involved a pendulum that swung between "thesis" and "anti–thesis." There were opposites, but they unfolded on the road of synthesis. He thought that the *Urquellen*, the original opposites, were universalism and particularism, and that out of these came liberalism and orthodoxy, individuality and authority, religion of personality and tradition, dominance of reason and dominance of feeling, tolerance and fanaticism, ethics and cultic life, prophet and priest. Each thesis/anti-thesis, Seligmann averred, mastered for a while and then gave birth to its opposite. Meanwhile, the synthetic historical path became increasingly enriched.[10]

With the Emancipation, it appears to me, the common source that enclosed the dialectic was removed. One source was Torah revelation. Guttmann observed (as Shadal in fact had written to Ranak in 1837!), and Leo Strauss elaborated upon the theme, that even the most radical medieval thinkers formally recognized and presumed the authority of revelation. They acknowledged that each word of Torah was absolute truth, that truth was contained within the confines of Torah, and that the freedom of philosophical speculation had Torah boundaries. Modern thinkers, by contrast, were involved with the theoretical meaning of Judaism, the centrality of religious thinking.[11] Max Wiener observed that the *Einheitskultur* of Judaism collapsed with the Emancipation. Before it, when Jews were separated from the non-Jewish world, their society was subordinated to a religious-national idea. Jews were one people, certain of their divine calling. Religion dictated distinct dress, food, thinking, and feeling. This unified condition broke with the advent of Emancipation. For the first time, the Jewish mind confronted the question, What does religion mean? What does our belief mean?[12]

Without the metaphysical basis of Torah or the *Einheitskultur*, nineteenth-century thinkers were left to operate sui generis. Each selected his own basis. Sometimes it was autobiographical (Maimon, Samuel Hirsch); sometimes the basis was a philosophical father-figure: Kant (Ascher) or Hegel (Formstecher) or Schelling (Einhorn); sometimes a societal demand (Lazarus). Without Torah or culture to provide an enclosed environment of discourse, these thinkers characteristically created their own delimiting contexts by telling us what their positions were *not*. Each had the truth, and those who disagreed resided beyond truth's border in the realm of falsehood. In the nineteenth century, it was *either* reason *or* revelation *or* moral feelings *or* ontological ethics *or* history. The pendulum mechanism was dismantled. There was no way to move, for example, from Steinheim's revelation to Formstecher's reason, from Einhorn's principle of historical centralization to Lazarus's ethics.

How did this happen? The story begins with Moses Mendelssohn. Simon Rawidowicz describes the "house" that Mendelssohn built. On the ground floor there was the general religion of mankind, with its eternal, universal, and necessary truths produced by human reason as revealed to it by God. All mankind could live on this floor. On the second floor there were historical, temporal truths, accepted by faith and supported by miracle and authority. These truths could change with circumstances, notably the move from the Land of Israel. Only Jews lived on this floor. Jews alone lived on the third floor as well, where there were eternal contingent truths provided by God and changeable by Him alone.[13]

Mendelssohn's "house" was a refuge for Jews of the Emancipation era. Instead of choosing between Judaism as it existed before, and Judaism as it unfolded thereafter, they could be medieval and modern at the same time. Along with Mendelssohn, one could be both a religious philosopher for whom the God-man correlation was rationally contiguous, and a traditional "revelationist" for whom legislation was revealed supernaturally. One could be a member of universal society and also a Jew enclosed by a wall of mitzvot, which alone led to universal truths. It did not take long for Christian thinkers to identify the problems in the "construction." They observed that the attempt to accommodate tradition and change simultaneously left a vacuum at the center and that the house would fall (Hamann [1784], Benedikt Stattler [1787], Kant [1798]).[14] But as far as Jews were concerned, with all the different opinions (see Schoeps and Michael Meyer),[15] Mendelssohn had the personal and intellectual stature to make his house de facto valid, at least for the moment.

But could such ambiguity and "talking from both sides of the mouth" last? In fact, it did not.[16] There was at least one important attempt to keep the fire of ambiguity alive—Isaac Reggio's *Ha-torah veha-pilosofiyah* of 1827.[17] But this "Italian Mendelssohn" was attacked from the right, in the name of tradition (curiously enough, by the "Russian Mendelssohn," Jakob Baer Levinsohn),[18] and from the left, in the name of *Wissenschaft,* by Jakob Goldenthal.[19] The book—albeit a substantive work—was all but forgotten. Instead, the thinkers/philosophers of the nineteenth century each took a "section" of the house and made it central to a new structure. In this way, ironically, Mendelssohn may be credited with preserving Jewish thought. The trauma of Emancipation could have stopped Jewish thought entirely, based as it was until then on Torah revelation and community. Instead, Mendelssohn kept all its elements alive and available—Torah, reason, history, ethics—until the crisis of Emancipation could settle down, there was time to reflect, and individual thinkers could come along and rebuild.

Let us look at these sui generis developments, with examples from the centers of reason, revelation, moral feelings, ethics, and history.

Reason

Salomon Maimon defined religion as the expression of gratitude and reverence toward the source of human benefits, that is, God. God for Maimon was the metaphysical idea of unidentified ultimate cause and, as such, perfect and infinite essence, the ideal of infinite perfection. Man should relate to this ideal through the idea of the power of infinite understanding. Through this idea, and reflection upon it, human consciousness could connect to this infinite ability and relate to it. Maimon described human perfection in terms of a priori, metaphysical enlightenment about the reality of perfect, infinite substance. For him, "The absolutely Perfect Being can reveal Himself exclusively as an idea to the reason" *(Das allervollkommenste Wesen kann sich bloss als Idee der Vernunft offenbaren)*. True, that is, covenantal, Judaism is founded solely in the nature of reason *(Dieses Paktum kann also nicht anders als in der Natur der Vernunft, ohne Ruecksicht auf einen Zweck gegruendet sein)*. What of tradition, legal and otherwise, with its appeal to revelation? According to Maimon, it was generally construed by those interested in blocking access to the metaphysical idea and establishing power for themselves, and it should be removed.[20]

For Salomon Formstecher, whose *Weltanschauung* and dialecticism came from the Hegelian Joseph Hillebrand of the University of Giessen, Hegel's successor at Heidelberg (and, despite what our historians say, not from Schelling), rational consciousness coincided with revelation. God posited His world-soul, in which spirit and nature resided in equilibrium, into the cosmos at creation. This constituted "prehistorical revelation." God remained conscious of the world-soul; its spiritual dimension was elevated by Him above its natural component. He revealed this power of self-consciousness to man upon creation and the onset of history, by presenting man with a choice between nature and spirit. God then revealed the power to Israel, by liberating it from the pagan mentality that was confined to nature and granting it a special awareness of world-soul and its spiritual possibilities. Beginning with the Patriarchs, an entire nation had unique access to divine revelation in history. According to Formstecher, Israel's history consisted of the increasing consciousness of the world-soul; in other words, of rationalizing revelation, of subjectivizing the objective world-soul, of bringing ontology into anthropology. There was no substantive difference to revelation, prehistorical or historical, and its rational apprehension. On the contrary, human consciousness was the purest way to enter the range of divine self-consciousness. To be sure, God's transcendental essence beyond time and space could not be known by man. But reason could probe revelation, and, in the process, the line that separated anthropology/subjectivity could become increasingly transparent. Ultimately, all of history would become a grand act of self-consciousness; all mankind would become the image of God.

Formstecher regarded Mendelssohn as the culmination of ever more rationalizing of revelation—a process that began with Abraham and the prophets, and proceeded through the rabbinic and medieval period—and as the threshold to the end of history. In Formstecher's view, revelation was not outside reason. Indeed, it fulfilled itself in rationality. History for him was the growth of self-conscious reasoning, the increasing spiritualizing of nature. Moral feeling would have no significant place in his system, nor would ethics, other than as a form of self-consciousness.[21]

Maimon and Formstecher had unreserved praise for Mendelssohn—even if they each incorporated him into their own approach—but David Einhorn did not. He appreciated Mendelssohn's contribution to making Judaism a part of the broad universe of human religious experience and to looking at Judaism ontically and objectively. But Einhorn was exasperated by Mendelssohn's contradictions—between freedom of religious conscience and reward/punishment, and between the reasoned God and the revealed God.

Einhorn burst forth and declared a new definition of Judaism—"Mosaism" as the "centralization of various existences, without capricious infringement upon any individual existence." The essence of Judaism now became a logical, rational theme with its own being—a theme apparently drawn from Schelling's philosophy of identity. All dimensions of Jewish experience were seen by Einhorn as stemming from and reverberating with this a priori principle. Thus, Mosaic theology "centralized" pagan naturalism (God within nature) with the theme of idealism (Platonic?) that the world was "other" than God, such that God was both transcendental (YHWH) and immanent *(Elohim)*. In the concept of man, creation out of nothing *(bara)* was centralized along with emanation *(assa)* into the concept of formation *(yatsar);* man was centrally *nefesh,* the simultaneous identity/opposition of body and spirit. Beyond the rational theme at the heart of Mosaism, Einhorn averred that the distinction between revelation and reason was subjective, and that reason could and should overcome this limitation. Revelation—the paradigm was Sinai—was the "moisture" of the earth, there to evaporate and descend like rain as reason approached it. History was there to provide time and material for reason to access revelation. Mitzvot were instruments for rational apprehension, disposable when this occurred. Ultimately, for Einhorn, reason would comprehend revelation; history would be properly utilized. At that point, all mankind would join Israel, and Israel's distinction will end. It was not as if Israel "owned" the truths of Sinai, they were ultimately available to anyone's reason. A planet, Einhorn pointed out, did not belong to the first astronomer to identify it.[22]

Revelation

Steinheim "dug his heels in" at the revealed center of Judaism. Having established a duality between the pagan mind, which developed God out of reason and understood the world in terms of causal necessity, and the Jewish mind, for which God was revealed as a transcendent being and the creator of the causal sequence, Steinheim deposited Mendelssohn, Formstecher, and Hirsch in the former camp. Mendelssohn belonged there, according to Steinheim, because he denied divine revelation in favor of a God-idea natural to man, because he derailed the revealed doctrine of God and made man's spirit into God. Hirsch—who in his *Die Religionsphilosophie der Juden* (1841) indeed inundates Holy Scripture, the God-man individual relationship, and religious history with philosophically dialectical human consciousness—and Formstecher belonged there because, as Steinheim read them, they enslaved Jewish existence and history to the logically necessary principle of dialectic, and they conditioned God's self-realization upon human consciousness.

Steinheim rooted himself in revelation and separated Judaism from reason and all its anthropocentric ramifications. The only function reason had was that of reining itself in. Steinheim maintained that reason should identify its limits in terms of understanding empirical reality, the future, and God, and clear the way for revelation. Judaism, indeed, could be identified in terms of opposition to reason. The revelation at Sinai was dramatic, and it was mutually exclusive with what man could know. Specifically, the shibboleths revealed at Sinai were that: (1) God was one, a simple unity, neither the unity of multiplicity nor the multiplicity of unity that reason formulated. (2) Man was free to respond to divine command, neither submissive to law nor obligated to self—which were the rational options. (3) The world was created, neither self-generated nor endlessly old, as reason might conclude. Revelational Judaism survived within Israel despite persecution and remained the same despite changes in reason and history. Sinai revelation burst into history and remained there, but was unaffected by history; history rather accommodated to it.[23]

Moral Feelings

Shadal (Samuel David Luzzatto) distinguished between the mentalities of "Atticism" and Judaism. Atticism was progressive; it stood for continual development. Judaism was antiprogressive; its doctrines were immutable. Philosophy was associated with the former. Shadal considered philosophy useless—after all the centuries, philosophers still agreed on little—if not dangerous to emotional well-being; it made some students depressed to the point of suicide. He attacked Rambam for displacing the Sages' emphasis on deed with the Aristotelian idea (for Rambam even the soul's immortality was determined by intellectual knowledge), instead of elucidating how Scripture and the Sages promoted righteousness by addressing compassion and delineating a system of reward and punishment. Shadal also attacked Spinoza, for identifying the ideal man with intellectuality at the expense of feelings, in particular the feeling of compassion; and for a concept of a world that was run by the necessities of natural law but not by a real creator, God, by divine providence, and with reward and punishment. Spinoza's miserable existence unto death was characteristic of the life offered by philosophy.

Shadal's Judaism, mutually exclusive with Atticism, was rooted in a morality based upon feelings and not reason. Its origins were identifiable with Abraham's revelation. For Shadal, this revelation involved Abraham's asserting autonomous moral consciousness and notably selfless compassion, and projecting moral feeling onto God to assure the concepts of divine imperatives, reward and punishment. Shadal's Judaism had to do with natural qualities, not metaphysical truths; it functioned according to natural sensitivities to agreeable/disagreeable outside impressions; to natural feelings of sympathy and justice, and the ways in which reason entered into the picture only to work with them.[24]

Ontological Morality

For Moritz Lazarus, Judaism was centrally an expression of morality. This morality was an ontological, cosmic reality that pervaded the universe. It was at moments prior to God, simultaneous with God, or secondary to Him. Taken altogether, it appears that Lazarus's morality was involved in a dialectical dynamic, one in which God and morality interrelated as concentric circles that alternated endlessly at the inner position. Thus, the moral world order for Lazarus emerged from the divine source that revealed it, and ethics were as unthinkable without God as was the physical world without sun; God emerged from hiddenness into an ethical context. Or, morality was in God and God's ethical acts were His autonomous assertions, yet God was subordinate to ethical imperatives. Or again, morality was absolute because it was in God, yet it also contained its own reality. For Lazarus, human existence belonged to the ontological ethical context. Man came into being after the ontic reality that was the source of all human endeavors, including the intellectual. The purpose of human life was to continue and to further morally creative activity—of which God was the prototype: "Because the moral is divine, therefore you shall be moral; and because the divine is moral, you shall become like unto God." As to the revealed laws of Israel, the Sinai legislation, Lazarus understood them in terms of already extant autonomous morality. For him, the laws were imperative because of the morality they contained: "Not because God has ordained it is a law moral, but because it is moral, therefore God has ordained it."[25] In the severe critique that Hermann Cohen leveled against *Die Ethik des Judenthums,* he did agree that the human spirit was grounded in God as the essence of morality, and that the concept of divine essence was identifiable with the concept of morality.[26]

History

Ascher thought that Mendelssohn undid himself *(Ich weiss nicht, welcher gleichgueltige Genius einen Mendelssohn leitete, seinen Gegner ueberwinden zu wollen, und sich doch selbst ueberwinden zu lassen).*[27] And what was Ascher's alternative? Heinrich Heine thought that Ascher represented the ultimate rationalist:

> The poor fellow philosophizes everything glorious out of life—sunlight, belief, flowers: [I had this nightmare, in which] the dead Doctor Saul Ascher entered my room [and told me], "Be not afraid, and do not believe I am a ghost. It is only an illusion of your fantasy, to believe you see me as a ghost. What is a ghost? Define it. Deduce the conditions for the possibility of a ghost. . . . Reason. I say reason."[28]

But even Ascher's reason is centered in history.

For Ascher, the essence of religion was the principle or idea of a being that was higher than man, and the relationship of man to that being. Religious history had three overall stages: In natural *(natuerliche)* religion the idea was the epitome of natural perfection, that is, idolatry. In revelational *(geoffenbarte)* religion—primarily Judaism but also Christianity and Islam—the idea, which for Judaism was the metaphysical and moral God, intervened in history. This intervention formed the basis for historical consciousness. In the third stage, that of rational *(vernuenftige)* religion, the idea was that of metaphysical source for human morality. For its part, Judaism's history went from a "regulative" to a "constitutive" situation. The regulative, which ran from Abraham through the prophets, involved laws that responded to human, social, and national needs. The constitutive involved inflexible laws that were imposed upon society (halakhah).

According to Ascher, the Napoleonic revolution heralded the world's passage into rational religion. He wanted Judaism to align itself to this progress. To do so, Judaism needed to divest itself of the constitutive layer, and restore the doctrines of faith (the "organon" that Ascher enumerated) of its original regulative existence. This would enable it to disseminate the original moral monotheism. By its very nature, Ascher's original Judaism was potentially coincident—in its morality, regulations, and, according to Schweid's interpretation, even rationality[29]—with European rational humanism. As part of the commitment to the latest stage of religious development, Ascher attacked the likes of Fichte, Arndt, and Jahn for their "*Germanomanie*" (Germanic mania), by which they wished to burn up Jewry along with everything foreign *(muss Brennstoff gesammelt werden und in dem Haueflein Juden wollten unsere Germanomanen das erste Buendel Reiser zur Verbreitung der Flamme des Fanaticismus hinlegen).*[30] The German antirational nationalistic paroxysm was incompatible with rational enlightenment.[31]

I would include Nahman Krokmal, the "Galician Mendelssohn,"[32] in the historical camp. His historiosophy is well known: All nations undergo tripartite cycles: (1) "growth," where the Absolute Spirit begins to assume the form of a national spirit *(Volksgeist)* with a special character—for example, Rome and its law; (2) "flowering," where the special character dominates and the nation is strong; (3) "atrophy," where the character continues at the expense of other necessary aspects of culture, and the *Volksgeist* erodes. After the cycle is completed the nation disappears from history, leaving only an imprint of the dominant character on the Absolute Spirit. While the Absolute Spirit is present in the cyclical dynamic and receives the positive residue, it is not in the *Volksgeist* itself. The nation, as such, is ephemeral. It is otherwise with Israel, which is steeped in the Absolute Spirit. With Israel's history, a new cycle develops after each atrophy. Israel does not leave the scene of history, because all of its experiences are part of the Absolute Spirit. As such, Israel's history is dialectical—it undergoes time-bound cycles but returns to the eternal base of spirit.

Ranak's historicism extended into his personal role in the development of Jewish thought and into his philosophizing. The last cycle, which began with Yavne, peaked with Maimonides, and declined with Shabbetai Zevi, had yet to be succeeded when Ranak entered the scene. Ranak analyzed the "poisonous" elements of Judaism—ecstasy, idolatrous attempts to crush evil, slavish obedience to commandments; and their polar opposites—denial of spirituality, doubts about sacred texts and venerated personalities, abandonment of pious acts—and thereby made it possible to eliminate them and start a new cycle. Aware of Absolute Spirit, Ranak helped to draw it once again into a cyclical historical experience. He gave new impetus to the dialectical history of the Spirit. Ranak also furthered that history within the discipline of philosophy. He resolved oppositions between theological faith and rational scientific study with philosophical theology; between logical philosophy and natural philosophy with the philosophy of spirit; between being and nothingness with being-in-and-for-itself. He resolved oppositions between attraction and repulsion, discrete and continuous quality, and finite and infinite, by simultaneously negating and retaining the polarities, opposing and identifying them. In these ways, he uncovered the underlying dialectical and dynamic forces connecting philosophy to the dialectical history of Absolute Spirit.

I offer this listing as a suggestion for debate. To demonstrate the *shevirat ha-kelim* completely, it would be necessary to show how each of these philosophers rejected the centers other than his own; and to show how the other nineteenth-century figures (Francolm the rationalist and Graetz the historiosopher come quickly to mind) belonged to the enclosed camps.

Before closing, it should be asked whether this process was beneficial. Simon Bernfeld wrote about how religious thinkers sometimes provided "quick fixes," which, after they wore off, left the people to suffer even worse than before. He observed how in every age of the Jewish religion, scholars and intellects have arisen to research the substance of religion and reasons for *mitzvot;* they expanded the conceptual and ethical dimensions of the religion. But sometimes the thinker offered something for his own time that could prove injurious to subsequent generations: "To what is this like? To a sick person who feels physically exhausted. Some medicines are taken, which indeed revive him temporarily. But then exhaustion returns, worse than before."[33]

Did our thinkers relate only to their circumstances, and thereby retard the progress of philosophy or even cripple it by the time the Rosenzweigs and Bubers entered the scene? On the contrary. In the multifaceted society of post-Emancipation Judaism, in the shattered *Einheitskultur,* Jews thought differently than before and differently among themselves, and the differences had to be explored all the way. Moreover, had Jewish religious philosophers operated within a single channel, each trying to outdo Mendelssohn, had the history been linear and Jewish thought monolithic, it is not inconceivable that, when the terrible blows of the twentieth century came, they would have destroyed the Jewish mind in its entirety. Ultimately, the diverse paths of nineteenth-century Jewish thought provided a flexibility, a variety of radically different reference points that would be needed when the Jewish world structure was shattered. Because of the *shevirat ha-kelim,* there still were reference points for the individual-without-a-society to invoke. Indeed, Krokmal's view of history was cited in the displaced persons camps in Germany;[34] Lazarus's ontological ethic was echoed in Leo Baeck's postwar statements in London;[35] Steinheim's revelation became meaningful for Moshe Schwarcz in Ramat Gan[36] and Heinz Moshe Graupe in Hamburg.[37] *Shevirat ha-kelim* represents not only the breakdown in the nineteenth century of traditional structures in both philosophy and Jewish life, but also the possibility, in the absence of such structures, of pluralistic and dynamic responses to the cataclysms of the twentieth century.

Notes

I remain ever-grateful to my teacher Eugen Kullmann for having drawn me into this field of interest, and nurturing me once I arrived.

1. Simon Bernfeld, *Daʿat Elohim* (Warsaw: Schuldberg, 1897); Max Wiener, *Jüdische Religion im Zeitalter der Emanzipation* (Berlin: Philo, 1933); Julius Guttmann, *Die Philosophie des Judentums* (Munich: Reinhardt, 1933), English translation: David W. Silverman, *Philosophies of Judaism: The History of Jewish Philosophy from Biblical Times to Franz Rosenzweig* (New York: Holt, Rinehart and Winston, 1968), Hans Joachim Schoeps, *Jüdischer Glaube in dieser Zeit. Prolegomena zur Grundlegung einer systematischen Theologie des Judenthums* (Berlin: Vortrupp, 1934), and *Geschichte der jüdischen Religionsphilosophie in der Neuzeit* I (Berlin: Vortrupp, 1935); Albert Lewkowitz, *Das Judentum und die geistigen Strömungen des 19. Jarhhunderts* (Breslau: Marcus, 1935); Jacob Agus, *Modern*

Philosophies of Judaism: A Study of Recent Jewish Philosophies of Religion (New York: Behrman, 1941); Itshak Heinemann, *Ta^came Ha-mitzvot Be-sifrut Israel,* 2 vols. (Jerusalem: Jewish Agency, 1942); Nathan Rotenstreich, *Ha-mahshavah Ha-yehudit Be-et Ha-hadasha* (Tel Aviv: Am Oved, 1945), English translation: *Jewish Philosophy in Modern Times: From Mendelssohn to Rosenzweig* (New York: Holt, Rinehart and Winston, 1968); Arthur A. Cohen, *The Natural and the Supernatural Jew: An Historical and Theological Introduction* (New York: Pantheon, 1962); Ya'akov Fleishmann, *Ba'ayat Ha-natzrut Ba-mahshavah Ha-yehudit* (Jerusalem: Magnes, 1964); Moshe Schwarcz, *Safa, Mitos, Amanut, Iyyunim Be-mahshava Ha-yehudit Be-et Ha-hadasha* (Jerusalem: Schocken, 1966); Emil Fackenheim, *Encounters between Judaism and Modern Philosophy: A Preface to Future Jewish Thought* (New York: Basic Books, 1973); Eliezer Schweid, *Toldot He-hagut Ha-yehudit Be-et ha-hadasha. Ha-mea ha-tesha esre* (Jerusalem: Keter, 1977).

2. Lewkowitz, *Das Judentum,* p. 2.
3. Schoeps, *Jüdischer Glaube,* p. 26.
4. Wiener, *Jüdische Religion,* pp. 118–20.
5. Schweid, *Toldot He-hagut,* pp. 342–49.
6. Schoeps, *Geschichte,* pp. 61–64.
7. Fleischmann, *Ba'ayat Ha-natzrut,* pp. 119–30.
8. Guttmann, *Die Philosophie,* pp. 350–52; Nathan Rotenstreich, "The Inner Imperative and Holiness," in *Jewish Philosophy in Modern Times,* pp. 43–51.
9. Schoeps, *Jüdischer Glaube,* p. 27.
10. Caesar Seligmann, *Geschichte der jüdischen Reformbewegung von Mendelssohn bis zur Gegenwart* (Frankfurt am Main: Kaufmann, 1922); 12.
11. Guttmann, *Die Philosophie,* pp. 259, 342. Leo Strauss, *Philosophie und Gesetz* (Berlin: Schocken, 1935).
12. Wiener, *Jüdische Religion,* pp. 5, 7.
13. Shimon Rawidowicz, "Ha-pilosofiyah shel *Yerushalayim,*" in *Iyyunim Be'-mahshevet Israel* II, Benjamin Ravid (Jerusalem: Mass, 1971), pp. 70–117.
14. Johann Georg Hamann, "Golgatha und Scheblimini. Von einem Prediger in der Wüsten" [1784], *Hamann's Schriften,* vol. 7, ed. Friedrich Roth (Leipzig: Reimer, 1825), pp. 17–70; cf. Ze'ev Levy, "Johann Georg Hamann's Concept of Judaism and Controversy with Mendelssohn's *Jerusalem,*" *Leo Baeck Institute Yearbook* 29 (1984); 295–329; Benedikt Stattler, *Wahres Jerusalem* (Augsburg: Rieger, 1787); Immanuel Kant, "Der Streit der Fakultaeten" [1798] in *Immanuel Kants Saemmtliche Werke,* vol. 7, ed. G. Hartenstein (Leipzig: Voss, 1868), pp. 369n–70n.
15. Hans Joachim Schoeps, "Die Begruendung der jüdischen Religionsphilosophie im System Moses Mendelssohns," in *Geschichte,* pp. 21–38; Michael Meyer, *Origins of the Modern Jew: Jewish Identity and European Culture in Germany, 1749–1824* (Detroit: Wayne State University Press, 1967).
16. In 1841, Schelling's favorite Jew, Meir Hirsch Loewengard, could say, "Mendelssohn noch, über den das neue Geschlecht die Achseln zuckt, war ein ebenso aufrichtig-frommen Israelit als ausgezeichneter Philosoph. Jedoch in einen Zeitraum vom ungefähr 50 Jahren haben wir schnell alle Phasen durchgemacht, vom bescheidenen Zweifel bis zum völligen Unglauben, und zu totaler Gleichgltigkeit nun wissen wir nich que faire?" *Beitrage zur Kritik der Reformbestrebungen in der Synagoge* (Stuttgart, 1841), as cited in Schoeps, *Geschichte,* p. 41n.
17. Isaac Samuel Reggio, *Ha-torah Veha-pilosofiyah* (Vienna: Schmid, 1827).
18. Jakob Baer Levinsohn, *Yehoshofat. Hu bikoret al sefer Ha-torah Veha-pilosofiyah leha-hakham Itshak Shmuel Reggio, ha-mekhune Yashar, ve-nilve lo od ketsat bikoret al inyanim zulato meha-mehaber ha-zeh* (Warsaw: Halter, 1883).

19. Jakob Goldenthal, "Beiträge zur Literatur der jüdischen Religionsphilosophie," *Allgemeine Zeitung des Judentums. Literararisches und homiletisches Beiblatt* 1, no. 35 (15 December 1838): 159–62, and no. 36 (27 December 1838): 163–66.

20. Salomon Maimon, *Lebensgeschichte,* mit einer Einleitung und mit Anmerkungen neu herausgegeben von Jakob Fromer, 2d ed. (Munich: Muller, 1911; originally published 1792–93), ch. 20; *Philosophisches Wörterbuch. Oder Beleuchtung der wichtigsten Gegenstände der Philosophie in alphabetischer Ordnung* (Berlin: Unger, 1791), ch. 27; *Kritische Untersuchungen über den menschlichen Geist. Oder das höhere Erkenntnis—und Willensvermögen* (Leipzig: Fleischer, 1797); "Hakdamat Ha-hakham Baʿal Giveʿat Ha-more," *Sefer More Nevukhim Leha-Rav Ha-gadol Ha-hoker Ha-elohi Ha-hakham Ha-kolel Rabbenu Moshe Ben Maimon zts"l. Im shene perushim nikhbadot medubar bam. Hema perush ha-Rav ha-hoker ha-mekubal ha-hakham ha-pilosof Moshe Norboni u-ferush "Give ʿat Ha-more,"* vol. 1 (Vienna: Schmid, 1828), pp. iii–vii.

21. Salomon Formstecher, *Die Religion des Geistes. Eine wissenschaftliche Darstellung des Judenthums nach seinem Charakter, Entwicklungsgange und Berufe in der Menschheit* (Frankfurt am Main: Hermann, 1841).

22. David Einhorn, *Das Prinzip des Mosaismus und dessen Verhältnis zum Heidenthum und rabbinischen Judenthum,* vol. 1 (Leipzig: Fritzche, 1854).

23. Salomon Ludwig Steinheim, *Die Offenbarung nach dem Lehrbegriffe der Synagoge,* vol. 1. *Ein Schiboleth* (Frankfurt am Main: Schmerber, 1835), vol. 2. *Die Glaubenslehre der Synagoge als exacte Wissenschaft. Über das Wesen und die Charaktermerkmale der Offenbarung* (Leipzig: Schnauss, 1856), vol. 3. *Die Polemik. Der Kampf der Offenbarung mit dem Heidenthume, ihre Synthese und Analyze* (Leipzig: Leiner, 1863), vol. 4. *Commentar zu den ersten fünf Capiten der Genesis. Fünf Monomachieen* (Altona: Bonn, 1865); *Moses Mendelssohn und seine Schule in ihrer Beziehung zur Aufgabe des neuen Jahrhunderts der alten Zeitrechnung* (Hamburg: Hoffman and Campe, 1840); "*Die Religionsphilosophie der Juden. Oder das Prinzip der jüdischen religiosen Auschauung und sein Verhältniss zum Heidenthum, Christenthum und zur absoluten Philosophie* . . . . von Dr. Samuel Hirsch," *Literaturblatt des Orients. Berichte, Studien und Kritiken für jüdische Geschichte und Literatur* 5 no. 20 (14 May 1844): 308–13; 21 (21 May 1844): 321–27; 22 (28 May 1844): 338–44; 23 (4 June 1844): 360–65; 24 (11 June 1844): 375–77; 25 (18 June 1844): 388–92; 27 (25 June 1844): 420–23; 28 (9 July 1844): 433–37; 30 (23 July 1844): 465–69; 31 (30 July 1844): 483–87; "Weder zur Rechten noch zur Linken," *Israelitischer Volkslehrer* 7 (1857): 54–191.

24. Samuel David Luzzatto, ["Criticism of Maimonides"], *Kerem Hemed* 3 (Prague, 1838): 66–73; "Mikhtav Me-et Shadal. Likhvod yedidi ha–yakar ha-maskil veha-navon kavod morenu Rav. I. H. Schorr shalom u-verakha," *Otsar Nehmad* 4 (1838): 108–11. "Briefwechsel über religiöse Zustände" (Letters to Reggio) *Israelitische Annalen. Ein Centralblatt für Geschichte, Literatur und Kultur der Israeliten aller Zeiten und Länder* 29 (19 July 1839): 227–28; 30 (26 July 1839): 235–37; and "Neged Shpinoza," in *Mehkare Ha-yahadut* (Warsaw: Hatsefira, 1912–13), pp. 198–221; *Yessode Ha-torah* (Lemberg: Ehrenpreis, 1880).

25. Moritz Lazarus, *Die Ethik des Judenthums,* vol. 1 (Frankfurt am Main: Kauffman, 1898), pp. 86–88.

26. Hermann Cohen, "Das Problem der jüdischen Sittenlehre. Eine Kritik von Lazarus' *Die Ethik des Judenthums*" [1899], in *Jüdische Schriften,* vol. 3 (Berlin: Schwetschke, 1924), pp. 1–35.

27. Shaul Ascher, *Leviathan. Oder über Religion in Rücksicht des Judentums* (Berlin: Frank, 1792), p. 240.

28. Heine Heinrich, "Reisebilder [1861] I. Die Harzreise," in *Heinrich Heine. Historisch-kritische Gesamtausgabe der Werke,* vol. 6, ed. Manfred Windfuhr (Hamburg: Hoffmann und Campe, 1973), pp. 103–4.

29. Eliezer Schweid, "Arbaʿah Degamim shel Historiosofiyah Be-filosofiyah Hayehudit shel Ha-me'ah Ha-tesha Esre," *Divrei Ha-kongres Ha-olami Ha-shishi Lemadaʿe Ha-yahadut* [13–19 August 1973] vol. 3 (Jerusalem: World Union of Jewish Studies, 1977), pp. 479–87.

30. Shaul Ascher, *Die Germanomanie. Skizze in einem Zeitgemälde* (Berlin, 1815), pp. 15–16.

31. Ascher, *Leviathan, Eisenmenger der Zweite. Nebst einem vorangesetzten an den Herrn Professor Fichte in Jena* (Berlin: Hartmann, 1794); *Napoleon. Oder über den Fortschrift der Regierung* (Berlin: Lange, 1808); *Die Wartburgs—Feier mit hinsicht auf Deutschlands religiöse und politische Stimmung* (Leipzig: Achenwall, 1818).

32. Joseph Klausner, *Historiyah shel Ha-sifrut Ha-ivrit Ha-hadashah,* vol. 2. *Ha-dor shel ha-romantika ve-hokhmat Israel* (Jerusalem: Ahiasaf, 1952), p. 148.

33. Simon Bernfeld, *Daʿat Elohim* (Warsaw: Schuldberg, 1897), p. 5.

34. Moshe Halpern, "Der sod fun unzer kiyyum," *Yeshurun* 6 (Munich, August 1948): 26–7.

35. Leo Baeck, *Der Sinn der Geschichte* (Berlin: Habel, 1946).

36. Moshe Schwarcz, "Mussag Ha–herut Be-dat Ha-pilosofit shel Schelling Uvedat Ha-torah shel Shelomo Steinheim," *Safah, Mitos, Omanut. Iyyunim Bemahshavah ha yehudit be-et Ha-hadashah* (Jerusalem: Schocken, 1966), pp. 89–140; "Pulmus Ha-pantiʾizm Veha-teologiah shel Shlomo Ludwig Steinheim," in *Hitagalut, Emunah, Tevunah, Kovetz Hartsaʾot,* ed. Moshe Halamish and Moshe Schwarcz (Ramat Gan: Bar Ilan University, 1976), pp. 119–30.

37. Hans Joachim Schoeps, Heinz Mosche Graupe, and Gerd-Hesse Goeman, *Salomon Ludwig Steinheim zum Gedenken. Ein Sammelband* (Leiden: Brill, 1966).

Part Two

Contemporary Jewish Philosophers in the Academy: Franz Rosenzweig and Emmanuel Levinas

Levinas, Rosenzweig, and the Phenomenologies of Husserl and Heidegger

RICHARD A. COHEN

THERE is a moment of exceptional humility in *Totality and Infinity.* In the preface, Emmanuel Levinas acknowledges a profound indebtedness to a book published forty years earlier, Franz Rosenzweig's *The Star of Redemption.* He writes: "We were impressed by the opposition to the idea of totality in Franz Rosenzweig's *Star of Redemption,* a work too often present in this book to be cited."[1] One can hardly imagine higher praise or the admission of greater debt.

The magnitude of indebtedness is even more striking when viewed in the light of a letter unknown to Levinas, written by Franz to his mother, dated 5 October 1921. Rosenzweig writes:

> I understand I was put in a [rabbi's] sermon yesterday and my book referred to as "the sublime book of a new thinker who lives in our midst." But it won't be really good until they use me in sermons without quoting me, and best of all, without even knowing that it is me that they are using.[2]

Franz's words to his mother are fulfilled by Levinas's words to his readers.

We might therefore begin to understand the place of *The Star* in *Totality and Infinity* by interpreting these private words by Rosenzweig in a public Levinasian way. "Really good" words, we would say, are not scholastic exercises, not recitations, but words freely used "without quoting," the speech or *saying* of a thinker whose living presence is always "new," always beyond what happens to be *said,* subject matter, contents, or themes. The new would not just be the novelty resulting from an author's craft or artistry, but the freshness of he "who lives in our midst," he who faces us *face to face.* "Best," to continue this reading, would be words used "without even knowing," words used without the shadows cast by reflection, without the echoes of mental life, without the distances of its caution, reserve, and irony. Genuine words would be those disrupting knowledge from outside its grasp, words that escape the superior and synoptic gaze of comprehension, words that make greater *demands* on knowing than knowing knows or demands of itself. Interpreted in this fashion, Rosenzweig's *Star* would be the "sublime" book, the overflow, that serves as both mount and "sermon" of *Totality and Infinity.* And it certainly is such a book.

Yet Levinas's thankful words force us to do more than discover the place, however cleverly detected, of *The Star* in the general economy of *Totality and Infinity.* Levinas forces us to do more because directly after acknowledging the incalculable debt *Totality and Infinity* owes to *The Star,* he acknowledges an even greater debt to Edmund Husserl's phenomenological method. The next sentence reads: "But the presentation and the development of the notions employed owe everything [*doivent tout*] to the phenomenological method." *Owe everything!* It cannot be accidental that right after acknowledging an immeasurable—or unmeasurable—indebtedness to Rosenzweig's *Star,* Levinas acknowledges an even greater indebtedness to Husserl's phenomenological method.

What is at stake here? Why *these* acknowledgments? Why this "timidity and audacity" (to take up the title of a talk Levinas gave on Rozenzweig in 1959,[3] one year before the publication of *Totality and Infinity*)? What timidity it is, after all, to be in such debt, to owe so much to these giants of early twentieth-century thought. What audacity it is, nonetheless, to admit to such a debt, to proceed on one's own in the face of two such thinkers. Why, more to the point, this unmistakable link between *The Star* and phenomenology?

To have an even preliminary feel for the weight of these two sentences within *Totality and Infinity,* we must be reminded that Levinas's preface is in no way a polite litany of acknowledgments. Neither, though it is tacked onto the front of an already completed book, is it a preliminary map or guide to the text that follows it. Nor, for that matter, is the preface a preemptive criticism, spoken from some laborious and superior vantage point achieved only by the book's conclusion, as if Levinas were surveying both text and reader like the adult whose condescending gaze looks down upon the innocent child at the start of an arduous education.

In its last sentence Levinas reveals the purpose of the preface: "attempting to restate without ceremonies what has already been ill understood in the inevitable ceremonial in which the said delights." The *said* here is the body of *Totality and Infinity.* It is both inevitably and, so it seems, quickly, ill understood, so quickly misunderstood that the very preface is already its corrective. Of course, the preface too, though it valiantly attempts to forestall the inevitable misunderstanding of the text, will with equal inevitability be itself misunderstood. To counter these misunderstandings without affirming some impossibly absolute word, some "magical" word that always rings true, Levinas links end and beginning. By joining beginning to end and end to beginning he sets in motion a circular and therefore unending reading of the text, a reading resembling nothing so much as the annual reading of the Torah in the Jewish liturgical year. Endless, but at no point for the sake of the text alone. Each time the text is ill understood, inevitably, quickly, something more is understood, something deeper—something not in the text, "beyond the book."

The preface continues, reanimates, emphasizes, the philosophical claim, life, truth, spirit—there are no magic words—that animates *Totality and Infinity,* however inevitable and quick the loss of whatever it is that drives this text, that is in it but not of it, Rosenzweig's *Star.* I use these particular verbs and nouns deliberately because on Levinasian "grounds" one must be wary of characterizing the achievement or accomplishment of *Totality and Infinity* in such traditional terms as "themes," "contents," "grounds," "essences," "theories," and the like. One must be wary, even and especially in view of the unavoidable peculiarity of speaking of contents, themes, and grounds that are neither contents, themes, or grounds, nor the negation of contents, themes, or grounds. It is precisely *this* distance from traditional philosophical positions—and the word "wariness," like all words, is not quite right either, thank goodness—that is already on display in the structural relation of the preface to the rest of *Totality and Infinity.*

If we take Levinas at his word, is it not strange, to say the least, for a preface *to come before what it continues*? How can what has not yet begun be continued? Can there be a beginning prior to the origin? If being has an origin, as philosophy has always maintained (regardless of whether philosophy can or cannot discover that origin), then what is the sense of "is" when one says that "there *is* a beginning prior to the origin"? Such a beginning would already be a challenge to the firstness of first philosophy, would already be a challenge to the "is" that attempts to discover its origin, the original, of itself, by itself, courageously, invoking all of history and nature, if that is what it takes to be free of outside help. Perhaps this peculiar structure is the first signal or the first shot of the revolution that is the true *work*—the accomplishment, the achievement—of Levinas's text: a pacific but fundamental inversion of philosophical discourse, an inversion of the order of justification and being. Is this not the sign or trace of the peculiar way that the "really good," to return to Franz's letter, enters philosophy? Is it not also and already a clue regarding the strange presence of Rosenzweig's *Star* in Levinas's *Totality and Infinity*? Surely if in the discipline of philosophy one were *to continue what has not yet originated,* "its" presence would be overwhelming at the same time that it could not be quoted.

Stepping back from the pursuit of these lines of inquiry, these intrigues, however fascinating or fruitful they may prove, let us for the moment just say that the glimpses they yield succeed in showing that Levinas's acknowledgments of indebtedness to both Rosenzweig and Husserl, far from being merely private or professional discharges of obligation, are in fact essential ingredients of his philosophy.

To lend further credence to this unassuming claim, and to gain a further but still preliminary insight into its significance, that is to say, insight into the relation between Rosenzweig's *Star* and Husserl's phenomenological method, we have to look at the specific context of these two sentences. We have to be reminded that the acknowledgment of indebtedness to Rosenzweig begins two paragraphs and follows one paragraph entirely devoted otherwise to phenomenology. The very first appearance in *Totality and Infinity* of the word "phenomenology" is in the paragraph directly preceding the appearance of Rosenzweig's name. Levinas's acknowledgment of indebtedness to Rosenzweig's *Star* is, in a word, sandwiched between two prolonged discussions of the phenomenological method. The two acknowledgments are not just linked by their contiguity and their hyperbole, but, as if to answer any further doubts about their conjunction, the gist of both is immediately played out: *The Star* vanishes and phenomenology looms large; it is but an island in a sea of phenomenology. Or, to change metaphors, *The Star's* place in *Totality and Infinity* recalls "those figures of Silenus in statuaries' shops," where a center of astonishing purity is hidden by a familiar image—a star encased by philosophy's familiar scientific pose.

There is yet another paradox. Just before announcing that his text "owes everything" to the phenomenological method, that is to say, in the paragraph preceding Rosenzweig's name, Levinas lashes out against one of the most fundamental tenets of the whole of phenomenology, namely, the idea that consciousness is always intentional consciousness. The soon to be praised method is fundamentally flawed. Against the idea fundamental to phenomenology, that consciousness is adequate to its objects, Levinas defends the existence and status of a more fundamental nonadequation, an extraordinary "relation" to the idea of infinity. All of *Totality and Infinity* is "about" this relation, which the text will later call an "unrelating relation."[4] Thirteen years later, in *Otherwise Than Being or Beyond Essence,*—where, still true to the earlier work, Rosenzweig and *The Star* do not appear at all—it is precisely this relation again that is "otherwise than being or beyond essence." It is already "at work" or "at play" or "in effect" or "operative" in a preface that comes both before and after a text.

Levinas's criticism of phenomenology occurs in the paragraph preceding the mention of Rosenzweig, and reads, with minor deletions, as follows:

> Consciousness then does not consist in equaling being with representation, in tending to the full light in which this adequation is to be sought, but rather in overflowing this play of lights—this phenomenology—and in accomplishing *events* whose ultimate signification (contrary to the Heideggerian conception) does not lie in *disclosing*. . . . The welcoming of the face and the work of justice—which condition the birth of truth itself—are not interpretable in terms of disclosure. Phenomenology is a method for philosophy, but phenomenology—the comprehension effected through a bringing to light—does not constitute the ultimate event of being itself.[5]

Only after this harsh indictment of phenomenology does Levinas acknowledge his debt to Rosenzweig's *Star of Redemption,* in the space opened by the indictment. The peculiarity or paradox thus increases: It is not only after having acknowledged an inordinate debt to Rosenzweig's *Star* but also after having attacked phenomenology at its roots, that Levinas acknowledges his massive debt to the phenomenological method. Only in the light of these peculiar preparations does Levinas finally proceed to a prolonged and relatively positive discussion of phenomenology, though at this point the reader may not quite know whether this discussion is more or less paradoxical, given all that has preceded it.

Rather than say that Levinas's acknowledgment of Rosenzweig is sandwiched between two separate discussions of the phenomenological method, it is more accurate to say that it *interrupts* one extended discussion of phenomenology. I use the term "interruption" deliberately here, not only to recall the dynamics of the living, face-to-face, conversation, which is so important to both Rosenzweig and Levinas, and not only to recall the sense in which Levinas takes skepticism to be a refutable but irrepressible interruption of philosophy,[6] in a conflict of epistemologies, but also and most importantly to invoke the manner in which knowledge itself is permanently ruptured not by *what* comes from another dimension, but by the *otherness* of another dimension, by the difference between that other dimension's slant onto knowledge, its *absolute* "opposition" to knowledge, if you will, and the slant of knowledge itself with its many but always relative oppositions. Again, here "is" the peculiar presence of the "really good," a good that is not real but is *really*, is neither ontic nor ontologic but emphatic.

Again let us take a step back from these heady developments to return to a simpler, more prosaic, point, to the fact obvious by now that the Rosenzweig sentence interrupts many sentences having to do with phenomenology and, indeed, to perhaps only restate the same claim, that it interrupts all the sentences of *Totality and Infinity.* Rosenzweig's name and the name of his book appear in only this one sentence, one out of thousands. The contributions of Husserl and Heidegger, on the other hand, figure explicitly or implicitly on nearly every page of *Totality and Infinity,* as one would expect from an author whose worldwide scholarly reputation came initially from several excellent expositions of the phenomenologies of these two philosophers.

Can it be that we are on the wrong track and this scarcity betokens insignificance? One sentence—is it possible, contrary to everything thus far indicated, including Levinas's own testimony, that this means that Rosenzweig is *not* important? We raise this objection, if it merits even this title, rhetorically, only in order to make a final preliminary point. A Jew (Levinas is certainly Jewish), or the Jewish people (*The Star* is certainly a book for the Jewish people), or a Christian, or anyone else, for that matter *humans,* who stand in solidarity with the fundamental humanism and monotheism of the West, however little these noble causes are in evidence, cannot be so jaded as to be impressed only by large numbers, as if *one*—the one above, and each and every one below—were not the most impressive of all numbers, or as if *two* or *three* did not already set in motion innumerable infinities. Levinas is meticulously true to his few words about Rosenzweig's *Star.* We never hear of Rosenzweig or *The Star* again! They are "invisible to history," to use an expression dear to both Levinas and Rosenzweig; they are *almost* lost in the "inevitable ceremonial in which the said delights." It is *almost as if* nothing had been said.[7] It is in this *almost* and in this *as if*—lighter than winged words, heavier than the universe—that a world of difference lies. Can one imagine a finer distinction, a more refined discretion, a greater dignity and trust, to be thus mentioned once and once only!

In view of these two peculiarities—(1) the eminent but brief appearance of Rosenzweig, like a shooting star, within an extended discussion of phenomenology, and (2) the allegation of *The Star's* exorbitant presence in absentia in *Totality and Infinity*—we are prompted to ask two questions. First, what connection is there for Levinas between Rosenzweig's *Star* and the phenomenologies of Husserl and Heidegger? Second, what is the deeper meaning of Rosenzweig's excessive presence and absence in *Totality and Infinity*? How can a thought be *too often* present? When quantity becomes quality, when excess becomes invisibility, are we not already in the presence of the idea of infinity? Though I will start with the question of the relation between *The Star* and phenomenology, it will become apparent that the two questions and their answers are inseparable.

In the main, the discussion before the Rosenzweig sentence is, as we have seen, critical of phenomenology, whereas the discussion afterward, as we have yet to see, is laudatory.

Returning to the criticism of phenomenology quoted earlier, where phenomenology's central methodological and structural notion of intentionality, the adequation of consciousness to its objects, is challenged in the name of the idea of infinity, one can see the logic whereby Levinas concludes his discussion with glowing praise for Rosenzweig's *Star,* more specifically for its "opposition to the idea of totality." Levinas's logic would be as follows: the primordial "*events* whose ultimate signification" exceed phenomenology are "the welcoming of the face and the work of justice." These two events, as events,[8] are precisely the central message of Rosenzweig's *Star,* its revelatory love of the neighbor and its redemptive call to save the world, a revelation and a redemption whose imperative force enables *The Star* to oppose the idea of totality.

Just as Rosenzweig strives to break up the classical philosophical equation of thinking and being, especially as found in the Hegelian dialectic, that is to say, in the dynamic identity (whether open or closed) of identity and difference, Levinas opposes phenomenology's fundamental idea of intentionality, the idea of a thoroughgoing correlation of consciousness and its objects. By defining consciousness as intentional from top to bottom, from its most transcendent to its most immanent significations, as intentional even in its own self-constitution, phenomenology sees no exit from the circuit of noema and noesis. The mercy and justice that Rosenzweig's *Star* sets up against the conceptual totalizing of "philosophy from Parmenides to Hegel" also inspire Levinas in his opposition to the noetic-noematic totality of phenomenology.

The inspiration of the concluding words of *The Star* is intended not merely as another philosophical discourse, nor merely as another philosophical intuition, but rather as a *call* from above. Rosenzweig has chosen his words deliberately, borrowing from the Bible, in order to *stir* his readers, not merely to persuade but to exhort them "to do justice and to love mercy," and "to walk humbly with thy God."[9] When concluding his text with these words, Rosenzweig explicitly warns his readers that love and justice are not to be taken as "goals," that is to say, as ideas in the Kantian sense. "To love mercy" is to aid the nearest one, the neighbor, and this (rather than the 613 commandments given on Mount Sinai, by the way) is the content or event of revelation. "To do justice," likewise, is to save the world, to complete it in and through history, to engage actively in hastening the Kingdom of God. "The Kingdom of God," Rosenzweig writes, "prevails in the world by being prevalent in the world";[10] neither revelation nor redemption are "goals," for they are "wholly today, and thus wholly eternal as life and the way."[11] They are the inwardly burning fire of Judaism, its life, and the outwardly spreading rays of Christianity, its way. Rosenzweig intends the imperatives of love and justice to be taken—here interpreting Levinas's criticism of phenomenology as a commentary on Rosenzweig—as precisely those "*events* whose ultimate signification (contrary to the Heideggerian conception) does not lie in *disclosing*." Loving mercy and doing justice, whether in their Jewish or Christian modalities, are the events—"beyond the book"—that exceed the phenomen-ology that is today's philosophical version of the German idealism criticized by Rosenzweig.

This answer draws Rosenzweig into Levinas's criticism of phenomenology. By orienting their thought in ethics and social justice rather than grounding it in disclosure, by remaining true to the concrete persons and demands of social life rather than to the constitutive requirements of the "life of the mind," Levinas and Rosenzweig together oppose the idea of totality—whether the sophisticated and complex totalities found in the modern German idealisms of Fichte and Hegel, or those found in the contemporary German idealisms of Husserl and Heidegger. Levinas and Rosenzweig oppose totality in fundamentally the same way.

Beyond this side of the Rosenzweig-Husserl relation which *Totality and Infinity* sets up and maintains, we must also account for the seemingly paradoxical conjunction of *The Star* and Levinas's *positive* appraisal of phenomenology. Having insisted *prior* to the Rosenzweig sentence that "phenomenology—the comprehension effected through a bringing to light—does not constitute the ultimate event of being itself," and having insisted that "the welcoming of the face and the work of justice—which condition the birth of truth itself—are not interpretable in terms of disclosure," we must ask how it is that *after* mentioning Rosenzweig, Levinas can assert that "the presentation and development of the notions employed [in *Totality and Infinity*] owe everything to the phenomenological method"? If Husserl and Heidegger are wrong about the status of intentional analysis, why does Levinas use it as his method? Why, furthermore, does he go out of his way to highlight his use of the phenomenological method in conjunction with his praise of Rosenzweig's *Star*? Certainly the textual contiguity, the shared excess, and the several speculations begun here suggest an important link between Levinas's two positive appraisals.

At this juncture it is time to note Rosenzweig's own neglect of phenomenology. *The Star,* after all, was published more than two decades after the publication of Husserl's *Phenomenological Investigations* (1899–1901), decades that saw this new phenomenology widely discussed in German philosophical circles. *The Star* was, in addition, written right after the publication of Husserl's *Ideas I* (1913). During Rosenzweig's formative and creative years, then, Husserl was recognized in German-speaking circles as Germany's leading philosopher. Nonetheless, despite the chronological, geographical, and professional proximity, Rosenzweig neither uses nor criticizes the phenomenological method. He never even mentions it. Although it is true that shortly after the publication of Heidegger's celebrated *Being and Time* in 1927, a text that totally ignores *The Star,* Rosenzweig, though quite ill and only able to communicate with the greatest difficulty, does devote a few pages to it, to what he generously takes to be its proximity to *The Star,* he still does not discuss or so much as mention Husserl. Phenomenology is neither present nor present in absentia in Rosenzweig's work—it is totally absent. This silence, however, speaks (though with quite a different voice than Heidegger's several silences).

Despite Rosenzweig's silence, we have nonetheless seen how Levinas could bring *The Star* to bear on a criticism of phenomenology, by opposing ethics and justice to the residual philosophical idealism of phenomenology. Now, in contrast, we are asking how Levinas can praise *The Star* in nearly the same breath with which he praises the phenomenological method.

The answer lies in grasping exactly what Levinas praises in phenomenology. Putting aside his role as loyal expositor, when he creatively appropriates phenomenology for his own purposes, he is no longer interested in the chimera of a pure phenomenological method. Although Levinas always prefers phenomenology in its Husserlian form, his own philosophical task is not the defense of that form against other alternative versions of phenomenology. In a word, one must distinguish what Levinas finds wrong and what he finds right about phenomenology. Because, like all of Husserl's great "students," Levinas has his own philosophy, one must discover his own phenomenology.

In the discussion that *concludes* with Rosenzweig, Levinas focused on the revelatory aspect of phenomenology, phenomenology as "the comprehension effected through a bringing to light," what he labels "the Heideggerian conception." This aspect, luminous phenomenology, intuitional, evidential phenomenology, is what Levinas criticized for not being able to reach, for covering up *in the brilliance of its light* what is truly primordial, that is, "the welcome of the face and the work of justice." Disclosure, though essential to phenomenology, as Heidegger saw even more deeply than Husserl, is inadequate to the "phenomena"—properly speaking, the "enigma"[12]—that interest Levinas: the events of ethics and justice. And these events, to repeat, are precisely what he has so gratefully learned from Rosenzweig's *Star.*

In the discussion that *commences* with Rosenzweig, however, Levinas's focus is on two different aspects of phenomenology: its concreteness and its break-up of representation. Directly after saying that "the notions employed [in *Totality and Infinity*] owe everything to the phenomenological method," he tells his readers what, in his eyes, this method is. He writes:

> Intentional analysis is the search for the concrete. Notions held under the direct gaze of the thought that defines them are nevertheless, unbeknown to this naive thought, revealed to be implanted in horizons unsuspected by this thought; these horizons endow them with a meaning—such is the essential teaching of Husserl. What does it matter if in the Husserlian phenomenology taken literally these unsuspected horizons are in their turn interpreted as thoughts aiming at objects! What counts is the idea of the overflowing of objectifying thought by a forgotten experience from which it lives. The break-up of the formal structure of thought (the noema of a noesis) into events which this structure dissimulates, but which sustain it and restore its concrete significance, constitutes a *deduction*—necessary and yet non-analytical.[13]

The focus now is on the nonformal, the "concrete" sources of the formal structures of thought, and on the way these "events," as Levinas (and Rosenzweig) calls them, break up and sustain the formal structures of thought.

To maintain this shift in focus and evaluation, Levinas makes an important distinction. He contrasts "Husserlian phenomenology taken literally," which he opposes in intellectual fellowship with

Rosenzweig, and "the essential teaching of Husserl," to which he is indebted even more so than to Rosenzweig for the "presentation and development of the notions employed" in *Totality and Infinity.*

It is by means of a heightened attention to the concrete sources of formal thought—the "essential teaching of Husserl"—that Levinas finds the all important double-edged *event,* the event both violent and nurturing that breaks up and sustains representation. First, starting with objective thought, there is a destructive side to the concrete: "the overflowing of objectifying thought," "the break-up of the formal structure of thought." This movement reinforces Levinas's alliance with Rosenzweig, reinforces their mutual "opposition to the idea of totality." Second, starting now with what *truly* comes first, there is a positive side to the concrete: the recognition that that which overflows and breaks up formal objectifying thought is at the same time that "from which it lives," that can "sustain and restore its concrete significance," that can "endow" it with meaning. For "Husserlian phenomenology taken literally," in contrast, the radicalness of its destructive work is undone by a reconstruction of the same formal objectifying thought at a deeper constitutive level. Like a Medusa's head, formal thought returns with a vengeance, reconstituting itself at deeper levels of consciousness, closer to and finally at the very heart of consciousness itself.

Now, even if one were to take exception to this line of thought, that is to say, even if one were to argue that "Husserlian phenomenology taken literally" is innocent, that it does not reestablish the primacy of formal objectifying thought, it would still be the case, by all accounts, that it reestablishes, according to its unshakable tenet, the primacy of intentional thought, the primacy of "thoughts aiming at objects." Levinas contests not only the formal objectifying character of absolute consciousness, but also the intentionality of consciousness. The coup de grace, however, is that to effect this contestation, to "prove" it, he enlists the evidence of phenomenology itself! Phenomenology, the latest and strongest form of philosophy as a science, destroys itself. Thus Levinas's contestation of philosophy, and through phenomenology his contestation of philosophy, takes the form of critique rather than criticism. Phenomenology is permitted to show its glory, its science, and at the same time, through this same success, it is made to display its breakdown, its wounds. Precisely as such, in its success and in its failure, in the failure of its success and the success of its failure, it is invaluable.

It is instructive at this juncture to note that the manner in which Levinas distinguishes between the essential and the literal in Husserl, between what one can learn and what one must guard against, reproduces his earlier 1930 reading of Husserl[14] in *The Theory of Intuition in Husserl's Phenomenology.*[15] Though the primary intent of this early work was to provide the French intellectual world with a faithful exposition of Husserl's theory of intuition, Levinas does manage here and there, already in 1930, to take an independent stand. The general criticism of phenomenology that permits him to take this stand is essentially the same as that found thirty years later in *Totality and Infinity.* That is to say, Levinas's criticism of phenomenology in 1930 and in 1961 is that Husserl founds representational thought on representational thought, that for Husserl consciousness is always and ultimately representational consciousness, a predicative synthesis. But it is instructive for our current discussion to note that in contrast to 1961, where, enlisting Rosenzweig, Levinas criticizes Husserl in the name of ethics and justice, in 1930, in the *Intuition* book, he criticizes Husserl under the influence of Heidegger, that is to say, in the name of being. Beneath representation he sees not more representation but presence to being, that is, an ontological thinking.

To be sure, Levinas was not a Heideggerian in 1930, nor is he one today. Though profoundly influenced then and now by the power of Heidegger's thought, influenced so far as to insist that all philosophy must "go through"[16] Heideggerian thought, Levinas has never been a Heideggerian. One interesting result of our investigation into Levinas's joint appropriation of *The Star* and phenomenology, as we shall see in a moment, is to clarify the precise nature of his ambivalence toward Heidegger. It is on this ambivalence that the general significance of phenomenology for Levinas will hinge. In 1930, in any event, his work evidences an ambivalence toward both Husserl and Heidegger. In his *Intuition* book, Levinas attributes to Husserl a theory of consciousness grounded in representation, *and* a theory of consciousness grounded in presence to being.[17] In so doing, he avoids mentioning Heidegger while crediting Husserl with being a Heideggerian! For those who know better, it is clear that Levinas is praising and blaming both thinkers at the same time.

The 1930 distinction between a representational foundation for consciousness and an ontological foundation for consciousness does not, however reproduce the 1961 distinction between a literal and an essential reading of Husserl's phenomenology—and not just because of its ambivalence. At best it half reproduces it. In both instances Husserl's phenomenological method is credited with breaking up the formal level of representation. Furthermore, in both instances Husserl is understood to have grounded representation on more representation, and to be found lacking for so doing. So much for sameness.

The difference between the 1930 and the 1961 accounts is far more striking, and with regard to the question of Rosenzweig's role, is far more illuminating. It is clear on any reading that Levinas was from the first dissatisfied with the foundations of Husserlian phenomenology. To assuage this dissatisfaction in 1930 he was tempted, albeit hesitantly, in a veiled manner, by the Heideggerian turn toward being, by Heidegger's reading of phenomenology as fundamental ontology. Levinas had just recently read Heidegger's brilliant ontological and hermeneutical appropriation of phenomenology in paragraph seven of *Being and Time*.[18] He was actually in Freiburg during the 1928–29 school year, attending the private philosophical discussions led by Husserl, who had officially retired from the university a year earlier, and also attending the celebrated seminars of Husserl's successor, Professor Martin Heidegger who, if he had not yet eclipsed Husserl, was surely the new and still rising star of German philosophy. What, then, convinces Levinas to turn away from Heidegger in his turn away from Husserl?

To answer this question, our account of Levinas's relation to Husserl and Heidegger requires one further nuance. In both *Totality and Infinity* and in his *Intuition* book, Levinas understands ontological thinking as an alternative and more profound *ground* for representational thinking. In both cases he sees that not more representations but the truth of being, truth as the disclosure of being, as Heidegger understood it, underlies representational thought. But despite this genuine and unbroken appreciation for Heideggerian ontology, there is still a wide gap separating his assessment of Heidegger and phenomenology in 1930 and in 1961. In 1930 Levinas opposes Husserlian representation with Heideggerian ontology. In 1961 he opposes both the Husserlian phenomenology, that is, the representationally grounded phenomenology, *and* the Heideggerian phenomenology, that is, the ontologically grounded phenomenology. In the name of "the welcoming of the face and the work of justice," Levinas now opposes Husserlian representation and Heideggerian disclosure, even though he takes Heidegger to be essentially correct, against Husserl, that ontological disclosure *is* the foundation of representation.

It is precisely the encounter with Rosenzweig's *Star* that enables Levinas to make his subtler and more fundamental critique of phenomenology. It turns out that his dissatisfaction with the foundations of Husserlian phenomenology stems from two sources, one more profound than the other. It is not until he encounters Rosenzweig's *Star,* because it is the more profound alternative, that he can fully assuage this dissatisfaction. *Heidegger's ontology permits Levinas to see beneath the representational character of Husserl's phenomenology, true; but the ethics and justice of Rosenzweig's* Star *permit him to see through the ontological character of Heidegger's regrounding of phenomenology.* Heidegger frees Levinas from Husserl and at the same time deepens his appreciation for phenomenology, but Rosenzweig frees Levinas from phenomenology by deepening his appreciation for ethics and justice.

Thus in the discussion of phenomenology in the preface to *Totality and Infinity,* which *commences* with praise for Rosenzweig's *Star,* the opposition between what is essential and therefore still acceptable in phenomenology, and what is literal and therefore unacceptable in phenomenology, will place both Husserl and Heidegger on the side of the literal. Now the literal means not just founding representation in more representation, a la Husserl, nor the founding of representation in ontological thinking, a la Heidegger, but the very idea or form of *Grund* (and its partner, *Abgrund*) as such—that is, the standard of *adequation,* the thinking of thinking as sustained by adequation. It is this difference between Levinas's earlier and later assessment of phenomenology that is the meaning of his acknowledgment of Rosenzweig's *Star* in close proximity to the phenomenological method. It is comforting to note, by way of biographical support for this thesis, that Levinas first read the *Star* in 1935.[19]

Under the influence of Rosenzweig's *Star,* Levinas will now oppose not just the formality and objectification of representation, an opposition also proposed by Heidegger, but the notion of *adequation* as such, whether of the intentional-consciousness sort proposed by Husserl, the correlation of noema to noeses, or of the existential-ontological sort proposed by Heidegger, the correlation of *Dasein* to *Sein.* It is also important to realize, in grasping this connection between Levinas's debt to Rosenzweig's *Star* and his positive evaluation of phenomenology, that he finds within phenomenology itself the resources for its own undoing.

In *his* reading of phenomenology—against both Husserl and Heidegger—Levinas finds not only the recognition of a movement of thought that breaks up correlation as such, whether formal or existential, but the recognition that this break-up comes from an irrecuperably nonadequate relation—an ethical relation—whose significance is prior to the significations established through intentional correlation. Underneath the structure of founded and founding that dominates both Husserlian and Heideggerian phenomenology, Levinas, along with Rosenzweig, asserts the primacy of *metaphysics,* the unquenched and unquenchable thirst for alterity, the always inadequate desire for the inordinate.

We can now see that when Levinas writes that the "notions employed" in *Totality and Infinity* "owe everything to the phenomenological method," he means that they are indebted to phenomenology for three interrelated movements or dimensions: (1) the turn to the concrete, (2) the break-up of the formal structures of representation, and (3) the recognition that the formal structures of representation "live from" and are "endowed" with significance by horizons unsuspected by intentional thought. It is the combined movement of all three of these components that Levinas calls the "phenomenological deduction."

What phenomenological deduction reveals is the truth of metaphysics, metaphysical truth: the priority of goodness and justice. It is as if the phenomenological deduction forced philosophy, per impossible, one step beyond its maximum capacities, as in a quantum leap, or the abutment of one topological dimension by another of a different order. Ethics and justice would no longer provide "principles" or "grounds" for philosophy, nor, certainly, would they be subsumed by philosophy, nor, worse, would they be excluded from philosophy altogether. Rather, philosophy, thought through to the end, to the end of its end, troubled by Husserl's phenomenological deduction, would acknowledge itself as a *mode* of ethics and justice. "Husserlian phenomenology," Levinas writes in the concluding sentence of the two-paragraph discussion of phenomenology that follows the acknowledgment of Rosenzweig's *Star,* "has made possible this passage from ethics to metaphysical exteriority."[20]

Having attained some insight into the metaphysical dimension that both undermines and nurtures philosophy *qua* phenomenology, we are now in a position (or "nonposition," Levinas would say) to appreciate the extraordinary absence and presence of *The Star,* its presence in absentia, in *Totality and Infinity,* to appreciate why this absence is necessary, and how it relates specifically to phenomenology. There are two sides to the absence of *The Star* in *Totality and Infinity,* and both of them, of necessity, have their parallels in *The Star's* relation to itself and in *Totality and Infinity's* relation to itself.

First, to say that *The Star* is present in *Totality and Infinity* only by being absent, that *The Star* "is" extraordinarily absent, that it is "otherwise than being," is another way of saying that phenomenology—to which *Totality and Infinity* owes everything—is precisely what permits glimpsing the true sources of thought, sources that lie outside of phenomenology and outside of thought altogether. Rosenzweig shows Levinas the way free from phenomenology, just as Schelling showed Rosenzweig the way free from idealism. It is not simple curious that in *The Star* and elsewhere Rosenzweig reveals his own hyperbolic modesty and audacity in relation to Friedrich von Schelling, giving him credit for having shown the way out of idealist philosophy. It is Rosenzweig's contention that had Schelling only completed his project of a positive philosophy, which was begun in *The Ages of the World* (1820), then *The Star* "would not have been worthy of anyone's attention except the Jews."[21] What he means is that the philosophical possibility of *The Star's* basic message comes from Schelling, from Schelling's argument against nineteenth-century Germany idealism, his argument that if thought through to the end, idealism can be made to glimpse its own true sources outside of idealism. Levinas is clearly making the same claim with regard to phenomenology. Both idealism and phenomenology can be made to see—not, however, with the necessity that makes for their own sight, the sight that can be blinded by its own light—or made to *suffer,* one should perhaps say, the *weight* of metaphysics, the superlative of the divine, which "appears" in the face of the other person and "unfolds" in the struggle for justice. Phenomenology, so Levinas claims by invoking the "opposition to totality" found in Rosenzweig's *Star,* reveals its own shortcomings, its own inadequacy.

Second, just as idealism was for Rosenzweig not just any philosophy randomly selected for criticism, but the essence of philosophy, philosophy itself, for Levinas it is phenomenology that is now philosophy's most rigorous form. If philosophy stayed put, if it never advanced, then Rosenzweig (or perhaps Schelling) could have done his critical work and we would all be finished with it once and for all. But philosophy does not stay put, even if it does not necessarily "advance" either. Just as idealism was yesterday's misunderstanding of metaphysics, corrected by phenomenology, phenomenology is today's misunderstanding of metaphysics (and, increasingly, phenomenology in our day has also become yesterday's understanding of metaphysics). We must understand that it is not just the text of *Totality and Infinity* that is inevitably ill understood and immediately calls for a preface. Neither, more broadly, is it just phenomenology or idealism that are always, inevitably, ill understood. These are merely the latest philosophical "ceremonies" in which goodness delights in expressing and losing itself. Philosophy itself, or, even more broadly, the world itself, both expresses and loses the metaphysical, the meta-physical. To reanimate the very same inspiration that animates *The Star,* then, Levinas must grapple with phenomenology rather than with nineteenth-century Germany idealism.

The necessary undoing of philosophy (which is itself, in another sense, *philosophy*; the unsaying of the saying that has become said) is historical in the sense that philosophy, like the world of which it is a part, takes on different historical forms, forms that both complete and at the same time disfigure the metaphysical. But at the same time the undoing of philosophy so understood is ahistorical. It is always the very same metaphysical claim—always absent, always overwhelmingly present, better than being, other than being—that undoes each and every philosophical form, undoes each and every "ceremony," undoes each and every provisional stopping place that takes itself too seriously, that is to say, that takes the genuine ethical and social claims of humanity too lightly. The undoing of philosophy is as eternal and as temporal as philosophy itself. "Thinking," Levinas has written, "has never been more difficult." Thinking, we could add, has at each time always been most difficult. But perhaps, let us add in a final suggestion, which returns to *philosophy* in another sense, the idea or life of *wisdom*—the "wisdom of love,"[22] Levinas writes—is how philosophy itself acknowledges this difficulty, thinking that which transcends thought itself.

Notes

1. Emmanuel Levinas, *Totality and Infinity,* trans. Alphonso Lingis (Pittsburgh: Duquesne University Press, 1969), p. 28.

2. Cited in *Franz Rosenzweig: His Life and Thought,* ed. Nahum N. Glatzer (New York: Schocken, 1967), p. 104.

3. Levinas's talk was given in September 1959, that is, before the publication of *Totality and Infinity.* It was published in *La conscience juive,* ed. Amado Levy-Valensi and Jean Halperin (Paris: Presses Universitaires de France, 1963), pp. 121–37, along with a record of the discussion that followed, pp. 137–49. It has appeared in English as "Franz Rosenzweig," trans. Richard A. Cohen, 29, no. 9 (November 1983); 33–40.

4. Levinas, *Totality and Infinity,* p. 295.

5. Ibid., pp. 27–28.

6. See the section on "Skepticism and Reason" in Emmanuel Levinas, *Otherwise Than Being or Beyond Essence,* trans. Alphonso Lingis (The Hague: Martinus Nijhoff, 1981), pp. 165–71. Also see the analysis of this section given by Jan de Greef in "Skepticism and Reason," in *Face to Face with Levinas,* ed. Richard A. Cohen (Albany: SUNY Press, 1986), pp. 159–79.

7. Levinas begins his 1957 article, "Phenomenon and Enigma," with the following quotation from Ionesco's *The Bald Soprano:* "In short, we still do not know if, when someone rings the doorbell, there is someone there or not," in *Collected Philosophical Papers,* trans. Alphonso Lingis (Dordrecht: Martinus Nijhoff, 1987), p. 61.

In a footnote to the same article Levinas acknowledges another intellectual debt, this time to Vladimir Jankelevitch, especially to his *Philosophie premier: Introduction a une philosophie du "Presque"* (Paris: PUF, 1954). "Our own project," he writes, "owes a great deal to his work." *Collected Philosophical Papers,* p. 63.

8. See Franz Rosenzweig, *The Star of Redemption,* trans. William W. Hallo (Boston: Beacon Press, 1972; Notre Dame: Notre Dame Press, 1985), p. 108: "And theology itself conceives of its contents as event, not as 'content'; that is to say, as that which is lived, not as 'life'."

The invisibility of great events is a "theme," touched on in this article, that is crucial in bringing Rosenzweig and Levinas together. Rosenzweig has written: "perhaps the great events in a man's life always begin undetected by human eyes," in *Kleinere Schriften* (Berlin: Schocken, 1937), p. 325, quoted by Else-Rahel Freund in *Franz Rosenzweig's Philosophy of Existence,* trans. Stephen L. Weinstein and Robert Israel (The Hague: Martinus Nijhoff, 1979), p. 64. Levinas: "The great 'experiences' of our life have properly speaking never been lived." See "Phenomenon and Enigma," in *Collected Philosophical Papers,* p. 68. I will return to this theme and these two claims elsewhere.

9. Rosenzweig, *The Star,* p. 424.

10. Ibid., p. 239.

11. Ibid., p. 424.

12. See Levinas, "Phenomenon and Enigma," in *Collected Philosophical Papers,* pp. 61–73.

13. Levinas, *Totality and Infinity,* p. 28.

14. In *Totality and Infinity* Levinas refers to his 1959 article "The Ruin of Representation," which will be published in English translation in a collection of Levinas's writings on Husserl, *Discovering Existence in Husserl* (Evanston: Northwestern University Press, forthcoming).

15. Emmanuel Levinas, *The Theory of Intuition in Husserl's Phenomenology,* trans. André Orianne (Evanston, Ill.: Northwestern University Press, 1973).

16. Emmanuel Levinas, *Ethics and Infinity,* trans. Richard A. Cohen (Pittsburgh: Duquesne University Press, 1985), p. 42.

17. Levinas himself admits to having given a Heideggerian reading to Husserl in the *Intuition* book; cf. *Ethics and Infinity,* p. 39.

18. Martin Heidegger, *Being and Time,* trans. John Macquarrie and Edward Robinson (New York: Harper and Row, 1962), pp. 49–63.

Although for our purposes what I have said is sufficient, it should be noted that for Heidegger the relation between phenomenology and ontology is more complex than indicated. Toward the end of paragraph 7 Heidegger writes: "Ontology and phenomenology are not two distinct philosophical disciplines among others. These terms characterize philosophy itself with regard to its object and its way of treating that object. Philosophy is universal phenomenological ontology, and takes its departure from the hermeneutic of Dasein." In a complete treatment of this question, then, care would have to be taken to distinguish between philosophy, phenomenology, ontology, and hermeneutics.

It is also of interest to note, with regard to what has been said about Levinas's relation to Rosenzweig and phenomenology, that toward the end of section 7 Heidegger acknowledges his indebtedness to Husserl, and at the same time takes a critical distance from his mentor. Heidegger's criticism is effected in the same way as Levinas later effects his, that is, by means of a discrimination between what is essential to phenomenology and what is not essential. "The following investigation," Heidegger writes, "would not have been possible if the ground had not been prepared by Edmund Husserl, with whose *Logische Untersuchungen* phenomenology first emerged. . . .what is essential in it does not lie in its *actuality* as a philosophical 'movement.' Higher than actuality stands *possibility*. We can understand phenomenology only by seizing upon it as a possibility."

19. See François Poirie, *Emmanuel Levinas: Qui êtes-vous?* (Lyon: La Manufacture, 1987), p. 121. Not knowing of this book, I asked Levinas in October 1987 when he had first read Rosenzweig's *The Star of Redemption*. His answer was the same: 1935.

20. Levinas, *Totality and Infinity*, p. 29.

21. Quoted by Ernst Akiva Simon in "Reflections of a Disciple," in *The Philosophy of Franz Rosenzweig*, ed. Paul Mendes-Flohr (Hanover, N.H.: Brandeis University Press, 1988), pp. 205–6.

A close examination of *The Star's* relation to the whole of Schelling can be found in Freund, *Franz Rosenzweig's Philosophy of Existence*.

22. Cf. Levinas, *Otherwise than Being or Beyond Essence*, pp. 153–62.

A Note Concerning Rosenzweig and Levinas on Totality

JOHANAN E. BAUER

"La lumière d'Israël est un cri à l'infini"
—Edmond Jabès

THE following remarks sketch the outlines of an argument rather than present a thorough development of the subject. Within appropriate brevity, my purpose is to sharpen the question concerning the extent of Rosenzweig's influence upon the Levinasian rejection of totality as presented in Richard Cohen's article. His perceptive analysis sustains the thesis that while the Levinas of *Théorie de l'intuition* (1930) opposed Husserlian representation from the point of view of ontological disclosure, the Levinas of *Totalité et Infini* (1961) was critical both of Husserl's phenomenology and of its ontological regrounding by Heidegger. The new critical stance was rendered possible by *Der Stern der Erlösung* that Levinas read in 1935 and that enabled him to deepen his "appreciation for ethics and justice."[1] Rosenzweig's significance for Levinas centers on the role that the former assigns to the "events" of revelation and redemption in their opposition to the "pantheistic concept of the All"[2] grounded in the identity—and thus adequation—of Being and Thought.

In the often quoted passage, Levinas openly acknowledges his deference to Rosenzweig: "L'opposition à l'idée de totalité, nous a frappé dans le *Stern der Erlösung* de Franz Rosenzweig, trop souvent présent dans ce livre pour être cité."[3] However relevant the recognition of *The Star's* impressive opposition to totality and of its "presence" throughout *Totalité* might be, in my opinion, neither the textual evidence nor the final philosophical positions legitimize R. Cohen's assumption that "Levinas and Rosenzweig oppose totality in fundamentally the same way."[4] Being impressed by Rosenzweig's opposition to totality may just mean the recognition of the intellectual audacity and originality of his undertaking, without necessarily implying agreement with the intellectual thoroughness displayed in the undertaking or with the final philosophical premises determining the opposition.

I would thus propose to distinguish Rosenzweig's "presence" in *Totalité* on two different levels. Obviously, Rosenzweig's profoundly Jewish gesture of rejecting *Identitäsphilosophien* or "closed system" had a deep impact on Levinas's intellectual development. But it is precisely in the name of the truth of this gesture that Levinas must depart at a deeper level and a decisive point, from some of Rosenzweig's main tenets. It is my contention that Rosenzweig undoes his audacious critique of totality by his own uncritical doctrine of God, and that Levinas has seen through this momentous failure. Rosenzweig's presence is thus not only that of a major Jewish-philosophical impulse, but also that of a great thinker worthy of being evaluated and eventually criticized by his own standards. *The Star* is also present in *Totalité* as a decisive but nonetheless unspoken object of criticism.

Rosenzweig's critique of the history of occidental philosophy—"von Jonien bis Jena"—with regard to the problem of totality constitutes without doubt a major philosophical accomplishment of this century. It must be recalled that for this task he found important support in the philosophies of Schopenhauer, the later Schelling, and Nietzsche. In the context of his argument leading to the affirmation of God's existence beyond the idealistic assumption of the identity of Thought and Being, Rosenzweig relies heavily on Schelling's later philosophy and especially on his treatment of God's nature. The postidealistic Schelling, criticizing "negative Vernunftphilosophie" from the standpoint of his own "metaphysischer Empirismus," realizes a fundamental turn towards the "positivity" of historical reality. However, in his attempt to save reality from the pretentions of an all-encompassing Reason, he seeks refuge in a sort of historicized pantheism granting no true *otherness* of the existing world vis-à-vis God.

Schelling expresses his fundamental conception succinctly when he writes: "Die Welt ist nur das suspendirte göttliche Seyn."[5] At the end of the process leading from nature through mythology and revelation to final redemption, God regains His being: "Die Aufhebung (des göttlichen Seyns) ist eine bloss temporäre, sie ist nur Suspension."[6] In this view, creation stands not in a relation of real alterity to God, but in one of polarity within a whole-in-becoming; redemption (that is, the *telos* of becoming) is essentially liberation from that to which the "Suspension" gave origin. Inasmuch as the reality of the world and its history is only an interruption of God's own being that can be repaired by reversing the process, redemption is truly only the undoing of creation; apparent otherness is doomed to be reabsorbed in God's all-embracing totality. Schelling's historicization of the Heraclitean *hen panta* is no alternative to totality, but its radical consummation. Here, the incarnational structures of thought originating in Christology played an important role; for it is Christology as the discourse on God-becoming-man that pleads for the abrogation of their mutual otherness.

At this point let us recall Rosenzweig's explicitly acknowledged indebtedness to the later Schelling and especially to his elaborations on the nature of God. In a chapter "Logic of Redemption," Rosenzweig writes:

> Thus redemption has, as its final result, something which lifts it above and beyond the comparison with creation and redemption, namely God himself. We have already said it: he is Redeemer in a much graver sense than he is Creator or Revealer. For he is not only the one who redeems, but also the one who is redeemed. In the redemption of the world by man, of man by means of the world, God redeems himself. Man and world disappear in the redemption, but God perfects himself. Only in redemption, God becomes the One and All which, from the first, human reason in its rashness has everywhere sought and everywhere asserted, and yet nowhere found because it simply was nowhere to be found yet, for it did not exist. . . . Here in the blinding midnight sun of the consummated redemption it has at last, yea at the very last, coalesced into the One.[7]

The content of this passage is confirmed in the penultimate chapter of *The Star:* "Its direct effect is confined to the redemption of God Himself. For God Himself, redemption is the eternal deed in which He frees Himself from having anything confront Him that is not He Himself."

Like Schelling's God, the God of Rosenzweig is also in need of redemption—of self-redemption, for the simple reason that creation exists. According to this "Logic," the disappearance of the "creational vis-à-vis" is the necessary condition for God's own final realization: God is *liberated* from that which He is not. Rosenzweig describes this process by paraphrasing the famous fragment 50 (Diels-Kranz) of Heraclitus in the context of an unequivocally organic metaphor; the All [*das All*] has grown into the unity of the One [*zum Einen susammen gewachsen*]. In God's own final becoming, the alterity of the other is abolished [*aufgehoben*]. At the End of Days, totality shall reign unpaired.

Even if Rosenzweig stresses the fact that God's self-redemption does not occur "in time," the underlying conception comes close to what could be described as "Theodramatik,"[8] and shows structural affinities to some aspects of gnostic mythology that had manifest repercussions on Christian theology in particular. Without pretending to blur constitutive religious differences, Rosenzweig developed, with the aid of Schelling, a form of speculation concerning God's "eternal becoming" that in a way endangers the significance of God's radical difference to the world as understood by prophetic monotheism. Rosenzweig was, of course, well aware of the fact that Schelling's overall Christian conception was nurtured to some extent by patterns and contents of thought originating in kabbalah and, via kabbalah, by some earlier strains of thought within talmudic Judaism. This perception undoubtedly eased Rosenzweig's reception of Schelling's theology. But the intricacies of *Wirkungsgeschichte* do not dismiss this reception from the charge of being uncritical.

Short of being able in this context to discuss in detail the chapter on "Separation et absolu" at the end of the first part of *Totalité,* I would at least like to mention some of the conceptual articulations organizing Levinas's reflection on totality. It will become clear that Rosenzweig's "logic of redemption" falls within the scope of the Levinasian criticism.

Early in the development of his main work, Levinas recognizes the great force of the monotheistic idea of creation in the fact that it is conceived of as being ex nihilo. Created existence does not simply "come out of the father," but is in relation to God, a wholly Other.[9]

> Affirmer l'origine a partir de rien par la création, c'est contester la communauté préalable de toutes choses au sein de l'éternité, d'ou la pensée philosophique, guidée par l'ontologie, fait surgir les êtres comme d'une matrice commune. Le décalage absolu de la séparation que la trascendence suppose, ne saurait mieux se dire que par le terme de creation, où, à la fois, s'affirme la parenté des êtres entre eux, mais aussi leur héterogéneité radicale, leur extériorité reciproque a partir du néant.[10]

Against the idea of totality encompassing the multiplicity of being in a closed unit, the monotheistic concept of creation sets an insurmountable gap of nothingness between God and His world in order to grant to the finite and fragile existence of created being irreducible alterity, not only in relation to the Creator, but also within the community of being. The separating nothingness, which no mediation can cancel (and thus ontologize), is the condition of possibility of religion, that is, "le lien qui s'établit entre le Même et l'Autre sans constituer une totalité."[11] This form of metaphysical relation that renounces the possibility of reducing Otherness to Selfhood, is at the very basis of Levinas's critique of occidental philosophy; against totalizing ontology, metaphysics acknowledges the insurmountable distance in the relation to the always transcending Infinite. Being essentially an "éclatement de la totalité," the relation to transcendence liberates the Self from the illusion of "egological" imperialism and from the seducing comforts of religious ecstasy. Thus, the forever unquenchable desire of the Self for Otherness is fundamentally different from necessity *(Besoin),* whose very structure consists in attaining satiety by the assimilation—and thus reduction—of the Other to Self. Inasmuch as a relation determined by desire can only exist by virtue of the acknowledgment of separation, totalizing unity would destroy relation by pretending to cancel separation.

Levinas's philosophy stands or falls with the idea of creation, which he conceives of as a retiring of the Infinite from ontological extension in order to leave space for a separate being. The God of the "décalage absolu" creates essentially by His infinite receding, that opens up the creational dimension where the Other can attain existence. Creation is thus a trace left "behind" of God's overabundant Goodness *(Bonté),* and not a burden from which He yearns to be liberated. In Levinasian context God is not in need of being redeemed from His richness.

It is significant that although Levinas does not present an elaborated theory of the idea of redemption in *Totalité,* he does touch briefly on the problem of messianic times, "où le perpétuel se convertit en eternel,"[12] by asking the question: "Cette éternité est-elle une nouvelle structure du temps ou une vigilance extrême de la conscience messianique?"[13] No answer is given within the framework of the book. However, the very terms of the question indicate that the messianic future ("le triomphe pur") is an event in and for creation. Inasmuch as the existence of creation does not lessen God, its disappearance could not imply His completion. Applying a recurrent metaphor of Levinas theologically, one could say that God is not "allergic" to creation, for He has no drive against *allos* (other). On the contrary, by creating, the Infinite exists in a divine way.[14]

Seen from this perspective, Rosenzweig's conception of God's self-redemption *(Selbsterlösung)* appears as an inadmissible incursion of totalizing ontology into the very heart of theology. After rereading Rosenzweig's long passage on the "Logic of Redemption" quoted earlier, one will better appreciate Levinas's critical preoccupation when he writes: "L'aventure qu'ouvre la séparation est absolument nouvelle par rapport à la béatitude de l'Un et à sa fameuse liberté qui consiste à nier ou à absorber l'Autre pour ne rien rencontrer."[15]

Notes

1. Richard A. Cohen, *Elevations: The Height of the Good in Rosenzweig and Levinas* (Chicago: Chicago University Press, 1955), ch. 10.
2. Franz Rosenzweig, *Der Stern der Erlösung* (Haag, 1976), p. 19; *The Star of Redemption,* trans. William W. Hallo (New York: Holt, Rinehart and Winston, 1971), p. 17.
3. Emmanuel Levinas, *Totalité et infini. Essai sur l'exteriorité* (La Haye: Nijhoff, 1980), p. xvi; (*Totality and Infinity* [Pittsburgh: Duquesne University, 1969]).
4. Cohen, p. 15.
5. Friedrich Wilhelm Joseph Schelling, *Philosophie der Mythologie* (Darmstadt, 1976), 2:92.
6. Ibid., p. 83
7. *The Star of Redemption,* p. 238.
8. The term has been used by Leo Baeck in his characterization of Christianity, which he considered as an outstanding example of "romantic religion." In spite of the obvious doctrinal differences between Judaism and Christianity, the application of the term to Rosenzweig may be considered legitimate on the basis of his own doctrine of divine self-redemption, for "Theodramatik" is in its essence the acting out of God's own self-redemption as a fundamentally "egotistic" process in which the divine "I" revolves around its own self. The stress that the following text puts on the connection between romanticism and self-redemption supports some of the views previously expressed, especially if one considers that Schelling's thought was regarded in nineteenth-century Germany as the most adequate philosophical expression of the romantic spirit:

> Es ist nur eine letzte und logische Consequenz, wenn er (der romantische Glaube des Christentums) schließlich in die Gottheit selber diesen Ichgedanken hineingetragen and ihr Wesen darin gefunden hat, daß sie sich selbst erlösen will. So hat es eine romantische Philosophie gelehrt. Aber liegt dasselbe nicht auch in allen den alten Mysterien Religionen schon und in Grunde auch im paulinischen Glauben? Die Auferstelung, die im Mittelpunkt jener alten Geheimkulte stand, ist im eigentlichen nichts anderes als die Selbsterlösung des Gottes. . . . Aus der egoistischen Erlösungslehre, wie die Romantik sie predigte, geht der Gedanke, daß das göttliche Ich um sich Kreist ganz folgerichtig hervor.

See Leo Baeck: "Romantische Religion," in *Aus drei Jahrtausenden.* (The book was published in 1938, but was burned by the Nazis and only a handful of copies remained; it was reprinted in 1958. See "Romantic Religion," in Leon Baeck, *Judaism and Christianity,* trans. Walter Kaufmann [Philadelphia: Jewish Publication Society, 1958] -R.J.)

9. Levinas, *Totalité,* p. 35.
10. Ibid., p. 269.
11. Ibid., p. 10.
12. Ibid., p. 261.
13. Ibid.
14. Cf. ibid., p. 77
15. Ibid., p. 268.

Levinas's Thinking on Religion as beyond the Pathetic: Reflections on the First Part of *Difficult Freedom*

EPHRAIM MEIR

MOST of the essays in *Difficile liberté—Difficult Freedom* were written between the end of World War II and the beginning of the sixties. They reflect Levinas's thinking as influenced by Husserl's phenomenological method[1] and Heidegger's philosophy,[2] but no less by Jewish writings ranging from biblical and talmudic literature through Buber and Rosenzweig.[3] *Difficult Freedom* belongs to Levinas's Jewish writings. In these, he continues to speak "Greek," translating Jewish wisdom into philosophical terms and "articulating in Greek the principles Greece ignored."[4] Even in his reading of traditional Jewish texts,[5] he remains a philosopher, explaining these texts with philosophical criticism. His philosophical reflections are unique in that they represent "wisdom of love in the service of love."[6] In *Difficult Freedom,* as in the rest of Levinas's writings, the tradition of Athens as love for wisdom is a function of the tradition of Jerusalem as wisdom for love.[7] Although his language remains "Greek" throughout his entire oeuvre, which seeks to clarify man's responsibility, his new thinking, very much like Rosenzweig's in *The Star of Redemption,* is often expressed in old Jewish words. Before we describe Levinas's thinking on religion as it comes to the fore in *Difficult Freedom,* we depict briefly his general attitude toward ethics and religion.

In an attempt to break away from Nietzsche's "Wille zur Macht," from the Darwinistic struggle for life and from the ontological persistence in being, Levinas describes Jewish life as "otherwise than being." In his thinking, which is basically a contestation of the ontological by the ethical and an attempt to link ethics and metaphysics, he holds that the Jewish books contain the demand to break with the imperialism of the *conatus essendi* (the effort to exist, or the ontological principal) in dispossession (*dépossession* or *déprise*) and subjection to the other (*asujettissement* or *sujétion*). Whereas Heidegger subordinates the existents to existence, the beings to anonymous being, Levinas depicts a movement of rupture with the "there is" *(il y a)*.[8] As against Heidegger for whom being itself appears in human beings who are concerned about their being, Levinas defines the human being concerned about the life of the other: man is capable of a dis-inter-ested life, not persisting in being or clinging to the inclination to be.

Judaism represents the possibility of a difficult freedom. In his entire work, Levinas—clearly inspired in this by Rosenzweig[9]—denounces the violence inherent in history and in a totalizing way of thinking. He criticizes man who thinks and acts as if he is master of the world, reducing the other to the self. Instead of the traditional ontology, which respects neither the individual nor the uniqueness of the other, he construes a new way of thinking in which the other is central, whereas time is reread as possessing the power of rupturing totality. In so doing, Levinas lays a basis for a morality in which man is constantly judged because he is responsible. Man's responsibility *(respons-abilité)*, inverting the apparent order of self and other,[10] is his difficult freedom. Jewish life is conceived as such a freedom, engraved on the tablets of stone.[11]

According to Levinas, the dimension of the Divine is revealed in the human face.[12] The eyes authoritatively demand not to kill. Eye to eye with the other, I feel the crisis, the judgment. Do I have the right to be? Am I not oppressing the other by being and persevering in being? Am I not usurping the other's place? Levinas even speaks of being the other's hostage, and of ethical maternity—being pregnant with the other. He talks about substitution, to be in the place of the other; the other is my business. Furthermore, I can substitute myself for the other, but no one can substitute for me. Taking responsibility appears to be a traumatic event. The other causes my dispossession. He is "opposition," radically (more than formally) different, teaching me his irreducible otherness. The other is more than and different from the representations I have of him. He is "face," not assimilable, not something that I can employ.

From man's face comes the imperative "Thou shalt not kill." The trace of God *(la trace)*[13] is to be found in this commandment: He is *illéité*, the in-finite in the frail face of the other. God is absent, as was experienced by Moses.[14] He is preeminently "otherwise than being." He is with the sufferers, and this is His *kenosis*, His disincarnation and glorification. God's *illéité* excludes satisfaction, because

His transcendence is an ethical one, ever demanding. In responsibility for the other, I come near to God. Therefore, for Levinas the relation to the other is metaphysics. The relation to God is not the satisfaction of a spiritual need; in that case, God would only be a function of the totalizing ego.

Judaism represents for Levinas a religion of responsibility where God remains holy, separated from the ego and irreducible to it. Fear of God shall not become fear of the self. Instead, God is perceived as present in the rupture of the immanent order of being and in the ethical answers to the demand coming from the face of the other. God is not in our image, not an extension of being interested in being. Because the other is preoriginal and an-archic, he resembles God.[15]

After this brief sketch of Levinas's general attitude toward religion and ethics, we now turn our attention to *Difficult Freedom,* wherein he conceives of the Jewish religion as a religion of responsibility, the ethical demand forming the essence of Judaism. Levinas here sheds light on the meaning of Jewish study, law and ritual, constantly surprising the reader in an effort to reformulate religious life in terms of an answer to the demand of the other, which opens the perspective of the infinite. In *Difficult Freedom* he discusses general themes concerning religion and ethics: he writes on law and love, letter and spirit, law and faith, law and freedom,[16] on justice, conscience, responsibility, education, patience, heteronomy and autonomy, atheism, enthusiasm; on utopia, magic, violence, the adventurous, the heroic and dangerous, on history, science, and philosophy.

Apart from these themes, there are specifically Jewish themes concerning religion and ethics, such as sacred history, Jewish chosenness, salvation and messianism, particularism without separation or exclusivity with toleration, Jewish prayer and ritual, the difficulty of the Torah, the hiding of God's face and, finally, the State of Israel. As noted already, Levinas—a prolific writer on Jewish life—remains a philosopher in his Jewish writings. He is not theologizing. Key philosophical ideas appear in *Difficult Freedom,* where Bible and Talmud are studied as well as problems of modern Judaism. As in his general writings, ethics comes before ontology and God is conceived in the ethical perspective.

Our focus of interest in this article is Levinas's attitude toward the relation between ethics and religion, as it appears in *Difficult Freedom.* Against all possible trivialization of religiosity in religious systems, he stresses the originality of religious existence, breaking away from natural egocentricity and establishing an existence-for-the-other. The idea of God comes to mind in the ethical relation,[17] without forming a proof for God's existence. This ethical relation, present in the talmudic order, is a rupture with the natural narcissistic attitude.

The very first part of *Difficult Freedom*[18] provides us with ample material allowing us to know and analyze Lévinas's attitude toward ethics and religion. We therefore will confine ourselves to a description and discussion of his articles gathered around the general theme "beyond the pathetic."

Rashi's commentary on Leviticus 10:2, about the prohibition against entering the divine sanctuary in a state of drunken enthusiasm, serves as the motto for the first series of articles, bearing the title "Beyond the Pathetic." In this way Levinas suggestively rejects pathetic enthusiasm *in religiosis*. He prefers the difficult freedom of entering into the asymetric, unequal relation with the other, religion being for him essentially ethical. In this perspective, attachment to the sacred is more materialistic than attaching value to bread and meat for everybody.[19] Judaism is considered to be the type of religion that calls upon the personal responsibility of man: man, irreplaceable, is chosen to realize a just society. It is the hunger of the other that is indeed "sacred."[20]

The first two articles, "Ethics and Spirit" and "A Religion for Adults," deal extensively with the problematics of the relation between religion and ethics. We therefore devote a careful, close reading to them.

In the first article, Levinas writes that for a long time Jews thought that religious situations gained their spiritual importance from ethical relations.[21] When Judaism entered the community of nations in the nineteenth century, moralism was perceived as the raison d'être.[22] Jewish atheists joining the liberal and social movements would testify to the divine tradition of a demanding justice.[23] On the other hand, the Jew who had just entered the general world and had begun to use the language and thought of the surrounding world, was already opposed to it. Judaism requires science but also rituals. The just cannot be ignorant. And Jewish ritual both preserves and breaks away from the impulse of the heart; it is "the passion suspecting its pathos, becoming again and again *conscience*."[24]

Further along in the article, Levinas writes about the face of the other resisting our grasp; and thus about the necessity of breaking away from violence through conversation, establishing face-to-face contact. Conscience is defined as the impossibility of invading reality, and religion should not be conceived differently. Violence is present when man performs an act as if he were alone. There is violence in the satisfaction of needs,[25] in war and in knowing; violence manifests itself in fear and trembling when the sacred drags us away from ourselves, in passion (the arrow in the heart of the loving one), in the intervention of the unconscious, and in recourse to the magic action of sacraments.

As does Eric Weill, Levinas sets reason and language against violence; conversation is the "wonder of wonder."[26] In talking, one ruptures the order of violence. The other isn't known, he is *salué;* he is saluted, appearing in the vocative, not in the indicative. Talking and listening are one. Looking at a look is being confronted by a demand. The other "regards you" (*vise,* related to visage, face). Things haven't faces so that one may grasp them, but a human being does have a face. The eyes are the most exposed part of the body, unprotected. Yet they resist possession. They demand: "Thou shalt not kill"—put positively: perform social justice.

Conscience is the rupture with a violent and natural existence, it is talking to the other. The violent one, who doesn't leave himself, only takes. His violence is sovereignty, but loneliness. And to undergo violence enthusiastically is to be possessed. Knowledge can also be violent when, in the act of knowing, one absorbs the object like food. The well-known proverb "know yourself"[27] makes man return to himself, like Ulysses to Ithaca, without reaching out.[28] But the face of the other, which cannot be assimilated, which resists becoming satisfaction, demands that I leave myself and break away from my usual way of living. A religion, Levinas concludes, should not be conceived otherwise. The Infinite isn't known, but given in the moral look.

The second text in *Difficult Freedom* was originally a speech delivered by Levinas at the monastery of Tioumliline, Morocco, within the framework of a congress on the subject of education. From the outset, Levinas writes on human autonomy, based upon supreme heteronomy. Judaism is not outdated, superstitious, or preparing the way.[29] It is "rabbinic," a particularism promoting universalism. Judaism further disenchants the world; it is a rupture with the idea of religion as enthusiasm. Instead of the numinous and sacred violently transporting man beyond his own power and will, Judaism stresses the freedom and the education of man. The God of the Jews is not a survivor of mythical deities. Jewish monotheism represents a rupture with a certain concept of the sacred.[30] Here Judaism is akin to philosophy.

Education for a Jew is instruction, and the ignorant cannot really be pious. Breaking away from the numinous concept of the sacred involves the risk of atheism, deemed to be better than piety for mythical gods. Levinas expresses appreciation for God who created man, affirming God after denying Him in myths and enthusiasm. Man is capable of hearing God from afar, from out of the separation, from within atheism. Monotheism is higher than atheism, but is not possible for those who have not reached the age of doubt, loneliness, and revolt.

God's presence is felt in the relation to man. The contact with an exterior being does not compromise man's sovereignty. On the contrary, the consciousness of the self is inseparable from the consciousness of justice and injustice. This is why, in Rashi's explanation, the Bible starts with the story of the creation before man receives the divine commandments: God created the earth, so that man cannot usurp it. The "normal" functioning of the I, transforming everything into "mine," is brought into question. To possess is always to receive. Therefore, one cannot think about the Promised Land in terms of property and ought to remember—when the first fruits are brought to the Temple—that one's forefather was a nomad. Self-consciousness is thus moral consciousness, and by relating to the other, one relates to God.

Consciousness of the self and consciousness of God come together in the moral relation. "Ethics is not the corollary of the vision of God, it is this vision itself. Ethics is an optical instrument." A desacralization of the holy takes place: what I know about God must be expressed ethically. In the holy ark where Moses hears God's voice, there are only the tablets of the Law. "God is merciful" means "Be merciful as He is"; the divine attributes are given not in the indicative, but in the imperative. Knowledge of God comes as a commandment, a *mitzvah;* knowing Him is knowing what one ought to do. Education as obeying the other Will is the highest instruction; the knowledge of this Will is the basis of all reality. Levinas stresses that the otherness of the other doesn't destroy one's freedom: it opens the beyond. God is accessible in His transcendency, without destroying man's freedom. It is justice that brings man closer to God.

Without justice, prayer and liturgy are nothing. Only the just one is pious. Ritual law is "the rigorous discipline tending towards this justice." There is only recognition of the face of the other when difficult rules are set upon one's own nature. Ritual acts are therefore necessary for the one who wants to elevate himself to God. The way to God leads ipso facto to man, and the way to man leads to a ritual discipline, a much demanding self-education. The words of Bala'am on Israel rising like a lion, refer in the talmudic interpretation to the power of a people capable of an everyday rite. This is not felt as a yoke; the law is not a yoke, but a joy. The originality of Judaism lies in the combination of much goodness and much legalism.[31]

The relation with the Divine coincides with social justice. Moses and the prophets did not talk about the immortality of the soul, but about the poor, the widow, the stranger, and the orphan. God does not abolish responsibility. When man commits a sin against his fellow man, a rite does not eradicate the sin. Even God Himself cannot substitute Himself for the victim: "The world where forgiveness is almighty becomes inhuman." Instead, God patiently waits for man's turning.[32] Traditionally, everything is in God's hand, except the fear of God.

To bring about a just society is, for Levinas, an eminently religious act.[33] In the talmudic treatise Taʿanit, the day of establishing a just society—a day that "receives rain"—is greater than the day of the resurrection of the just, than the day on which the Torah was given, and than the day of the creation of heaven and earth. Realizing this, society has priority over all possible relationships with God—redemption, revelation, and creation. The implementation of such a society has to do with Jewish messianism.[34]

The universalism of Judaism becomes clear when one considers the role of ethics in the religious framework. Judaism is universal in its linking the divine to ethics. In this context, election is not a privilege, but a responsibility;[35] it is the nobility of entering into an unequal relationship, of being responsible. I am obliged to relate. And the more just I am, the more severely I will be judged. Moral conscience is thus consciousness of election. One has to demand more from oneself than from the other.[36] This position, "apart from the nations," is realized in Israel. Thus, for Levinas Israel is a moral category, rather than a historical entity—even if Israel historically was faithful to this concept. He refers to Rabbi Meir who once said that a pagan who knows the Torah is the equal of the high priest,[37] which proves that the notion of Israel differs from every historical, national, local, and racial notion.

Before landscapes and towns, the Jew discovers man. Somehow exiled in this world, he finds meaning in the world because of human society. The earth is not owned, but belongs to God. Man starts out in the desert living in tents. Jewish existence is freedom from landscapes and architecture, from sedentary forms of existence.[38] The festival of Tabernacles commemorates this, and the prophet

Zachariah foresees that in messianic times this will be a festival for all the nations. The world becomes, in Jewish perspective, intelligible in the human face, not in houses, temples, and bridges. The Jewish freedom from places makes values of rootedness secondary, and institutes other forms of faithfulness and responsibility. Morality creates freedom from history, a right to judge history.[39] Man does not have to grant to anonymous history the right of judgment. Justice is above culture, ancestral ground, architecture, and arts. In justice, the Jew encounters God. All this becomes clear in the story of Hillel, who refused to recognize as a judge the murderer of a murderer. Ever occurring violence is not the sentence of history; history itself is not a judge. No historical event can judge a conscience; this supports the theological saying that God alone is Judge.

We now briefly refer to other short articles appearing in the first part of *Difficult Freedom* before we proceed to discuss Levinas's concept of religion.

In a short article, "Judaism,"[40] written for the *Encyclopaedia Universalis,* Levinas reflects on subjects with which we are already familiar, but also on several new issues. Is Judaism a nationality or a religion, a fossilized civilization or a passionate desire for a better world? For Levinas, Judaism belongs to the Jewish people who are descendants of the people of the Sacred History. Therefore, the creation of the State of Israel with the aim to find again the creative inspiration of old is inconceivable without the Bible.[41] Levinas refuses to accept the reductionism of the nineteenth-century "Science of Judaism." In Judaism, one is called to follow the Most High in caring for the other. One should suspect the myths of accomplished fact, the compulsion of customs or of territory, and the Machiavellian state with its reasons of state. Man is elected to be responsible; he is necessary in God's plan. His uniqueness lies in the responsibility he displays for the other. The other may ask from me what I may not ask from him. Man is thus a creature who can be saved "without falling into the egoism of salvation."[42] God needs man; he is God's plan within being. Being chosen is being called, the awareness of an indisputable assignment *(une assignation irrécusable)* from which ethics springs. Man can do what he has to do; he can bring about the messianic reign in history, for God demands of him an extreme humanism. But the most characteristic aspect of Judaism is the famous yoke of the law, the ritualism maintaining a distance from nature and a presence for the Most High.

The last-mentioned theme is taken up again in "The Pharisee Is

Absent"—the Pharisee being the preeminent Jewish type for Levinas. Here again he denounces audacious and shameless enthusiasm, which, he holds, is not the purest way to establish contact with God. The naiveté of spontaneous movements and unreflected reactions constitutes the charm of wild beasts and young children; human life does not owe its dignity to them.

To enthusiasm, Levinas opposes the "severe tenderness" of the Pharisee, fighting a battle of reasons against reasons, a battle without anger, bringing peace on earth. In the Pharisee there is much obedience and much sovereignty. Against the idea of pure grace, Levinas posits the hard work of questions, ever more fruitful after each solution. The Pharisee heralds a paradise where all the joys are made of eternal efforts. Concerning the biblical passage where Moses talked to God face-to-face, the sages remarked that disciple and Master studied the same talmudic lesson. The Pharisee takes water from the well, but does not mistake himself for the well; God stays outside, remains exterior. In a romantic time when Jews only understand hasidic stories, there is the "miracle of exteriority": man is capable of listening to what comes from outside. This is knowledge, or Torah. The sublime forms of the human are not pathetic anymore.

The next to last text that we will describe is "Means of Identification."[43] Here Levinas writes that one does not "adhere" to Judaism, for that suggests the possibility of estrangement. One is born a Jew; one doesn't become one. Of course, someone may become a Jew, but thereafter it is as if no conversion had taken place. To be a Jew is to be what one is, prior to all allegiance. One cannot "adhere" to whatever is human. Certain Jews say "Jew" where one would expect "mankind." Here is an identity, founded on an adherence that preexists any form of allegiance, and that can be expressed in verifiable terms. As Hayyim Volozhiner writes in *Nefesh ha-Hayyim* (1824), the Jew is accountable and responsible for the whole edifice of creation. Jewish identity is patience[44] and the fatigue of a responsibility, a stiff neck that—like Atlas—supports the universe.

After having noted that rooting Jewish identity in Zionism risks confusing it with nationalism, Levinas points out that the Western mentality, to which the Jew has become assimilated, refuses to adhere to anything unless an act of adhesion is performed: one must not spontaneously accept one's own nature, but look at oneself from the outside, ponder about oneself. One has to use universal speech. Judaism, too, has to use the language of the university, namely, philosophy and philology.[45] Civilizations like Judaism owe their excellence not to their originality but to their high degree of universality.

It is thus not enough to inventory what Jews think and feel today. One cannot choose in which ways to be conscious of something; the Jew has to go back to the forgotten, difficult ancient texts. This "worm-eaten old Judaism" is to be preferred to the transient Judaism of the Jews. The books—"the ember glowing beneath the ashes" (Rabbi Eliezer)—are the flame within history, without burning up history.

Finally, the text on "The Ark and the Mummy" treats of the destiny of the Jewish people, which is conceived as beyond history. With their supranatural history, Jews participate in the world: they want to create a type of man living in a demystified, disenchanted world.

Levinas again returns to the concept of "enthusiasm" which, he argues, is being possessed by a god. Yet Jews do not want to be possessed; they want to be responsible. Their God is the master of justice who cannot forgive a sin committed against another man. There are many prohibitions within Jewish ritual life that have guaranteed the Jews' independence of spirit. Most contemporary Jews have distanced themselves from this disciplined and not-easy life. Only a minority continues the difficult life of freedom linked to many so-called outdated, anachronistic, customs.

Levinas draws our attention to the midrash that tells how people wondered at the sight of the Israelites, traveling in the desert with two arks—one containing Joseph's bones, the other the ark of God. The Jews answered: "This is the coffin of a dead one and that—the ark of He who lives eternally." They explained to the astonished passersby that the one who rests in the coffin accomplished what is written on the tablets of the law, which rests in the second ark. The living God, Levinas concludes, accompanies His liberated people in the desert only if the mummy of the one who obeyed His law also travels with them.

We now reflect on the writings that have been summarized.[46] The several articles from the first part of *Difficult Freedom* make it clear that Levinas's thinking largely leans on the prephilosophic element of the Jewish tradition. His philosophical thinking is pervaded by a biblical spirit. In biblical and talmudic sources, conversing and being responsible appear to form the real relation with the other. For Levinas, those texts are fundamental to experiencing the humanity of the human being, to the rupture with being. The other is the stranger, the widow, and the orphan to whom I am obliged. Much as in the Jewish sources, Levinas stresses that the other is the poor one and at the same time my master. I am both strong and his servant. My relation with the other is one of dissymetry. The first word issuing from the face of the other, "Thou shalt not kill," is a commandment, causing a rupture in being. The other counts on me, appeals to me to treat him as absolute, resistant to every possible reduction. I am called on; the obligation can never be satisfied, but grows further when fulfilled. Duty is infinite.

Through the answer "Here I am" *(hineni)* to this unlimited ethical appeal to the never-ending command to sanctify himself, man testifies to the Infinite. The Infinite is "attested." In Jewish mystic texts one starts with "you" and ends with "he." One is able to bear witness to God.[47] As in the prophetic literature, the access to the face means access to the idea of God, the relation to the Infinite remaining a "desire."[48] The desire for the other challenges the sovereignty of the ego. There is fear of God in the fear of the other, an effect in which man does not return to himself.[49] In Jewish writings one finds ethical testimony; the clear conscience of my being-there is put into question by the suffering one who solicits my help.[50]

In the article described here, Judaism, with its laws and rituals as a discipline inclining toward justice, is an ethical community, a particular community with a universal dimension.[51] Judaism disenchants and demythologizes the world. The numinous that violently transports man beyond his own powers and will is incompatible with the sovereignty, the freedom, and the education of man. The God of Israel is not one of the mythical deities; His holiness does not eliminate man's freedom.

Breaking away from the numinous concept of the sacred implies the risk of atheism, which attests to the radical non-naiveté of Levinas's religious thinking. According to Levinas,[52] monotheism must take into account the legitimate demands of atheism. The God of the Jews is a God of adults, manifesting Himself in the emptiness of the childish heaven. It is a God who, by hiding His face, is present in His demands for man's full responsibility. In Judaism, direct contact with the sacred is lacking; the mediation of reasons and of a teaching, of the Torah, is always required. Further, in Judaism, man is a free and separate being, denying God in the numinous and in myths. Thus a place is created for consciousness and philosophy. Instead of the violence of possessing or being possessed, Judaism breaks away from ecstasy and enthusiasm, introducing the consciousness of the self, which is inseparable from the consciousness of justice and injustice. Judaism introduces a depossession of the "I", and a life in response to the other. This ethical relation is the vision of God; "Ethics is an optical instrument." The access to the face makes God accessible.

For Levinas, man is a free being. But the consciousness of the self is, immediately, consciousness of the moral self; and the moral self is dependent on the other. In religious terms: man sanctifies himself by obedience to a heteronomous will. Saintliness is the characteristic of the person who, in his being, is more attached to the being of the other than to his own.[53] The divine will is revealed in the face of the other. This will is not destructive to freedom, but appeals to it. The face is not a force, but an authority. Rightly, E. Wyschogrod writes.

> For Levinas, heteronomy is not the imposition of a divine will, but a revelation through the appearance of other persons. The notion that the other does not compel but solicits, is consistent with traditional Jewish thought yet does not impose itself as an alien will destructive to freedom. Levinas' attempt to save human freedom, while maintaining that human action depends upon the recognition of heteronomy, rests upon understanding the term in its authentic sense as non-violent and therefore non-compelling. He thus avoids the coerciveness attached to the Kantian interpretation of heteronomy, while still affirming heteronomy as an absolutely passive principle of alterity which founds moral action.[54]

For Levinas, the preeminent Jewish type is the Pharisee, as noted. Contact with God is not established through enthusiasm but through "severe tenderness," without merging oneself with God. Through the Pharisee's constant study of Torah, he is capable of listening to what comes from the outside, and this is "the miracle of exteriority." Levinas, living the crisis of the twentieth century, again underlines the "exceptional destiny" of Judaism, returning to the rabbinic texts that "develop the law of strict justice."[55] But this Jewish particularism, as he conceives it, is at the same time a concretization of the universal. At the center of Jewish religion is the demanding appeal of the other calling into question one's spontaneity and making consciousness and knowledge possible:

> The realization of the just society is ipso facto an elevation of man to the company with God. . . . Ethics is an optical instrument to the divine. . . . The divine can only manifest itself in relation to one's neighbor. The incarnation is not possible and not necessary for the Jew. The formula is after all from Jeremiah: "To judge the cause of the poor and the unfortunate, is this not to know Me says the Eternal" (22:16)[56]

Ethics does not prepare for religious life, nor does it follow from it; it is religious life itself. The old distinction between observant and nonobservant Jews, according to Levinas, was valid in the Diaspora, where rites preserved Judaism. In Israel, by contrast, the question of who is religious and not would be answered by distinguishing those for whom the state must embody justice, from those for whom the state per se is the end. Ritual would be reborn in the vitality of action and thought.[57]

Levinas's conception of Israel's election is also noteworthy: far from contradicting universalism, it is a *function* of universalism.[58] Israel is a moral category; "one must make Israel."[59] Judaism emerged for all of humanity, as expressed in the talmudic story of the patriarchs and their wives resting in the same cave as Adam and Eve. Being elected is not consciousness of exceptional rights, but of exceptional tasks; it is the prerogative of moral conscience itself. I alone am responsible, irreplaceable in assuming responsibilities. The Jewish concept of election, far from being anterior to a universalism where all differences are blotted out, includes this abolition of differences as a condition, yet indispensable to it.

Two questions must now be posed. What is Levinas's relation to the Jewish ethical monotheism of the nineteenth century; and who are the Jewish thinkers whose thoughts show affinities to Levinas's reflections on ethics and religion in the first part of *Difficult Freedom*? We will try to provide answers to these questions.

Levinas highly esteems the Jewish moralism of the nineteenth century that breaks with the irrational, the numinous, and the sacramental.[60] The reception of the stranger is not a corollary, but the very content of faith. Faith is a responsibility that cannot be declined.[61] But at the same time, and without falling in the pitfall of fundamentalism, he points to the relevance of ritual law for a life of obligation to the stranger. Further points of difference between nineteenth-century ethical monotheism and Levinas is his emphasis on ethics that leads to a redefinition of the sacred and the secular, and his view of humanism as insufficiently human.[62] Because Judaism was secularized as humanism, Jewish education became religious instruction on abstract ideas, forming the one slight remaining distinction separating Jews from the surrounding society; and, finally, this last distinction also dissolved.

The crisis of humanism in the twentieth century led to another conception of Jewish education, "a need of *kashrut.*" Levinas conceives Jewish education as an "antihumanism" commencing from a better attention to the human, and shattering the dichotomy between law and freedom. There is a Jewish unrest in regard to several kinds of liberation, laying bare the misery within the illusions of happiness and the meager happiness of the satisfied. Love and law, spirit and letter, are held together. The wisdom of the law does not reflect or proclaim European culture; it teaches real humanism, maintaining a distance from the self and nature. The law embodies freedom in order to assure freedom. Judaism is thus a particularism without separation from universal man,[63] a resistance, refusing to continue the war in the war against war. The Jewish stiffneck, "the supernatural part of the Jewish anatomy," is true freedom.[64]

Finally, Levinas's thinking differs from that of the Jewish ethical monotheists of the nineteenth century because the latter were hardly interested in Hebrew and rabbinic studies. By reducing Judaism to what everybody knows, they lost sight of the particular Jewish wisdom.

With all the conspicuous differences between Levinas and the nineteenth-century Jewish ethical monotheists, he may nevertheless be interpreted as a descendant of post-Kantian German Jewish idealism, giving—like Kant—priority to practical reason.[65] Levinas refers to Hermann Cohen,[66] in whose vision Jewish religion is the domain for ethical action according to a God-given moral order. But Edith Wyschogrod rightly observed that Levinas "rejects an interpretation of prophetic futurism which makes the political arena the sphere of its operation."[67] Wyschogrod further analyzed[68] the points upon which Cohen and Levinas converge and differ. She argues that Levinas, in his concept of man, corrects Cohen's view with the help of Heidegger's phenomenological approach, whereas he puts forward a Cohen-like view in order to correct Heidegger. Levinas shares with Cohen the assumption that the moral self cannot be explained in accordance with psychological laws. Furthermore, pity and compassion, which are the primal form of human love for Cohen, play an important role in the thinking of Levinas: Men are poor, subjected to the contingencies of economy; and the stranger, different from oneself, appeals to me. But "what for Cohen is an inequity in economy becomes for Levinas a constitutive inequity between self and other."[69]

A further parallel between Cohen and Levinas is "the view that prior to the recognition of other persons as moral data, social existence is violence. But the end of social existence is peace, not as a mere cessation of violence but as a new existential condition which both Cohen and Levinas refer to as Messianism."[70] For Levinas, Cohen's view that a person is known in pity and compassion is truer than Heidegger's view that the other person—the object of concerned solicitude—remains secondary to the primacy of being. But Levinas finds Cohen's vision methodologically problematic, since "conceptual necessity rather than phenomenological 'eliciting' determines the character of the moral self."[71] And whereas for Cohen the relation to God is required to transform man into a unique individual, for Levinas the relation to God is already established in the intersubjective human encounter.

Wyschogrod also wrote[72] that while Kantian ethics requires strict autonomy of the absolutely good will—the will being its own law—Levinas insists on the strictly heteronomous rule, considering the other as the transcendent source of all moral value. In the words of *Difficult Freedom,* human autonomy rests on a supreme heteronomy."[73] And in contrast to Kant, who subordinates inclination to reason, Levinas rehabilitates inclination as an affect procuring an immediate and instinctive attachment to the good. Motive and duty, separable in Kant, are united in Levinas's notion of "desire."[74]

The articles assembled in the first part of *Difficult Freedom* do more than allow us to juxtapose Levinas with Kant and Cohen. We might also point to his affinity to Buber, for whom the existent is similarly established in relation, and for whom the eternal Thou becomes accessible in the dialogue with the human thou. But here again, the differences between Buber's and Levinas's thinking are significant,[75] as is already clear from the latter's conception of God as *illéité* and his definition of the relation as fundamentally asymmetric and nonspiritualistic.

In the section we have described, Levinas's reflections seem particularly close to those of Leo Baeck.[76] For both thinkers, Judaism is the classical religion where ethics occupies a central place, in contrast to religions of the romantic type where man is only the passive instrument of divine wonder-working. The enthusiastic, sentimental admiration of heroes and saintly men, and the primacy of supernatural salvation over justice, are replaced by imitation of God through fulfilling difficult laws. Like Baeck, and contrary to F. Schleiermacher, Levinas does not base religion on the *Gefühl schlechthinniger Abhängigkeit,* because man's realization of authentic freedom in study and action forms the *locus theologicus* of his encounter with God. Man is not magically saved *jensites von Gut und Böse* (Neitzsche) by faith in mystery and sacraments, but by entering into the ethical order. Judaism, struggling against "the intoxication of enthusiasm,"[77] unromantically stresses man's freedom and his ethical responsibility, through following never-to-be abolished laws, distrusting the wonder-working powers of sacraments, or magical formulas like Luther's "sola fide." Because of the accent on universal ethical responsibility, Judaism cannot claim to be the only saving religion, as becomes clear in the saying of Rabbi Meir quoted earlier.

The ethical demand is also the basis for Jewish tolerance: The Jewish faith is tolerant because Jews bear the whole weight of the others.[78] Instead of utopian flight to the heavens or, on the contrary, the very earthly casuistic approach where everything depends on circumstances and considerations, Levinas again appreciates the denigrated "moralism of the Old Testament," showing us the freedom engraved on the tablets of the law. His God is not the God of fear and trembling, but of Mount Sinai.

We would like to close with a critical note.[79] By refusing to root religion in the drunkenness of irrational enthusiasm, Levinas's philosophy has the advantage of restoring to modern man the possibility of rational discourse about the infinite Other. Does enthusiasm necessarily vehemently transport man beyond his own powers and will? Is it unthinkable that enthusiasm is balanced by reason, channeling wild streams of energy and purifying enthusiasm from its pathos? Might enthusiasm not be conceived as tempered by an asceticism that restrains and transforms it into a permanent force enabling man to work more efficiently? In that case, enthusiasm—etymologically, "being-in-God"—would not be in contradiction to human reason. Furthermore, in well-conceived enthusiasm, man experiences nonidentity and therefore the end of an autarchic life—experiences toward which Levinas cannot remain indifferent.

The Dutch essayist C. Verhoeven, in his book *A Philosophy of Enthusiasm*, includes an analysis of Plato's view on enthusiasm (in his *Io* and in the *Phaedrus*), and of Hegel's secularization of the same notion, the Hegelian "Begeisterung." Verhoeven explains how the source of enthusiasm is external, inspiring the enthusiastic man and overwhelming him. Enthusiasm possesses an element of passivity; man recognizes that there is more than his mastery over his life, more than his own initiative, and he accepts his dependence. But at the same time, enthusiasm contains an active element. The poet *(poiètès)* does *(poiein)* something, and in what he does, something happens. The other, radically different from the same, remains exterior but represents a source of activity. Understood in such a way and brought into the social context, enthusiasm is no longer violent, but rather is an ever-to-be-cultivated, necessary, condition of life. Could a so-defined enthusiasm not be the source of religion?

The conclusions emerging from our reading and understanding of the first part of *Difficult Freedom* that deals with the relation between religion and ethics, may be formulated in a few sentences.

For Levinas,[80] true religion does not dream of a distant utopia and does not seek the sacred in fear and trembling. Utopian man wants unjustly, refusing the conditions of life. True religion, on the contrary, suspects mystical ecstasies and does not flee from concrete situations; rather, it chooses ethical action in this world. Devoutness as theopatic absorption, to the exclusion of all human loves and human needs is replaced by an adult religion where God's trace is found in the other's appeal to one's irreducible responsibility.[81] The Jewish books declare a war against the sacred and the sacraments, refusing magical salvation and recognizing the necessity of a law. For Levinas, the revelation of the monotheistic God coincides with the awakening of conscience.

Notes

1. Levinas's phenomenology is unique in that it is based on an ethical a priori, present in the face of the other. But one may ask if his description of the face is the description of a phenomenon, something that appears. The face does not appear: it appeals. Levinas once said that he uses the phenomenological method to free himself from phenomenology. See R. Bakker, *De geschiedenis van het fenomenologisch denken,* Aula-boeken 1974 (Utrecht-Antwerp: Spectrum, 1977), pp. 480–81; S. Strasser, "Antiphénoménologie et phénoménologie dans la philosophie d' Emmanuel Lévinas," *Revue philosophique de Louvain,* 75, no. 25 (February 1977): 101–24.

2. Levinas considered Heidegger together with Plato, Kant, Hegel, and Bergson as one of the five great philosophers in history. But at the same time, he never forgave Heidegger's life-long silence on the death camps and the gas chambers, nor the sympathy he displayed for the National Socialist movement, as is clear from Heidegger's 1933 speech on the occasion of his nomination as rector at Freiburg, and from his 1936 encounter with Löwith in Rome, wearing the swastika on his arm. In E. Levinas, *Ethique et infini. Dialogues avec Philippe Nemo* (Paris: Fayard/ France Culture 1982), p. 84: hereafter *EI;* translated by R. Cohen as *Ethics and Infinity: Conversations with Philippe Nemo* [Pittsburgh: Duquesne, 1985]; Heidegger's philosophy is called "ontology without morals."

3. In the following, we use the third edition, from which some essays of the first edition have been dropped, whereas others are added. In a preliminary note to the third edition, Levinas explains that texts were omitted because of their lack of sharpness or actuality and that other texts, faithful to the original inspiration, were added. See E. Levinas, *Difficile liberté. Essais sur le judaïsme.* 3d ed. (Paris: Albin Michel 1976; originally published 1963), hereafter cited as *DL*. An English translation by S. Hand, is *Difficult Freedom. Essays on Judaism* (London: Athlone Press, 1990).

4. E. Levinas, *L'au-delà du verset. Lectures et discours talmudiques* (Paris: Minuit 1982), p. 234: "Nous avons la grande tâche d'énoncer en grec les principes que la Grèce ignorait. La singularité juive attend sa philosophie. L'imitation servile

des modèles européens ne suffit plus." In an interview with S. Malka, Levinas pointedly said that the work of the Septuagint is not finished. See S. Malka, *Lire Lévinas* (Paris: Ed. du Cerf, 1984), p. 107.

5. *DL,* pp. 87–139. In *DL,* Levinas reflects on "rigid texts more alive than life itself" (p. 9).

6. Levinas, *Otherwise Than Being or Beyond Essence,* trans. A. Lingis (The Hague: Nijhoff, 1981), p. 161.

7. In *DL,* pp. 249–52, Levinas writes that the logic of the Greek brings an understanding between men. But one must agree to speak. According to Plato, we cannot oblige the other to enter into talk. Monotheism, the word of the one God, is the word to which one must respond. This word obliges. Because of the monotheists who made the divine word heard, Greek universalism and its economy of *solidarity* is made possible.

8. See the title of Levinas' work *De l'existence à l'existant* (From the existence to the existent) (Paris: Vrin, 1947), translated by A. Lingis as *Existence and Existents* (The Hague: Nijhoff, 1978).

9. See *DL,* pp. 53–281. Regarding the radically ethical interpretation of Rosenzweig's notion of "eternal" Israel taking distance from the world, (see C. Chalier, *Pensées de l'éternité. Spinoza, Rosenzweig* (Paris: Éd. du Cerf, 1993), pp. 133–41.

10. *DL,* p. 10.

11. According to the words of *Pirké Avot* 6,2 which serve as a motto of the entire book.

12. For an analysis of the face, see Levinas, *Totality and Infinity: An Essay on Exteriority,* trans. by A. Lingis (The Hague: Nijhoff, 1979) (hereafter *TI*).

13. God's trace is not the trace that can be deduced and reconstrued until one discovers God. He remains Alterity, the in-finite Other.

14. Exodus 33: 18–23.

15. E. Levinas, *En découvrant l'existence avec Husserl et Heidegger* (Paris: Vrin, 1967), p. 174. This work is translated by R. Cohen and M. B. Smith, as *Discovering Existence with Husserl* (forthcoming).

16. Discussing these themes, Levinas also defines his position toward Christianity. He notes (*DL,* pp. 282–83) that Judaism is necessary for the future of a humanity who does not expect anything anymore, in the conviction that it is saved. The Jew reminds the conformists that they are not living in the best of worlds. Although critical of certain manifestations of Christianity and refusing for Judaism "the dignity of relics" (*DL,* p. 246), he does not forget the Christians' longtime "vicinity" (*DL,* p. 225) with Judaism, the existence of "a common language" (*DL,* p. 25; in a text like John 4:12 where God is said to reside among men when they love each other, Levinas sees the inspiration of the "Old Testament," *DL,* pp. 76–77) and the sharing with Judaism of "a state of unrest" (*DL,* p. 15). On p. 26, Levinas commemorates the Catholic priest, Chesnet, who recited Jewish prayers at a place where Nazis wanted to bury a Jewish friend like a dog.

17. See E. Levinas, *De Dieu qui vient à l'idée* (Paris: Vrin, 1982).

18. *DL,* pp. 11–85.

19. *DL,* p. 19.

20. "La faim d'autrui . . . est sacrée" (*DL,* p. 10). Levinas does not accept the spiritualistic attitude in certain circles where care for housing, clothing, and food is called "materialistic." See his criticism of Buber, "Martin Buber and the Theory of Knowledge," in *The Levinas Reader,* ed. S. Hand (Cambridge: Basil Blackwell, 1989), pp. 59–74, esp. 72–73. In *DL,* p. 36, Levinas notes that the relation to the other is not one of spiritual friendship, but realizes itself in the establishing of a

just economy. Further, the relation to the other is not reciprocal; the other is higher. From the vulnerable nudity of the face comes the demand, the primordial appeal "Thou shalt not kill," traumatizing and decentering the ego and demanding of the ego responsibility. A Roman once asked Rabbi Akiba: "Why doesn't your God, the God of the poor, feed the poor?" Rabbi Akiba answered: "In order that we may escape damnation." In *DL,* pp. 45–46, Lévinas explains that one cannot approach the widow, stranger, orphan, and beggar "with empty hands."

21. *DL,* p. 15.

22. Ibid.

23. *DL,* pp. 16–17. Writing on Léon Brunschvicq (pp. 63–71), Levinas notes that there exists an atheism that is nearer to God than the mystical experiences and the horrors of the sacred (p. 71).

24. "La passion se méfiant de son pathos, devenant et redevenant *conscience.*" *DL,* p. 17.

25. See R. Burggraeve, *From Self-Development to Solidarity: An Ethical Reading of Human Desire in Its Socio-Political Relevance according to E. Levinas,* trans. C. Van Hove-Romanik (Louvain: Center for Metaphysics and Philosophy of God, 1985), who opposes desire as the fulfilling of one's own needs, with the unconditional goodness as "desire," demanding ever more goodness. Burggraeve rightly emphasizes that the heteronomous responsibility by and for the other is insatiable (see n. 48). But modern psychology may show more other-centered tendencies than those present in the Freudian-Lacanian concept of man as presented by Burggraeve.

26. *DL,* p. 19. Talking is not primarily speaking about objects, but establishing a heteronomous relation with the other, irreducible to an object. It takes place in the face-to-face relation. This direct relation is original, preceding the egocentric self-development. It is a movement back "zu den Sachen selbst."

27. This Greek saying appeared on the temple of Delphi and was frequently used by Socrates. See "Paix et proximité," in *Emmanuel Lévinas,* ed. J. Rolland, Les Cahiers de La nuit surveillee 3 (Lagrasse: Verdier, 1984), pp. 339–46, esp. p. 340. Knowledge is part of man's interest. For Levinas, to be is: to be interested, to take part in the situation of inter-esse. In thinking as in acting, man behaves as if he is master of the world by reducing the other to the self. Knowledge as assimilation (*comprendre* being near to *prendre*) thus reinforces loneliness; by knowledge man perseveres in being. The social, on the contrary, is beyond ontology; see *EI,* pp. 45–54. The antipode of the interested man taking part in the world (much as Korah in Numbers 16:1) is Rabbi Akiba who refused to take a part of the Torah. He compared himself with a man inhaling the perfume of the citron, nothing of the citron being lost. Rabbi Akiba also compared himself with somebody who draws from a spouting well or somebody who lights a flame from a flame. See *DL,* p. 50. In this way Rabbi Akiba appears as an example of a dis-inter-ested life, a life of "otherwise than being," a life where the most natural becomes the most problematic (*EI,* p. 120).

28. Ulysses, returning home after his multiple adventures, is contrasted by Levinas to Abraham, whose words "Here I am" in Genesis 22:1 (also in Exodus 3:4 in Moses' mouth) cause him to abandon his egoism, and he does not return.

29. Levinas refers to Buber who once said that for Jews the Old Testament is neither old nor a testament.

30. Levinas retells the story of Abraham destroying the idols of Terah, and leaving one who would be, in his father's eyes, responsible for the massacre. Terah did not believe that an idol destroys idols. Elsewhere (*DL,* pp. 75–76) he writes that Judaism, refusing to be an exalting, inflaming faith, strives for a humanity without

myths that introduce in the soul the impure element of magic and sorcery, the drunkenness of the sacred and of war. Levinas quotes Brunschvicq: "Can the God of the wars of religion be the God of religion?" Judaism denounces the ambiguity in the exaltation. The so-called stubborn attachment to the letter is refusal of what one calls too easily "spirit." Judaism has to do with moral interiority, not with dogmatic exteriority. The supernatural in Judaism is not obsession, because contact with the Divine comes through the ethical.

31. Levinas quotes Psalm 119:19–20, in Chouraqui's rendering: "Mon âme se brise de désir pour tes jugements à chaque instant."

32. It is this patience, waiting for man, which constitutes God's grace. Burggraeve, *Self-Development to Solidarity*, pp. 90–91 n. 131, thus wrongly regrets that Levinas gives insufficient attention to the question of a gracious God. Lévinas's view on man's infinite, substitutional responsibility leads neither to hubris nor to self-contempt. Instead, Levinas writes about mercy that softens but does not suspend the rigor of the law. See *DL*, p. 46.

33. For Y. Leibowitz, on the contrary, morality is an "atheistic" category. See Y. Leibowitz, *ʾEmunah, historia ve-ʾarakhim. Maʾamarim ve-hartzaʾot,* (Jerusalem: Academon, 1982), p. 172. Similarly, Søren Kierkegaard, stressing the unbridgeable gap between God and man, denies that true religion requires social justice before everything else. Kierkegaard, together with the Kotzker, has been criticized for not having been involved sufficiently in the sociopolitical dimension of religious existence. See A. J. Heschel, *A Passion for Truth* (London, 1973), p. 108.

34. According to Levinas, a man who wants to be worthy of the messianic future has to accept ethics even without the promise of the messiah. Ethics is important without a happy ending, without rewards and assurances, and without the history of salvation. Levinas write that man is perhaps only worthy of the consolations of religion when he is able to live without them (*EI*, p. 117).

35. Leibowitz also holds this functional conception of election. See *ʾEmunah,* pp. 117–18.

36. I am elected to answer, I alone. It is my vocation. This, for Levinas, is the principle of the individualization of man. In Dostoyevsky's words; "Everyone is guilty before everyone else and I more than all the others" (*EI*, pp. 95, 97–98).

37. Also *DL*, p. 186 n. 1. On p. 247 Levinas notes that the principle of the participation of the just of all nations in the world-to-come is not an eschatological vision, but the idea of the sharing of an intimacy without reservation.

38. Levinas's reflections on the "wonder" of the Jewish freedom from places reminds us of Sartre's analysis of French antisemites who think of themselves as the legitimate possessors of the patrimonial ground and of French culture, and perceive of Jews as not belonging to the real French fatherland. See J.-P. Sartre, *Réflexions sur la question juive* (Paris: Gallimard, 1954), pp. 29–30, 97–101.

The theme of Jewish freedom from places, and recognition of the face of the other as the meeting place with God reappears in the article "Heidegger, Gagarine and Us" (*DL*, pp. 323–27). The article criticizes Heidegger's negative view of technology and explains technology and science as positive powers, desacralizing and demystifying nature. Judaism would be typical of this demystification: the other is face, he looks at me/regards me and demands that I not reduce him to a part of my centripetal totality. Against the view that modern technology would be dangerous, Levinas writes that the enemies of the industrial society are mostly reactionaries who forget or hate great hopes. Technology causes sedentary, particularistic, civilizations to collapse. But for Heidegger, man is *Dasein,* rooted; man has to open himself to the light of the large landscapes, to walk through the fields, to discover again the mystery of things. Being itself would be manifested through these experiences. What seems to be added by man would already be present in the splendor of the world. The work of art would reflect ante-human splendor. Humanity would bring man back to nature, with its founding human language. This Heideggerian theory is qualified by Levinas as "the eternal seduction of paganism." Judaism would be the exact opposite; in the purity of what one calls "vandalism," Judaism destroys the sacred bushes. When man is planted in a landscape, and is tied to a place, this brings a division in humanity between autochthones and strangers. Technology, less dangerous than the genii of the place, frees one from the Heideggerian world and the superstitions of the place. This does not imply that man has to go back to nomadism. It opens the possibility of meeting man outside his "situation," and permits the human face to shine in its nakedness.

Elsewhere Levinas underlines the importance of technology and science in man's respect for the other. See also "La souffrance inutile," in Rolland, *Emmanuel Lévinas,* 329–38, esp. 331–32 where the cry or sigh of the suffering one is conceived of as an "original appeal for help." Technology in general and in medicine is not necessarily a result of the *"Wille zur Macht"*; it belongs to a civilization called to nourish people and ease their suffering.

Judaism is the brother of the message of Socrates, who preferred the town where people are encountered, to fields and trees. Judaism was always free from places. There is only the Sacred Land which vomits out unjust inhabitants. (About this archaic bond between people and land, see also M. Buber, *Israel und Palästina. Zur Geschichte einer Idee* [Zurich: Artemis, 1950].) The Bible does not contain many descriptions of nature. Landscapes are described in elementary terms. Israel is the "land of milk and honey," one feeds oneself from the land. When it is said that Abraham planted a tamarisk in Beersheba, the Talmud immediately destroys the dream that a place contains the meaning of being. Tamarisk, *eshel,* means: to serve the other in feeding him, giving him drink, and lodging him. Levinas finally notes that Christian piety is rooted in and nourishes itself with landscapes and with familial, tribal memories. Christianity conquers humanity. But Judaism demands the destruction of idols, demystifying the universe by technology. Judaism, in disenchanting nature and opposing universality to imagination and passion, discovers man in the nakedness of the face.

39. For this freedom from history, see C. Chalier, n. 9 above.

40. This text is translated by Hand in *The Levinas Reader,* pp. 250–52.

41. For Levinas' reflections on the State of Israel, see n. 63.

42. Elsewhere (*DL,* p. 74), Levinas quotes Léon Brunschvicq: "Tant que vous ne penserez qu'à votre salut, vous tournerez le dos à Dieu. Dieu est Dieu, pour celui-là seul qui surmonte la tentation de le dégrader afin de l'employer à son service."

43. This text is translated by Hand; *The Levinas Reader,* pp. 263–66.

44. In *DL,* pp. 217–19 Levinas writes on the virtues of patience in an era when the adventurous, the dangerous, and the heroic are exalted, and fast, efficient action is praised. In a time where headlong youth is seen as the best part of life and slow maturation is barely tolerated, where violence is proposed as a way of salvation, patience takes on great value. According to Levinas, patience, not resignation, stems from a great piety.

45. Here Levinas stresses that Judaism is parallel to contemporary life and consciousness; elsewhere, he emphasizes that Judaism goes against it.

46. See also E. Wyschogrod, *Emmanuel Levinas: The Problem of Ethical Metaphysics* (The Hague: Nijhoff, 1974), pp. 163–67.

47. *EI,* pp. 101–7.

48. *EI,* pp. 86–87. Levinas distinguishes "desire" from need. Desire cannot be fulfilled, and nourishes itself on its own hunger, increasing after being satisfied. See *EI,* pp. 86–87.

49. As against Heidegger; *EI,* p. 118.

50. *EI,* p. 116.

51. See D. Lazar, "Universality and Particularity in the Thinking of Emmanuel Levinas" (Hebrew), *Shdemot* 81/82, (Tammuz, 1982): 190–98.

52. See "To Love Torah More Than God," *DL,* pp. 201–6.

53. R. Bernasconi and D. Wood, eds., *The Provocation of Levinas: Rethinking the Other* (London: Routledge, 1988), p. 172.

54. Wyschogrod, *Levinas,* p. 165.

55. *DL,* p. 227.

56. *DL,* p. 223.

57. *DL,* p. 306.

58. *DL,* pp. 245–48.

59. *DL,* p. 147: "Il s'agit de faire Israël." Each subject is thus "chosen" to be broken open by the other, to lose its place and to come under accusation. In this sense, election is not exclusive for the people of Israel.

60. *DL,* pp. 15, 17, 146.

61. Levinas quotes Rabbi Eliezer Hakappar: "The grave is not a refuge, because in spite of yourself you were created, and in spite of yourself you are born and live, and in spite of yourself you die, and in spite of yourself you will have to answer before the King of the kings of the kings." *DL,* p. 243.

62. See "Antihumanism and Education," *DL,* pp. 385–401.

63. In contrast to S. Dubnow's conception, Jewish nationalism is seen by Levinas as Israel's nonegoistic retreat into itself, a function of human universalism. The State of Israel is an occasion to realize a just world, "a search for the absolute and a purity," *DL,* p. 230. In "State of Israel and the Religion of Israel," *DL,* pp. 302–308, Levinas writes that Judaism is above the state, and that it has already realized the notion of the spirit expressed in the modern state. Belief in God does not stimulate justice, it is realizing justice. The Jews, Levinas continues, were the only people to define themselves by a doctrine of justice, but at the same time they were unable to apply it. This has changed, and the opportunity to realize Jewish social law forms the uniqueness of Israel where the state is subordinated to justice, as once justice justified the Jews' presence in the land. There will be religion if the great Jewish books are not forgotten.

64. *DL,* p. 143.

65. Wyschogrod, *Levinas,* p. 160 n. 2, 207.

66. Levinas, *Théorie de l'intuition dans la phénoménologie de Husserl,* Bibliothèque de'histoire de la philosophie, (Paris, 1984), p. 17. This work, which first appeared in 1930, has been translated by A. Orianne as *The Theory of Intuition of Hussserl's Phenomenology,* Northwestern University Studies in Phenomenology and Existential Philosophy (Evanston, Ill., 1973). See also *TI,* p. 71.

67. Wyschogrod, *Levinas,* p. 160 n. 2.

68. E. Wyschogrod, "The Moral Self: Emmanuel Levinas and Hermann Cohen," *Da'at* 4 (1980): 35–58.

69. Ibid., p. 42.

70. Ibid., p. 45.

71. Ibid., p. 48.

72. Wyschogrod, *Levinas,* pp. 207–8.

73. *DL,* p. 25.

74. Wyschogrod, *Levinas,* pp. 208–9.
75. See n. 20.
76. L. Baeck, *Aus drei Jahrtausenden* (Tübingen: J. C. B. Mohr, 1958), pp. 42–120; see also pp. 121–40.
77. The expression appears in *DL,* p. 304.
78. *DL,* pp. 241–44. For Levinas, in "Religion and Tolerance," the meaning of Judaism is perhaps that tolerance is possible without religion losing its exclusivity. That Jews are not missionaries and do not shut themselves off from the world stems not from an attitude of vanity, but from a demand toward themselves. Judaism is intolerant not toward doctrines, but toward immorality. Idolatry is fought, not for its errors, but for the immorality inherent in it. According to Rabbi Judah (Sanhedrin 63b), although idolatry is absurd, man gives himself to it because it justifies public debauchery. Jewish religious wars are aimed against this immorality. Levinas notes that the moral conscience of the humble servant guarantees peace more than doctrinal unanimity. Judaism, seized by the Absolute, does not turn to others in imperialistic expansion, devouring those who refuse. It burns to the inside, bringing Jews the infinite responsibility. In the words of Amos (3:2): "Only you I have elected among all the families of the earth. Therefore I call you to account for all your sins."
79. Here we make use of some ideas in C. Verhoeven, *Een filosofie van het enthousiasme. Essay* (Antwerp: De Nederlandsche Boekhandel, 1982).
80. See "Place and Utopia," in *Difficult Freedom,* pp. 99–102, (*DL*) pp. 143–47.
81. For a description of this excessive devoutness, see W. James, *The Varieties of Religious Experience: A Study in Human Nature* (Middlesex: Penguin Books, 1985), pp. 343–48.

Part Three
The Uses of Jewish Ethical and Political Thought

Jewish Ethics and the Crisis of Philosophy

GILLIAN ROSE

THE issue of Jewish ethics has been broached in two fundamentally different forms: by Aharon Lichtenstein, in his article "Does Jewish Tradition Recognize an Ethic Independent of Halacha?"[1] and by Eugene Borowitz, in his article "The Authority of the Ethical Impulse in Halacha."[2]

The difference between the two formulations of the initial question posed from *within* Judaism reflects, I shall argue, the breakdown of ethics *outside* Judaism. Therefore, I propose an inversion: there may be halakhah beyond halakhah, and only then an ethics.

The argument, to which I devote the elaboration it requires elsewhere,[3] will be sketched here in four stages. First, the breakdown of ethics in the modern state and the conceiving of law in modern philosophy will be thematized. In second and third place, the two formulations of the question in terms of tradition and authority will be compared and contrasted, and the types of questions as well as their content will be foregrounded. Finally, the meaning of the conclusion that there may be halakhah beyond halakhah and only then an ethics, should emerge in a way that is no longer perplexing.

The development of the modern nation-state has led to the breakdown of ethics and the conceiving of law generally. If we view modernity in the light of contemporaneity, using "contemporaneity" as Fackenheim proposes, to mean the Holocaust and its aftermath, natural law has been replaced by natural rights just as civil society is separated from the state. "Natural" and "human" rights do not protect their bearers but leave them vulnerable to the dictates of the state.[4] If we view contemporaneity in the light of modernity, modern philosophy has been superseded by social theory. This conceptual split leaves both philosophy and social theory without intellectual initiative, precisely because it separates ethics from the conceiving of law. The political and intellectual predicament outlined here characterizes the non-Judaic situation as much as the Judaic. Therefore the implicit assumption that Judaism is concerned with law (halakhah) whereas non-Judaism is concerned with ethics, is unsustainable.

This double thesis needs developing. Instead I offer a brief excursus on the conceiving of law since Kant.[5] In his practical philosophy Kant separated legality from morality, so that legality is the realm of heteronomy, whereas morality is the realm of autonomy. The will is heteronomous or legal when it accepts the law out of interested motives, such as fear of punishment or hope for gain whether material or spiritual. The will is autonomous or moral when it accepts the law out of sheer reverence and is utterly disinterested, with no hope of reward or gain. "Legality" belongs to the laws *(sic)* of necessity; "morality" belongs to the law of freedom. "Law" in Kant is split demonstrably in these four ways: legality/morality; necessity/freedom. These antinomies in the conceiving of law in Kant may be said—quite simply yet dramatically—to have led to the breakdown of philosophy and the rise of social theory.

In philosophy, Hegel's phenomenological philosophy of history shows how Kant's categorical, unconditioned split between morality and legality is conditioned. It has arisen in the modern state, which itself separates inner morality from the development of ethical life so that greater moral or subjective freedom invariably goes together with less objective or ethical freedom. In classic sociological theory, Max Weber also exposits that the increase in individual rights in modern societies may be accompanied by an increase—not a decrease—in domination. In his great work *Economy and Society* (1922), he distinguishes between modes of domination as modes of authority to which social action is typically and meaningfully oriented as long as legitimacy is maintained and routinized. The three main types of authority—traditional, charismatic, and legal-rational—are analytically distinct but always copresent to a greater or lesser degree. The main exemplar of legal-rational authority is modern bureaucracy, which, with its inherent tendency to rationalization, separates instrumental means from the evaluation of substantive goals, and increasingly inhibits the reformulation of ethical and political ends. Durkheim in his main works, *The Division of Labor in Society* (1893) and *Suicide* (1895), attributes the breakdown of social (i.e., ethical) cohesion in societies based on contract and administrative law to what he calls *anomie* (a-nomos, without a law), a condition from which he judged, on the basis of statistics, the Jewish communities to be exempt.[6]

Steven S. Schwarzchild has argued[7] that the priority of practical reason in post-Kantian philosophy shows that Judaism is qualified to lead the way in this convergence of philosophy and Judaism on ethics. But, as my argument so far seeks to demonstrate, it is Kant's emphasis on the priority of practical reason or subjective freedom that has itself *undermined* ethics. It is this *disjunction* between the moral discourse of rights and the systematic actualities of power in modern societies and states—that is, the disjunction between "morality" and law—that has given rise to the separation of philosophy and social theory, overlooked and presupposed in Schwarzchild's argument. Even within sociology the disjunction is perpetuated in the spectrum of competing approaches to the conceiving of law and the reinsinuating of ethics into science: from law defined normatively as sanction, to law defined ideal-typically as meaningful orientation.

My argument is therefore that the relation of law and ethics is as problematic outside Judaism as it is within it. As this excursus has, I hope, begun to establish, outside Judaism the disjunction of law and ethics arises from the modern idea of freedom inherited by sociological reason from philosophy. This modern idea of freedom according to which "man belongs to freedom: freedom does not belong to man"—that is, human potentiality is discerned within the holistic actuality of freedom—is distinct from the traditional inquiry into free will versus determinism, where freedom may or may not be an attribute or capacity of the soul. I borrow and adapt here Heidegger's striking aphorism on modern freedom from his commentary on Schelling's *On Human Freedom* (1809),[8] giving it a historical and political twist in a social setting he would not own. However, it will be objected, there is no such modern, subjective or holistic notion of freedom in rabbinic, halakhic Judaism. Yet, I would argue, the major statements of Judaic modernism, from Samson Raphael Hirsch's *The Nineteen Letters on Judaism,*[9] the founding work of cultural neoorthodoxy, to Joseph Soloveitchik's mitnagged *Halakhic Man,*[10]—the former neo-Hegelian, the latter a Cohenian neo-Kantian—have explicitly struggled with and, in some less explicit sense, incorporated the modern problematic of freedom into their respective restatements of halakhic Judaism.

It is on the basis I have outlined that I open the comparison between Lichtenstein and Borowitz's questions concerning ethics and halakhah. Lichtenstein asks whether Jewish tradition recognizes an ethic independent of halakhah, while Borowitz questions the authority of the ethical impulse in halakhah. Two intrinsically different modes of address are posed here. On the basis of Weber's distinctions, it appears that Lichtenstein questions the ethical legitimation of halakhah as traditional authority, whereas Borowitz questions the ethical legitimation of halakhah as legal-rational authority. Prima facie, Lichtenstein asks whether halakhah is *equitable* by inquiring into the *status* of equity within halakhah, whereas Borowitz asks whether halakhah is *egalitarian* by inquiring into the *flexibility* of halakhah. Lichtenstein focuses on the ethical potential *within* halakhah, whereas Borowitz focuses on the ethical potential *of* halakhah. Yet, paradoxically, as I shall show, it is Lichtenstein who demonstrates the flexibility of halakhah, while it is Borowitz who demands that ethics be as "categorical" (unconditioned) as halakhah, and not a secondary kind of imperative, "its own way," the position he attributes to Lichtenstein;[11] and it is Borowitz who inquires into the *status* of women.

Conversely, outside Judaism, it is the appeal of halakhic contestation that does not posit an end to law, within or beyond history, that is *not* categorical or unconditioned, that increasingly solicits attention, albeit half-understood, from the works of Levinas, Jabes, Blanchot, Derrida, Lyotard—not a Judaism where ethics would be as categorical as halakhah. Non-Jewish thinking picks up an idea of halakhah that resolves the relation of law and ethics by leaving it precisely broken or open, while reformed Jewish thinking is aspiring toward an ethic that is itself unstable and unresolved in its relation to law. Each idealizes the potentialities of the other and fails to locate its own fate in the actual discordancies of modern political and intellectual life. As a result, we become witnesses of a convergent aspiration without a third on which to converge. It makes just as much or just as little sense, therefore, to ask if the idea of halakhah might found ethics, as it does to ask if there is an ethic independent of halakhah.

Lichtenstein considers several preliminary definitions of ethics in his article: *lex naturalis, derekh eretz,* natural morality. Although the rabbis were explicitly opposed to natural law thinking, Lichtenstein concludes that all rationalizing of halakhah implicitly presupposes natural morality. The contemporary concern is whether halakhah, either *din,* specific statute, or the whole of Judaism as an ethical system, needs an additional ethical supplement. To avoid the simple equation of law with morality, which would imply that no instance of uncertainty concerning "what ought I to do" need arise, Lichtenstein proceeds to consider *lifnim mishurat hadin*. This means, literally, "beyond the line of the law." It was transformed by Nahmanides from the negative, condemnatory judgment that destruction befell those who, within the limits of Torah, failed to act "beyond the line of the law," into the suprapositive counsel of perfection: "Ye shall be holy" and act beyond "the line," that is the strict demands of the law. This morality of aspiration is supralegal but not optional. Lichtenstein scours the traditional sources to bring out the range of connotations of this unique idea of "supralegality," from an actionable, rigorous obligation to supreme idealism. *Lifnim mishurat hadin* is gradually delineated as a situational or contextual morality. By contrast with a formal ethic that is categorical and fixed, *lifnim mishurat hadin* balances universal and local factors in any specific case, instead of assimilating each case to the mean average of the category or class under which, strictly speaking, it falls. Overall, this discussion supports Lichtenstein's defense of halakhah as multiplanar and not deductive. The penumbral regions of *mitzvot* or *din,* specific or strict statute, are continually complemented and never completed with *lifnim mishurat hadin.*

It is the noncategorical status of this equitable element that Borowitz takes issue with. He argues that the supralegality of *lifnim mishurat hadin,* presented by Lichtenstein as "imperative in its own way," amounts to no more than a vague species of command, and is all of a piece with Judaism generally, which manages to be highly ethical as a whole, yet leaves the ethical qualified by leaving it unqualified. He agrees that there are varying levels of authority within rabbinic Judaism but argues that the ethical impulse is so restricted or denied that it can provide no remedy for issues such as the status of Jewish women. The much vaunted flexibility of halakhah is sacrificed when such an issue arises, even though a solution is crucial to its continuing legitimation and future survival. Instead, the cumbersome resistance of rabbinic Judaism proves its formal, outmoded reliance on human rather than divine authority, which it shares with other fallible social institutions.

Borowitz is right to raise the changing status/role of women as a crucial test for halakhah, according to which the category of "woman" has always been explicit. But the remedy he proposes is bizarre: that ethics "ought to come as a categorical or unmediated imperative,"[12] even though he has argued against Schwarzchild's Cohenian fusing of legality and morality,[13] and accuses contemporary rabbinic Judaism both of excessive formality[14] and of excessive tampering with the imperative quality of the Torah's ethical behests.[15]

Instead of searching for a conception that would render both ethics and law more flexible, or questioning the conditions that drive them apart and rigidify them, Borowitz imports the Kantian categorical ethic back into Judaism—the same ethic that has itself been fundamentally questioned by modernity, and displays the qualities of absoluteness, unconditionality, formality, and imperativeness that he otherwise deplores in the idea of law. This way of enlarging the idea of halakhah with an ethics imperative in an unquestionable sense coincides with the very mode of halakhic judgment rejected by Lichtenstein. Furthermore, Lichtenstein does not subordinate ethics to law as "imperative in its own way." He sets out the universal and local jurisprudence at stake throughout the sources in a variety of carefully related expositions.

Yet, I would—and will—continue to dispute by arguing that neither Lichtenstein (on substantial grounds) nor Borowitz (on formal grounds) will be able to remedy, say, the changing status of women without confronting more generally the modern problematic of freedom together with its conceptual and political antinomies. Judaism, with its substantial writing about women in the talmudic tractates of the Third Division, *Nashim,* cannot dissemble its assumptions and impositions. This does, indeed, constitute a significant difference from the non-Judaic positing of formal equality, which veils and perpetuates substantial ethical inequality.

Once the Judaic approach is defended as, potentially, a more flexible basis for change, it would, nevertheless, become as formal as the position with which it is contrasted, whether the defense is mounted within Judaism or from without. For what determines the meaning of law and ethics is not what is posited, or even how it is posited, by its jurisconsults, rabbinic or other, but how it is configured within the modern separation of state and civil society, which reappears in the separation of philosophy and social theory with which both Judaic and non-Judaic ethics are infected. To avoid this repeated idealizing and discrediting of ethics within Judaism, including current pluralistic versions, and between Judaism and non-Judaism (for which Rosenzweig and Levinas must bear much of the blame), would involve recognizing the preconditions of these reversals in the social and political history that they attest. Otherwise this benighted century will end up with the same stubborn and sentimental law and ethics from which it seeks to extricate itself. The status *(sic)* "woman" will continue to explode any surety it is made to stand for on the way.

Notes

1. Aharon Lichtenstein, "Does Jewish Tradition Recognize an Ethic Independent of Halacha?" in *Modern Jewish Ethics: Theory and Practice,* ed. Marvin Fox (Ohio: Ohio University Press, 1975), pp. 102–23.

2. Eugene B. Borowitz, "The Authority of the Ethical Impulse in Halacha," in *Studies in Jewish Philosophy,* ed. Norbert M. Samuelson (Lanham, Md.: University Press of America, 1987), pp. 489–505.

3. Gillian Rose, *Dialectic of Nihilism: Post-Structuralism and Law* (Oxford: Basil Blackwell, 1984); *The Broken Middle: On Our Ancient Society* (Oxford: Basil Blackwell, 1990).

4. See Hannah Arendt, *The Origins of Totalitarianism* (New York: Harcourt Brace Jovanovich, 1983).

5. See Rose, *Dialectic.*

6. *The Division of Labor in Society* (1893), trans. George Simpson (New York: Free Press of Glencoe, 1964), p. 159.

7. "Authority and Reason contra Gadamer," in Samuelson, *Studies in Jewish Philosophy,* pp. 161–90; "Modern Jewish Philosophy," in *Contemporary Jewish Religious Thought,* ed. Arthur A. Cohen and Paul Mendes-Flohr (New York: Scribners, 1987), pp. 629–34.

8. Martin Heidegger, *Schelling's Treatise on the Essence of Human Freedom* (1936), trans. Joan Stanbaugh (Ohio: Ohio University Press, 1985), p. 9.

9. Samson Raphael Hirsch, *The Nineteen Letters on Judaism* (1836), ed. Jacob Breuer (Jerusalem: Feldheim, 1969).

10. Joseph B. Soloveitchik, *Halakhic Man* (1944), trans. Lawrence Kaplan (Philadelphia: Jewish Publication Society of America, 1983).

11. Borowitz, "Ethical Impulse," p. 492.

12. Ibid., p. 500.

13. Ibid., p. 495.

14. Ibid., p. 503.

15. Ibid., p. 502.

Teaching Leo Strauss as a Jewish and General Philosopher

MICHAEL L. MORGAN

THIS article is an attempt to understand in what sense Leo Strauss is a Jewish philosopher, in what sense he is a philosopher generally speaking, and in what sense he might be both. It will deal, first, with the Jewish context of Strauss's thinking and the way in which he identifies and reflects on serious options for modern Jewish self-understanding. Second, it will consider Strauss's understanding of the crisis of modernity and how it complements his consideration of Jewish options in the modern world. Finally, it will discuss the conflict between philosophy and theology that Strauss discovers as he turns to premodern writings to understand classical religious and philosophical thought. The Jewish context of Strauss's thinking will be shown to be important for an understanding of what he is doing; he provides an excellent example of how Jewish experience and reflection can lead to powerful, general reflections on moral and political philosophy and their role in modern life. But, at the same time, it is doubtful that in the end Strauss is in fact, or could be, a Jewish philosopher.

Strauss's Jewish Thought

In his impressive reflection on Strauss's life and thinking, Allan Bloom has said that "Leo Strauss' thought . . . had its source in the real problems of a serious life. His intellectual odyssey began with his Zionism."[1] Bloom's judgment carries the important truth that Strauss's thinking has its origin in his reflection on his situation as a Jew and his attempt to understand his own Jewish life. And it may be true, biographically speaking, to locate the nub of Strauss's Jewish reflection in his Zionism. But in order to understand his Jewish thinking fully one must begin not with a solution but rather with the problem; for Zionism, in one form or another, was surely a solution to a problem, and Strauss saw it in this way. Bloom sees this too, for he notices that "assimilation and Zionism were the two solutions to what was called 'The Jewish Problem'."

Strauss himself is both more precise about this and less precise. There is a Jewish problem, which concerns the possibility of Jewish life within the world. Traditionally, Jews took that problem to be insoluble by human means; ultimately God would have to solve it. With Spinoza, however, two modern, human solutions revealed themselves: political Zionism and, what Strauss called, assimilationism. That is, the problem of exile and suffering for Jews could be solved by abandoning the impotence of a completely otherworldly trust and assuming the responsibilities and challenges of self-government, or by "assimilating" to the state religion, the civil religion of a liberal democracy. The Jewish predicament, therefore, could be resolved by human means—or at least seemed to be humanly resolvable—either by the establishment of a Jewish state or by total participation in a liberal democratic state. Both would put an end to exile, in a sense, and to Jewish suffering—or so one might have thought.

Strauss would identify several options for Jews in the modern world. Along with assimilationism and political Zionism, he would notice cultural and religious Zionism, modern rational Judaism, Jewish existentialism, and orthodoxy. What is especially interesting and subtle about Strauss's treatment of modern Jewish life and thought is that he does not simply identify and display these options. Rather he outlines a Jewish intellectual itinerary. He begins with an account of the modern Jewish situation, the predicament of modern Jews, and spells out the possible strategies for coping with that predicament and for resolving the Jewish problem, tracing options for possible solutions as they arise, and identifying their weaknesses. He would ultimately find his way to a return to premodern Jewish rationalism and thence to traditional Judaism and its confrontation with philosophy, by which Strauss means that type of moral and political thinking rooted in the Greek philosophical tradition.

As Strauss shows, the outcome of this reflection, this dialectical line of thinking, is no comfortable resolution. Rather it is the recognition of a fundamental opposition in Western thought between two conceptions of the good life and its foundations. He frequently remarks that the very life of Western civilization is "the conflict between the biblical and philosophic notions of the good life," and hence "a fundamental tension" exists that cannot be resolved as much as acknowledged and lived.[2]

There are a number of things to be said about Strauss's conception of the Jewish predicament and how it gives rise to Jewish reflection on its solution. The key texts are the "Introduction" to *Philosophy and Law (Philosophie und Gesetz)* and the "Preface" to the English edition of Spinoza's *Critique of Religion.*

In the "Introduction" Strauss sets out the quarrel between the Enlightenment and orthodoxy in order "to arouse a prejudice in favor of" Maimonides' form of medieval rationalism.[3] That is, Strauss delivers a critique of Enlightenment rationalism based on the notion of the self-sufficiency of reason, in order to expose the strengths of medieval rationalism. First, he tries to show the effectiveness of the Enlightenment commitment to reason in opposition to creation, miracle, and revelation. Then, Strauss shows that the existential disposal of rationalism and its return to orthodoxy is only a qualified one. In the end, one comes to realize that the attack of the Enlightenment was a failure; one set of presuppositions confronted another. Traditional thought was based on belief in a set of ideas that could never be refuted by reason alone. As beliefs they could be discredited only by a complete system that excluded them, and the complete system turned out to be idealist.

But, if Strauss is right, idealism in the end historicizes even the new science on which the Enlightenment is based; "it understands modern natural science as a historically conditioned form of 'world interpretation' along with others."[4] Ultimately, then, the upshot of these reflections is the realization that the controversy over revelation and orthodoxy becomes a quarrel between systems of belief. The modern existential response involves the recognition that life involves a special kind of response to one's natural situation and its threats and risks; religion is opposed as a palliative device. This new form of bravery is called "probity" and "it forbids every flight from the horror of life into consoling illusion."[5] This, Strauss says, is the truth of the quarrel between Enlightenment and Orthodoxy, between reason and revelation; this existential recognition incorporates the "intellectual probity" that refuses any mediation between the two and that recognizes the two as revelation and atheism. If these are the only alternatives, then either there is no resolution, or one is forced to ask whether modern rationalism is the only form of rationalism. Must reason always oppose revelation? Isn't medieval rationalism, such as that of Maimonides, outmoded just as Aristotelian cosmology is outmoded? Strauss suggests an alternative; that the centrality of law might make Maimonidean rationalism retrievable and hence true. In short, is a Judaism rooted in Torah true and recoverable?

In the "Introduction," written in 1935, there is a suggestion that the Judaism of Maimonides, based on Torah, might be true and immune to the subsequent attack of modern rationalism. In the "Preface," written in 1962, this suggestion is deepened. Later, I think, it is abandoned in favor of the view which I set out earlier and will elaborate later, that there is a permanent, fundamental tension between reason and revelation, between philosophical and biblical conceptions of the good life.

The "Preface" is Strauss's attempt to explain the intellectual route that led him to an examination of Spinoza's *Tractatus Theologico-Politicus*. Strauss tells us that his sustained reflection led him to understand existentialism as a voluntaristic rejection of transcendence, of religiosity, on the basis of "intellectual probity." It is, he says, an act of will that disposes of religion while also disposing of philosophy. The "atheism from intellectual probity" is the final and deepest justification of Spinoza's critique of religion. Hence, the final victory is orthodoxy's, for philosophy can only dispose of it through an act of self-renunciation, whereby rational reflection takes its stand against revelation, but only as an act of will based on belief.

Strauss then makes an ominous remark: "Other observations and experiences confirmed the suspicion that it would be unwise to say farewell to reason."[6] First, the outcome of this suspicion was the thought that premodern rationalism may not have succumbed to self-destruction the same way that modern rationalism did, and this led to a new study of old writings with a view to how they were written. Second, this suspicion also led Strauss to read Spinoza in a new way. Finally, it leads us to ask how differently Strauss understood the theologico-political predicament that initiated these reflections. I want to focus now on this last point and on the various ways in which Strauss came to understand the modern Jew's theologico-political predicament.

Strauss's remark, is ominous, I think, because it focuses on the difference between his situation in 1925–28, and his later situation over which Nazism cast its dark and dominating shadow. Strauss begins the "Preface" with these famous words: "This study on Spinoza's *Theologico-political Treatise* was written during the years 1925–28 in Germany. The author was a young Jew born and raised in Germany who found himself in the grip of the theologico-political predicament."[7] One is moved to wonder what exactly that final phrase means; and Strauss immediately begins to say something about it by identifying the regime, the Weimar Republic, as a liberal democracy with certain features, among them its weakness. Weimar, contrasted with the epoch of classical Germany, was a weak advocate of human rights, of freedom and tolerance, impotent to withstand any resurgence of German national longing and will. As

Strauss explores elsewhere, Weimar is a victim of the crisis of modernity, of a notion of the diminished state that honors private differences and convictions but is unable to withstand the power of vital, national will and all the animosities and hatreds that it brings. Existential voluntarism, historicism, and relativism poorly equip people to withstand such tendencies. Perhaps reason can. It is no wonder that after the fall of Weimar, when the desires and capabilities of Nazism became apparent, Strauss came to worry about the abdication of reason. As he put it in those ominous words, "other observations and experiences confirmed the suspicion that it would be unwise to say farewell to reason."

What then was the "theologico-political predicament" of this young Jew in the liberal democracy of Weimar? It was, I take it, the predicament of being a Jew in a liberal democracy in the modern world. It was the problem of reconciling his religiosity with the world of reason, freedom, tolerance, and so forth.

Was this *Spinoza's* theologico-political predicament? In a sense it was, for Spinoza sought a conception of religion that was compatible with his notion of the best state, a civil religion suitable for a liberal democracy. But Strauss came to see the weaknesses of liberal democracy and the crisis that Weimar suffered. Hence, his predicament was more complex than Spinoza's for, in subsequent years, he could not risk a reconciliation that would ill equip the citizens of the state to oppose Nazism and totalitarianism. He could not be satisfied with modern political philosophy and its implications; nor could he be satisfied with modern forms of Jewish self-understanding.

In the end, Strauss's theologico-political predicament is the "fundamental tension" between philosophical and biblical conceptions of the good life and the holding of one view while being open to the challenges of the other; it is, in other words, the very character, the vitality, of Western civilization. This tension is unresolvable and yet endurable. Hence, for the young Strauss the predicament was one thing, but for the older Strauss it was another. To put it summarily, the theologico-political predicament was, for Strauss, threefold: first, one of understanding Judaism in a way that met the demands of the crisis of liberal democracy and of modern rational critique; second, one of doing this while safeguarding oneself against the threats of Nazism; and, finally, one of recognizing that the biblical and philosophical views of the good life, their moral and political conceptions, are distinct, incompatible, and in conflict.

The "Preface" is a subtle piece of argumentation, closely reasoned, and intricately dialectical. In it, Strauss begins with his account of the predicament, with special attention to the weaknesses of Weimar and the nature of the Jewish problem. He then considers a variety of Jewish responses to that situation, from the creation of *Wissenschaft* to political Zionism, cultural and religious Zionism, rational religion, religious existentialism a la Buber and Rosenzweig, and finally to an "unqualified return to Jewish orthodoxy."[8] Indeed, Strauss's reflections lead him to "wonder whether an unqualified return to Jewish orthodoxy was not both possible and necessary—was not at the same time the solution to the problem of the Jew lost in the non-Jewish modern world and the only course compatible with sheer consistency or intellectual probity."

But doubts began to occur, and they began to take the shape of Spinoza, so that Strauss, in the 1920s, had come to the conclusion that "orthodoxy could be returned to only if Spinoza was wrong in every respect."[9] As Strauss asserts in the "Introduction" to *Philosophie und Gesetz,* Spinoza's attack on orthodoxy is unsuccessful or, to be more precise, only successful in existentialism, in the atheistic will to reject traditional religious belief as incompatible with "intellectual probity," a courageous confrontation with human anxiety that does not flee into illusion. But, as we noted earlier, Strauss's judgment is that the Spinozist refutation succeeds only by self-renunciation or self-destruction. Hence, Strauss's early study of Spinoza had taken him to be successful; later he came to see him as less so, and hence he felt compelled to return to premodern writing to see if reason could not be retrieved.

A close study of Strauss's "Preface" involves and uncovers most varieties of serious modern Jewish thought and does so at a subtle and deep level. But most important, it poses the question of what the "theologico-political predicament" of the modern Jew is, in all its diversity and depth. And it raises the question of how Jewish thought, Nazism, and an understanding of modern political and moral philosophy are importantly interrelated.

Political Philosophy and the Crisis of Modernity

Strauss, in a variety of places, characterizes what he called "the crisis of modernity" or "the crisis of Western civilization," to which the crisis of modern political philosophy is closely related.[10] The nature and existence of this crisis, as Strauss elaborates it, has been the subject of much discussion,[11] and that discussion has intensified recently with the publication of Allan Bloom's controversial *The Closing of the American Mind,* a critique of American higher education largely based on Strauss's critique of Western civilization, American liberal democracy, and so forth. We need not engage in either a detailed description of Strauss's critique or an evaluation of it. The issues—the nature of political philosophy; its relation to political science, to the history of political thinking, and to moral philosophy; and Strauss's intellectualist account of the impact of modernity via Machiavelli, Hobbes, Locke, and so on through Nietzsche—are important but complex and would take us far from our concern. My reason for introducing this cluster of issues at all is that they are essentially related to his Jewish thinking, on the one hand, and to his return to the classics, on the other.

Strauss takes Machiavelli and Hobbes to be the founding fathers, as it were, of the modern crisis of Western civilization and ultimately of liberal democracy in the West. A host of crucial shifts characterizes this crisis. They include the shift from the primacy of the notions of duty and obligation to the primacy of the notion of rights, from the primacy of whole to that of the parts, from the state or nation to the individual, from teleology to mechanism, from nature to history, from finitude to infinity, from truth to meaning, from an expressive relation between the state and a conception of the good life to an instrumental relation between the minimal, protective state and a variety of conceptions of the good life.[12] The fundamental failings of modern political thought and modern civilization concern its relativism, historicism, and ultimately its moral diversity. Strauss's criticisms, variously discussed in the article and books cited here, are not unlike those of Arendt, the Critical School, and others, including MacIntyre. The chief villains, for whom Strauss nonetheless has a deep respect, are Nietzsche and Heidegger.[13]

Strauss's understanding of modern political philosophy and of the crisis of the modern world led him to seek a return to the premodern or classic political writings of the West. His dialectical assessment of the possibilities for modern Jewish life and thought and his critical assessment of modern society and political thinking suggested to him the same strategy, an inquiry into classical thinking about Western moral, political, and religious life. On the one hand, Strauss the Jew was led to reread premodern Jewish rationalism and its sources, the Bible. On the other, Strauss the political philosopher was led to reread the classics of political philosophy. For our purposes, we can conceive of this two-pronged program as a single one.

Not only did these two routes lead to the same program, a rereading of the classics; the routes are also closely related themselves. What we have already said about Strauss's Jewish thinking suggests three points at which his thinking through his Jewish situation and his critical understanding of his modern political situation overlap.

First, they overlap because Strauss's reflections begin in a predicament that is precisely the predicament of someone with religious attachments and commitments in a twentieth-century liberal democracy; and the liberal democracy is the highest point of Western civilization, with significant strengths but outstanding weaknesses. That is, a central feature of Strauss's predicament is the fact that it is located in a liberal democracy, in a state that stems from Machiavelli and Hobbes, through Locke, Rousseau, and Kant. One might put it schematically. The modern liberal democracy is based on several notions: tolerance of a variety of conceptions of the good life, the centrality of rights, the primacy of the individual, and the separation of political conduct from moral purpose and frequently from moral assessment. These and other ideas are the legacy of these thinkers. They contribute to the crisis of liberalism, its relativism, its separation of the public and the private, and its vulnerability to hatred, domination, and so on. Modern liberal democracy promotes the surreptitious use of power behind the facade of rationality and persuasion. In short, the situation of origin for Strauss's Jewish reflections incorporates the presuppositions of just that liberalism that is in the midst of a crisis of its own. Hence, no successful Jewish reflection can ignore this context.[14]

Second, Strauss often says that the continued existence of the Jewish problem, the problem of the Jew in the modern world, of suffering and persecution, of integrity and assimilation, is an indication that the human condition remains unredeemed. It is an unsolved problem, a sign of incompleteness, of flaw. One is reminded of Rosenzweig's justification for Christian persecution of the Jews, namely that the Jews are a constant reminder of the Church's unfinished task and hence of the Church's failure. The synagogue, the distinctiveness of the Jewish people, is a historical emblem of being on the way, of not yet, of failure of achievement, of a redemption still to come. Strauss appropriates this teaching and makes it his own. Moral-political thinking from the Jewish point of view is, by Strauss's lights, fitting; the Jewish point of view is a peculiarly appropriate perspective from which to view the predicament of moral and political life.

Finally, Strauss notes that the historical locus of the crisis of Western civilization, of liberal democracy, and hence of political and moral philosophy, is that regime of total negativity, Nazi Germany.[15] That is, Nazism displays one outcome, perhaps the most appalling, of relativism, scientism, and historicism. It is no wonder that Strauss links Nazism with Nietzsche and Heidegger, albeit in no simplistic way. Hence, as we noted earlier, one might be tempted to accept the existentialist disposal of religion and revelation as dishonest or lacking in "probity," that new kind of bravery, until one realizes that existentialism reduces alternatives to matters of will and power. One should not, Strauss cautions, be too quick to win the rejection of religious orthodoxy if the cost is the self-destruction of reason. Is it surprising that Strauss worries about the replacement of duty, obligation, and law with rights, freedom, and positivism of all varieties?

Strauss associates the decline of Western civilization with the loss of the modern concept of progress:

> the idea of progress in the modern sense implies that once man has reached a certain level, intellectual and social or moral, there exists a firm level of being below which he cannot sink. This contention, however, is empirically refuted by the incredible barbarization which we have been so unfortunate as to witness in our century. We can say that the idea of progress, in the full and emphatic sense of the term, is based on wholly unwarranted hopes.[16]

At least one of the implications of Auschwitz, then, is that human hope is undone. More was actual than was possible. Arendt and Jonas were right. Moreover, as Strauss goes on to show, this barbarization is the outcome of "a gradual corrosion and destruction of the heritage of Western civilization." Nazism is one outcome of modernity, of a revision of Western civilization that has destroyed the notion of progress; there is no such thing as betterment. Political and social institutions are instrumentalities, available as tools of domination for those with will enough and power enough to commandeer them for their purposes. Nazism is the epitome of a world that has three characteristics. It is anthropocentric rather than theocentric; all meaning and purpose originates in the human subject. It is a world with a new moral orientation, centered on rights that are rooted in freedom and passion, rather than on reason and virtue and obligation. Finally, it is a world that has discovered history, where all truth is bound to situation and context, where the only determination is temporary and historical, and where the eternal is replaced by the temporal.[17]

Hence, it is not accidental that Strauss came to believe that the predicament of the modern Jew in a liberal democracy, and the crisis of modern political philosophy and Western civilization, both pointed in the same direction. At one point, Strauss puts it this way: "The crisis of modernity . . . leads to the suggestion that we should return. But return to what? Obviously, to Western civilization in its premodern integrity, to the principles of Western civilization."[18] At another place, he indicates why such a return is necessary: Adequate contemporary analysis of our social and political life requires understanding our presuppositions, assumptions, and hypotheses, and these are illuminated, brought to light, by an examination of classical political philosophy.[19] In order to assess our current understanding of political and moral life and the social sciences that provide our access to it, we need a prescientific understanding of social, political, and moral life. This, Strauss argues, can be obtained from the ancients where we can see at work the "common sense understanding of political things."[20]

On the one hand, then, in order to uncover the truth about moral and political life one needs to return to the ancient political and moral writings where the common sense understanding of political-moral phenomena is exposed. On the other hand, in order to arrive at an acceptable understanding of Judaism and Jewish life, one needs to return to premodern Jewish writings and the primacy of Torah in Jewish life and thought.

The Biblical and Philosophical Conceptions of the Good Life

What is the conception of the good life articulated in the biblical world, and can we return to it today?[21]

Thomas Pangle, in his introduction to *Studies in Platonic Political Philosophy,* focuses on the theologico-political predicament as the center or nerve of Strauss's thinking.[22] In a letter written by Pangle and Orwin in response to Myles Burnyeat's critical review of the volume,[23] Pangle makes a special point of registering as a shortcoming in Burnyeat's treatment his omission of any discussion of the role of Athens and Jerusalem in Strauss's thought. Burnyeat never really responded to this criticism. But Pangle is surely right, as we have tried to show; the outcome of a return to the classics, for Strauss, is a profound recognition of the tension between philosophy and religion, between Athens and Jerusalem. Pangle's analysis focuses on the role of Socrates and Plato with regard to this issue. My own perspective is somewhat larger and pays special attention to the role of Strauss's Jewish roots.

At one level, Strauss was vitally interested in and concerned about the relationship between politics and morality. Morality, broadly conceived, is about the good life, its constituents and goals. Different moral perspectives, some religious and some not, have differing views about what the good life is, whether it should focus on actions, personality and character, relationships, goals or purposes, and so forth. Political philosophy, broadly conceived, is about morality when it is elaborated within a social context. Hence, a primary question that should be raised by political philosophy is how political arrangements, roles, and institutions are related to moral views. Is a given political arrangement committed to and even expressive of a particular moral view? Or is it neutral with regard to a variety of moral views and organized to facilitate their implementation? To use a terminology from Charles Larmore, who has discussed these issues with regard to Locke, Rawls, and others,[24] sometimes moral views are also political views, sometimes they are not. At times, that is, civil and political institutions express a certain moral view and conception of the good life; at times they do not, but rather facilitate the citizens' implementation of a variety of such views or conceptions. As Larmore puts it, with respect to morality, some states are expressivist, some are simply facilitators.

In Strauss's view, the modern political enterprise, insofar as it sponsors liberal democracy, is committed to the modus vivendi view of the state; it is not itself committed to any particular conception of the good life but regulates affairs so that its citizens can, in private, engage in their lives according to their own conception of the good life. In antiquity, this was different. In the Greek polis as well as elsewhere, there was a continuity between the individual and the state. Morality and politics were part of the same cloth: to put it differently, morality was diffused throughout the individual's life, at every level. In Larmore's terminology, the ancient state was an expressivist state; it facilitated and represented one conception of the good life and what was good for humankind.

Given this distinction, Strauss adds a further discovery. A careful reading of the philosophical tradition and of the Bible reveals two conceptions of the good life that share certain features—a concern for justice and the like—and yet are significantly different. Their difference concerns the role of speculation, study, knowledge, and openness. In the Greek tradition, the ideal is speculative, exploratory and theoretical; in the biblical tradition, the ideal is practical and active, even legal. The outcome is two distinctive conceptions of the good life, of the human ideal, but both within a general understanding of the political as expressive and not merely facilitating. One of Strauss's conclusions is that in the modern world, liberal democracies, when properly organized and administered, may be the best that we, in history, can do, given the insoluble and irreconcilable disagreement between the biblical and philosophical conceptions of the good life.

But the conflict remains; it is the fundamental tension, which I referred to earlier. It is, I believe, the deep sense in which we live and have always lived in a theologico-political predicament. What this phrase really means, then, is that we live in a civilization in which (1) biblical and philosophical conceptions of the good life are permanently in conflict, and (2) political life can either express a moral view or remain neutral with respect to one's conception of the good life. Clarity and self-consciousness about these matters leads to the best form of life of which we are capable, a life of vitality but irresolvable tension. This is what Strauss means by the conflict between Athens and Jerusalem, and this is the most profound theologico-political predicament that he finally comes to recognize.[25]

A careful reading of Strauss reveals, I think, that this is what he has in mind. Pangle's point is that he finds the whole business already present in Socrates' life as portrayed by Xenophon and Plato. I think that Strauss already sees it reflected in the Bible, in his account of the early chapters of Genesis in "Jerusalem and Athens." Strauss believes that an open and honest reading of the classics of both dimensions of our tradition, the biblical and the philosophical, yields the same message—the perennial tension between Athens and Jerusalem, between reason and revelation, between "a life of autonomous understanding" and one of "obedient love."[26]

The three Chicago lectures that Strauss gave in the early 1950s certainly reflect this. There Strauss says that "the one thing needful according to Greek philosophy is the life of autonomous understanding. The one thing needful as spoken by the Bible is the life of obedient love." In other words, philosophy conceives of the best life as independent and cognitive; the Bible views it as dependent and affective. Strauss then proceeds to argue that both agree about the importance of morality or justice, although they tend to treat morality somewhat differently. But

> they disagree as to what completes morality. According to the Greek philosophers . . . it is understanding or contemplation. Now this necessarily tends to weaken the majesty of the moral demands, whereas humility, a sense of guilt, repentance, and faith in divine mercy, which complete morality according to the Bible, necessarily strengthen the majesty of the moral demands.[27]

Strauss associates this with the difference, as Maimonides portrays it, between a commitment to creation and divine omnipotence, on the one hand, and a commitment to eternity, on the other. In the one case, man's way in the world is ultimately dependent on his own knowledge of the world's way, that is, Nature. In the other, it is dependent upon a relationship with God, that is, a covenant with Him. This, Strauss says, is "the core, the nerve of Western intellectual history, Western spiritual history . . the conflict between the biblical and the philosophic notions of the good life . . . this unresolved conflict is the secret of the vitality of Western civilization." The result is that

> No one can be both a philosopher and a theologian nor, for that matter, some possibility which transcends the conflict between philosophy and theology, or pretends to be a synthesis of both. But every one of us can be and ought to be either one or the other, the philosopher open to the challenge of theology or the theologian open to the challenge of philosophy.[28]

Philosophy grounds itself on a commitment to epistemological certainty, whereas revelation is rooted in and confirmed by reliable tradition, prophecies, and miracles. In the end, there is no way that the two can be reconciled, no matter how vigorous the attempt. "It is impossible for Reason, for philosophy, to assent to revelation as revelation."[29] Indeed, as Strauss comes to realize, revelation and reason, Jerusalem and Athens, are so dissimilar that all mutual refutations are question-begging: "All alleged refutations of revelation presuppose unbelief in revelation, and all alleged refutations of philosophy presuppose already faith in revelation. There seems to be no ground common to both, and therefore superior to both."[30]

But Strauss then makes an admission reminiscent of a point we discussed earlier, of the way in which existentialism comes to appreciate orthodoxy as an alternative and less honest and courageous system of belief. He points out that, ultimately, philosophy "must admit the possibility of revelation"; this means that philosophy must admit that it "itself is possibly not the right way of life." But under these circumstances, "the choice of philosophy is based on faith. In other words, the quest for evident knowledge rests itself on an unevident premise."[31] This admission, moreover, has a twofold impact. First, it shows that the fundamental and permanent conflict between philosophy and the Bible, when acknowledged by the former, seems to be catastrophic for philosophy, which is based on reason and not on faith. Second, it should lead us to probe more deeply exactly how philosophy requires reason, for as long ago as Aristotle it was recognized that all knowledge cannot be demonstrative—which is another way of saying what Aristotle, Descartes, and others have recognized, that reason is heterogeneous, and that all reasoning need not rely on faith of one sort or another.

Centrally, then, Strauss raises the question whether one can be a religious thinker and a philosopher at one and the same time. Moreover, his recovery of the ancients and his rereading of the tradition suggests that this is simply impossible without a deep inner tension. Hence, in the end, Strauss himself can be either a Jewish thinker or a philosopher, but not consistently both, and not a Jewish philosopher, for that is an oxymoron pure and simple. This might be our conclusion—or, alternatively, one might have doubts. Rather than take Strauss at his word, one might be led to reengage the traditional texts and the issue itself, and ask once again this serious and deep question about the relationship between philosophy and religion, between Athens and Jerusalem. For a variety of reasons studying Strauss is a valuable exercise, and perhaps there is no better reason than this.

Notes

1. Allan Bloom, "Leo Strauss: September 20, 1989–October 18, 1973," *Political Theory* 2, no. 4 (November 1974): 379.
2. See "Progress or Return? The Contemporary Crisis in Western Civilization," *Modern Judaism* 1, no. 1 (May 1981): 44–45; "The Mutual Influence of Theology and Philosophy," *Independent Journal of Philosophy* 3 (1979): 111.
3. Leo Strauss, "Introduction," in *Philosophy and Law* (New York: Jewish Publication Society, 1987), p. 3.
4. Ibid., p. 14.
5. Ibid., p. 18.
6. Leo Strauss, "Preface" to the English Edition of *Spinoza's Critique of Religion,* reprinted in *The Jewish Expression,* ed. Judah Goldin, (New York: Bantam Books, 1970), p. 383.
7. "Preface," 344.
8. Ibid., pp. 348–62.
9. Ibid., pp. 362–63.
10. Among other writings, see the introduction to *The City and Man* (Chicago: University of Chicago Press, 1964), pp. 1–12; *Natural Right and History* (Chicago: University of Chicago Press, 1953), pp. 1–80; "Political Philosophy and the Crisis of Our Time," in *The Post-Behavioral Era,* ed. George J. Graham, Jr., and George W. Carey (New York: David McKay, 1972), pp. 217–42, adapted from Howard Spaeth, ed., *The Predicament of Modern Politics* (Detroit: University of Detroit Press, 1964); "The Three Waves of Modernity," in *Political Philosophy: Six Essays by Leo Strauss,* ed. Hilail Gilden (New York: Bobbs-Merrill, 1975), pp. 81–98; "Progress or Return?" pp. 17–45; *What is Political Philosophy?* (Glencoe, Ill.: Free Press, 1959), chs. 1, 2.
11. See, for example, John Gunnell, "Political Theory and Politics: The Case of Leo Strauss," *Political Theory* 13, no. 3 (August 1985): 339–61; *Political Theory: Tradition and Interpretation* (Cambridge: Winthrop, 1979).
12. I have tried to itemize the main features of the shift to modernity, as Strauss sees it. There is much to disagree with. For example, Strauss sees a shift from obligation to rights, but his understanding fails to be nuanced and sensitive to premodern examples of the notion of rights. He never gives a deep enough account of the kinds of rights, the relation between rights and obligations, and the role of rights in antiquity.

13. In an important passage in the "Preface," in the course of describing the weakness of Weimar Germany, and hence of modern liberal democracy, and the "precarious situation of the Jews in Germany," Strauss refers to Goethe, Nietzsche, and Heidegger ("Preface," pp. 347–48).

14. This is a thought that makes one wonder seriously about the *desiderata* for a viable Zionism or a viable liberal Judaism today.

15. Nazi Germany was the only German regime, indeed the only regime ever anywhere, Strauss says, whose sole purpose was murderous hatred of the Jews—which I take to mean, of a particular group. See the famous passage in the "Preface," 347. Arendt, in *The Origins of Totalitarianism* (New York: Harcourt Brace Jovanovich, 1983) spoke of the death camps as the laboratories for totalitarianism in which the essence of total domination was practiced, to make actual more than was possible. Strauss's memorable statement of the negativity of Nazism makes a similar point.

16. "Progress or Return?" p. 29.

17. Ibid., pp. 27–33; cf. *Natural Right and History,* pp. 9–34. Strauss also considers Communism as an epitome of another sort of possibility for the modern world; see *The City and Man,* pp. 4–6; "Political Philosophy and the Crisis of Our Time," pp. 220–21.

18. "Progress or Return?" p. 33.

19. "Political Philosophy and the Crisis of Our Time," pp. 226, 229; *The City and Man,* pp. 8–12.

20. *The City and Man,* p. 12; cf. "Political Philosophy and the Crisis of Our Time," p. 226, "an elaboration of the pre-scientific primary citizens' understanding of political things."

21. The central texts are the "Preface" to the English translation of the Spinoza book, "Jerusalem and Athens" (1967), and the three lectures given at the University of Chicago in the early 1950s, published as "Progress or Return?" and "The Mutual Influence of Theology and Philosophy."

22. "Introduction," pp. 1–27, esp. 18–23.

23. Myles Burnyeat, "Sphinx without a Secret: review of Strauss, *Studies in Platonic Political Philosophy,*" *New York Review of Books* 32, no. 9 (30 May 1985), pp. 30–36.

24. Charles E. Larmore, *Patterns of Moral Complexity* (Cambridge: Cambridge University Press, 1987), chs. 3–5.

25. The key figure in Strauss's account of the philosophical way of life is Socrates. He exemplifies the desire for knowledge, the interrogative and critical character of reason, and the intellectual openness of philosophy. The biblical view, on the other hand, is based on revelation and is hence closed by a body of fixed legislation, of a code of life. There is, of course, much to object to in this account of Athens and Jerusalem.

26. "Progress or Return?" p. 33.

27. Ibid., p. 37.

28. Ibid., pp. 44–45; cf. "The Mutual Influence," p. 111.

29. "The Mutual Influence," p. 116.

30. Ibid., p. 117.

31. Ibid., p. 118.

Part Four
The Holocaust: Philosophical Perspectives

Philosophical Considerations and the Teaching of the Holocaust

EMIL L. FACKENHEIM

I will begin with a personal remark.[1] It was not until the time of the Six-Day War (1967) that I ventured as a philosopher to confront the Holocaust, but since that time I have been unable to turn away from it. Many people think I have a Holocaust complex, and my reply is: you have a non-Holocaust complex. That is to say, you pretend it didn't happen, or pretend it was something other than it was.

The Holocaust is not really a Jewish subject; just as I like to think that antisemitism (including the crime of the perpetrators) is not a Jewish subject. Germans should be studying it, and indeed they do. However, we cannot make distinctions such as "Jewish subject," "German subject"—for we cannot separate the history of the victims from the history of the criminals, and from the history of the bystanders.

There are enormous numbers of people occupying themselves with the Holocaust one way or another, but I have come to the conclusion that, in most cases, when they deal with the subject, they change it. I hardly have to mention vulgarizations—which are enormous; and I will not dignify distortions such as "Lebanon is another Holocaust." But we must take seriously changing the subject in a way which blunts its singularity. There is the Holocaust, and there is Vietnam, and there is Cambodia, and so on. I would be the last person to deny that there are similarities, but the honest way of dealing with these is to do research dedicated to the similarities and the differences. To turn from the Holocaust to Cambodia is to change the subject, which is all right provided that the change of subject is recognized.

Often the change of subject is more subtle. There is now an enormous literature about what Americans did, or rather did not do, during the Holocaust. There is also an enormous literature about the responses of the *Judenräte,* that is, the victims. All this is important. It is also about the Holocaust. Still, I call it changing the subject if it turns the focus away from the main issue, which is the behavior of the criminals. I don't think we can assess American behavior fairly unless we first focus on how the Nazis exceeded every possible norm in persecuting Jews. Again, when Hannah Arendt described Adolf Eichmann as banal, she was then able to divert attention from him in order to attack the *Judenräte*—without understanding their situation. If she had paid more attention to the diabolical cunning and thoroughness of the criminals, she might have made it unnecessary for Isaiah Trunk to write a whole book about the *Judenräte.*[2] There is no choice for anyone dealing with any aspect of the Holocaust, but to focus attention on the criminals.

When Raul Hilberg wrote *The Destruction of European Jews,*[3] he did not let the criminals off the hook. But he made one mistake; he wrote one chapter about the Jews and the *Judenräte.* All the Jewish critics focused on that chapter, and ignored the great merit of the book, namely that Hilberg concentrated on the criminals, more than anyone else—except Claude Lanzmann in his wonderful film *Shoah.* Both Hilberg and Lanzmann reached the same conclusion on an important point, which Hilberg expressed by saying that he attended only to the small questions, for fear of giving too small an answer to the big question. The "small" questions concern *how* they did it, the "big" question is *why.* Never once in his film does Lanzmann ask the criminals he interviewed why they did it, and with good reason.

Somebody once tried to ask this question. Surely there was no greater expert on the murder of the Jews than Franz Stangl, the commandant at Treblinka. Gitta Sereny spent day after day interviewing that man (all honor to her, for how is it humanly possible to sit next to that man and treat him like a human being?), and finally got round to the big question.[4] She asked Stangl: "Why did they murder the Jews?" (She didn't say: "Why did *you* murder the Jews?" because he would have had all sorts of excuses.) Why did they—somebody else. Stangl replied: "They wanted their money." That was too small an answer to the big question! The Germans had already taken all their money. Many historians approach the big question and invoke terms such as madness or insanity. I maintain that this is also too small an answer to the big question.

At this point, I want to say a word about the relationship between history and philosophy, with regard to the Holocaust. One must paraphrase Plato: either philosophers must become historians, or historians must become philosophers. Since that is beyond hope, I would plead for the closest possible cooperation between the two on this particular subject. Now, what does a historian do? I think a historian does two things. First, he establishes facts. (But establishing facts in itself raises philosophical problems, because the neo-Nazi revisionists have established their own facts regarding the Holocaust.) Beyond establishing facts, the historian also tries to explain them. What does the philosopher do? He reflects on this and asks, What constitutes a historical explanation?

I used to teach the philosophy of history, and I did so without paying any attention to the Holocaust. As did other philosophers. One general philosophical theory of historical explanation—no longer quite so widespread—may be called positivistic, because it is based on the dogma of the unity of the sciences. In the sciences, one has explained something if one has discovered a law. According to the positivist theory, if history explains anything there must also be a law somewhere.

There are, of course, great differences between science and history. One difference is that the scientist aims to find laws, whereas the historian wants to explain particulars, so he can infer laws; he rarely seeks to formulate them. The second difference is that science establishes accurate laws, whereas one cannot have accurate laws of human behavior. Yet a third and crucial difference is that the scientist can repeat experiments, whereas the historian cannot repeat World War I.

Santayana's notion that those who don't learn from history are bound to repeat it is, in my view, a half-truth, since history never repeats itself. Sometimes we wish it did, because then we would become wise by studying history. I think the wisest man to deal with the Nazis was not a professional historian but an amateur, Winston Churchill. Positivist philosophers insist that if you say that *a* led to *b* or, more extreme, that *a* caused *b,* you imply a law. However, it is not possible to predict future events from past history.

So much for what is called the "covering law theory of historical explanation." I will now try to apply it to the "why" of the Holocaust. Before doing so, however, I have to specify this "why" more fully. I am not going to ask why the Nazis perpetrated the Holocaust but, rather, why they persisted in perpetrating it even when the Third Reich was collapsing.

I will give three examples: (1) Eichmann diverted trains desperately needed at the Russian front to send more Jews to Auschwitz. (2) A less well known example concerns the so-called death marches. When the Russians were approaching Auschwitz, the natural thing for the SS to do would have been to flee for their lives; or, if they had to murder Jews before fleeing, they could have blown up the place. Instead, they death-marched their victims westward, trying to torture and humiliate them until the very end. (3) When Hitler was in his bunker, he had given up everything; his *Weltanschauung, Lebensraum,* master race—all went down the drain. There were only two principles that remained inviolate, and he expressed them in his last testament: one was that the Führer is always right; the other was that the Jews are the poisoners of the world. In extremis, Hitler in effect said that the Germans, unworthy of their Führer, deserve to perish, yet must survive for one purpose only—to murder more Jews in the future.

I will try to apply the covering law theory to this case. It begins reasonably enough. You could have some lawlike statement: given economic distress, there will be social disruption. I'm quite sure if there had been no great depression, there would have been no Hitler; but there was a depression in America, too, and it produced Roosevelt. A depression is, then, a necessary but not a sufficient condition. One might then seek a second law. Given defeat, and resentment over its effect as produced by the Treaty of Versailles, with the addition of economic disruption, a Hitler can emerge. It makes a certain amount of sense. According to A. J. P. Taylor, if there had been no depression, Stresemann would have handled the situation; but given the combination of the two conditions, depression plus resentment over defeat, you have Hitler. Taylor doesn't say a word about the Holocaust; he manages to present a continuity of German history at the price of no Holocaust.

I suggest that the covering law theory has to bring in yet a third factor, and this is beloved of liberals (especially if they are Jewish), namely, the scapegoat theory of antisemitism. They love it because, as Sartre says, today the Jews are scapegoats, tomorrow it's someone else. Thus, one concludes, given the first two conditions plus an age-old hatred of a group of people needed as a scapegoat, you have explained the Holocaust.

But is this true? It may be plausible for the beginnings of the Nazi movement. George Mosse[5] has made the convincing case (to me at least) that when, in the early days of the Nazi movement, the Socialist and Nationalist wings threatened to fall apart, Hitler made adroit use of antisemitism (which both sides shared). We may therefore suggest that the scapegoat theory of antisemitism is important, as long as the persecution of the Jews is both public and a means to an end. But then comes the Holocaust, which is supersecret, and thus doesn't make sense according to the scapegoat theory. What is the Holocaust *used for* if it is supersecret? We clearly have to conclude that perhaps the scapegoat theory is not adequate.

One may still believe that for some reason the murder of the last Jew is essential for the victory of the Reich. But when we come to the extreme examples just described, even this makes no sense. The murder of Jews is more important than the survival of the Reich?

The historian starts out by saying that antisemitism is a means to the Nazi Reich; now he sees the Nazi Reich as the means to murdering more Jews! Faced with this turnabout, he would have to say that, given sufficient stress, the people engaged in the enterprise eventually come to believe absolutely in their own propaganda; they would rather die than give up their beliefs or even question them.

To me that is not an explanation, because what it amounts to is saying that they were all crazy; and that is too small an answer to the big question. Of course, some may hold that they were all robots obeying Hitler. Bettelheim's famous theory is that they lacked autonomy.[6] I say that Nazism and the Holocaust are more complex than is imagined in the Freudian textbooks of pre–World War II Vienna. Survivors don't like Bettelheim, and no wonder. Somewhere he writes to the effect that the victims who went to their deaths unresistingly had something in common—a lack of autonomy—with the victimizers who followed orders no matter what. What an insult and what a distortion! Hannah Arendt is not too far from this, yet she herself mentions Eichmann's invoking of Kant's categorical imperative. He followed the Führer *freely,* that is, autonomously. It thus appears that the covering law theory of historical explanation has reached its limits.

There is a modified version of that theory, put forward by a friend and colleague of mine, William Dray.[7] He states that laws of historical explanation do not explain *why* anything was necessary; only *how* it was possible. This makes good sense. It allows for freedom in history, for decision making, for responsibility. It also admits that lawlike generalizations explain history only up to a point. Thus the three lawlike generalizations given here show that the Holocaust was possible; it would have been impossible without them. They do not show why it became actual. But that is the central question. Why did they do it?

I once asked Raul Hilberg this core question. He heaved a sigh and said: "They did it because they wanted to do it." Of course, Hilberg knows very well that that is no answer, because the next question is, Why did they want to do it? And not only that; one doesn't do everything one wants to do. The main point is that somebody decided to do it. There was the Wannsee Conference, and no sensible and honest historian can doubt that Hitler had something to do with that decision. The denials by such as David Irving are not to be taken seriously.

There was, then, a *decision* on the part of someone. This leads us to the only real alternative theory of historical explanation. Its most distinguished representative in recent years has been R. G. Collingwood, who was almost alone at the time; therefore his book *The Idea of History* has become more famous than it deserves.[8] His idea is dubbed "idealist" for no better reason than his thinking that decisions and the reasons people have for making them do much to determine history. This is an excellent point. It also implies that *somebody* is responsible for what has happened in history.

Collingwood's favorite case is Caesar crossing the Rubicon, obviously a major decision. Collingwood says that we must discover his reasons for doing it. Sometimes this may not be possible, but if ever a historical figure was a rational agent, it was Julius Caesar. So when he made his decision, he anticipated the likely consequences, and changed Roman history. To this Collingwood adds an important point. Once one has discovered the reason for an agent's decision, it is absurd to go on looking to psychology for laws of motivation; if one does that, one does not treat the agent as a rational being.

So far, so good. But, once again, it never entered Collingwood's mind to ask why Hitler decided on the Holocaust. Now I want to progress carefully from the Rubicon to Auschwitz, so I first go from Caesar to Bismarck, and we thus move into German history, which is a little closer to our subject. However, the case of Bismarck is more complicated than that of Caesar. Like Caesar, Bismarck was a rational agent, and we can find excellent reasons why he made his decision to unite the German states. In retrospect, Bismarck was a prudent and responsible statesman. Seeing that a pan-German Reich, including Austria, would invite external conflict, he chose a small Reich. But then came Hitler, who annexed Austria and undid everything that Bismarck did, and for this reason alone invited chaos and catastrophe for Germany—to say nothing of the world.

If, however, we want to know why Bismarck did what he did, the question is more complicated than just looking for his reasons. There had been a nationalist fervor in Germany ever since Napoleon destroyed the Holy Roman Empire at Jena and Auerstadt. Without this, I think Bismarck might not have united Germany at all. He might have been happy with Prussia, just as Hegel was happy with Prussia, and for the same reason: Hegel was afraid of German nationalism. But, given this nationalist turmoil, Bismarck had to do something. Thus, when we ask how he reached his decisions, we must take into consideration nationalist sentiment and the fervor behind it. Nonetheless, whatever we may call that sentiment and that fervor, they are not sufficient reasons.

I now move from Bismarck to Hitler: Why did he decide on the Holocaust? Our first reaction is that this is a case close to Caesar because Collingwood's model works best when one deals with an individual. There was probably rarely—if ever—an action that was as much determined by a single individual. We can certainly say, as somebody wrote, "No Hitler, no Holocaust." We can also say, "No Hitler, no Nazi Reich."

Yet on second thought the Rubicon is far removed from Auschwitz. First, everybody was not just blindly obeying Hitler; this is simply not true. As already mentioned, when Arendt treats Eichmann as a robot who doesn't think, as banal in his evil, she doesn't understand him and what's more she testifies against herself, for she herself reports how, at the Jerusalem trial, Eichmann invoked Kant's categorical imperative.

Some obscure Nazi philosopher whose name I have forgotten reformulated the categorical imperative as follows: if the Führer knew what you were about to do, would he approve? This is, of course, a scandalous distortion of Kant's categorical imperative, but no one can say that anyone acting on this was just a robot. Eichmann did what he did because he asked himself that question. Whether he actually got orders from Hitler, I don't know; that it is unimportant for our present purpose is shown by the second case we have listed—the death marches. We can be absolutely sure that Hitler then no longer gave any orders; he was sitting in his bunker. Nonetheless, at Auschwitz members of the SS in effect asked themselves, Would Hitler approve if he knew what we did? So we do not have just one man making a decision, as in the case of Caesar. We might state that there was only one individual who was irreplaceable—Hitler; but there were many quasi Hitlers, and to call them heteronomous, whatever Bettelheim might think, is false. They identified with Hitler's will, and *they made it their own.*

Now we come to the climax of the question, in terms of Collingwood's theory. In extremis, was there still a reason when Hitler and the many quasi Hitlers no longer made the murder of Jews the means to the greater glory of the Third Reich, but rather reversed the relation and made the Third Reich, or what was left of it, a means to the murder of more and still more Jews? There was no reason, but rather the opposite. Thus, for the second time, we come to madness. A historian who resorts to this terminology is quite right, except for one thing: mass madness is not an explanation. It is merely an admission that explanation has come to an end.

Once again one reaches a dead end—or would do so, were it not for the Nazi *Weltanschauung.* When Hitler was not yet in power, he had a follower, Herman Rauschning, who turned anti-Nazi when he discovered that Nazism was not old-fashioned nationalism, but a revolution of nihilism. There is an element of truth to that term, which one learns from Eberhard Jaeckel's fascinating *Hitler's Weltanschauung.*[9]

Jaeckel shows, contra Rauschning, that Hitler did have a *Weltanschauung* in which he believed. It was composed of several elements: (1) There is a need for German *Lebensraum.* This can be achieved by an alliance with Italy and England. England already has its *Lebensraum* in the colonies; and to Italy, Germany will leave Africa. The Third Reich will expand eastward, at the same time destroying the Bolsheviks who are the enemies of the British and Italians as well as the Germans. According to Jaeckel, this is the essence of Hitler's *Weltanschauung;* in addition to the fact that (2) there must be a Führer who is always right, and Hitler is he; and (3) the Jews are the poisoners of the world.

I inherited my copy of Jaeckel's book from a friend who had the habit of underlining important passages. He hardly underlined anything anywhere, except in one chapter that was underlined throughout. That chapter showed that Jaeckel contradicts himself when he says that the need for *Lebensraum* was the *Weltanschauung* in which Hitler believed; he himself shows that Hitler was prepared to give up everything, except for two things: the Jews were the poisoners of the world, and the Führer was always right. What happened when England didn't play the role assigned to it? Why, Churchill was the slave of the Jews! What happened when the Russians were winning? Well, Bolshevism wasn't Jewish after all, and Stalin represented the real master race. Here is the nihilistic element that Rauschning had detected, climaxing with Hitler's wishing for the death of the German people who had been unworthy of him.

Hitler wrote in *Mein Kampf* (which I take very seriously) that he didn't really find himself until he found a *Weltanschauung* that he never had to change, that was the "granite" foundation of everything he did. He blamed the Kaiser's defeat in World War I on his lack of a *Weltanschauung.* I therefore ask, What remained granite-like until the very end? Only two things—the Führer is always right, and the Jews are the poisoners of the world. And one then asks, How do we know the Jews are the poisoners of the world? (Himmler thought there were some nice Jews, though he also thought they should all be murdered.) Because the Führer is always right! And how do we know that the Führer is always right? (After all, everything he did turned out wrong.) We know it because the Jews are the poisoners of the world. So, for yet a third time, we must consider Hitler's *Weltanschauung* in terms of madness, for a self-enclosed system immune to every external challenge is the essence of madness.

But we do have a new element—the role of a *Weltanschauung* in German history. I think that, as a German, Jaeckel is too close to understand this. I have heard him argue, quite rightly, that the Holocaust was the heart of the Nazi *Weltanschauung,* but when he tried to explain the "why" of the *Weltanschauung* and its hold on so many Germans, he explained that it was a lack of enlightenment, a "superstition." What an anticlimax! As if enlightened Ph.D.s had not been among the murderers; as if Reinhold Niebuhr had not said, many years ago, that antisemitism is a social disease that needs more than a little enlightenment.

What conclusion can we come to? I can only end with an appeal to the historians: we can't understand the phenomenon if we don't understand what *Weltanschauung* means in German history. First we must understand what it meant in its origins, and at the greatest height of German culture. What it came to mean in its great perversion was a case of *corruptio optimi pessima;* if ever that saying had a justification, this is it.

When Kant destroyed metaphysics—and in Germany this was nearly universally believed—*Weltanschauungen* took its place. The first great post-Kantian philosopher, Fichte, said in 1797 that there are two possible *Weltanschauungen* between which a person must choose, and one cannot prove either of them. What characterizes a *Weltanschauung?* First, it has to be coherent. Everything has to fit into it. Realism and idealism are equally coherent. This much we also find in Marxism, which is a minor version of a German *Weltanschauung.* But, unlike Marxism, Fichte's vision is cosmic in significance. When Fichte said that when a person chooses freedom the whole universe holds its breath, he ascribed to human freedom a cosmic significance. But, he said, I can't prove it because there's an opposite view which says that freedom is only an illusion; and the two cannot refute each other. Then how does one verify it? Only by committing oneself with one's whole life to the one or the other.

Two years later, another great philosopher, Schleiermacher, who by now uses the word systematically, finds yet a third, equally cosmic, *Weltanschauung* that calls for a commitment, and that is the religious *Weltanschauung.* The feeling of absolute dependence upon a force beyond man is the ultimate prism through which one views everything; but one cannot prove it or refute it. The following year, Schelling came along with yet a fourth *Weltanschauung,* the esthetic world view: Truth is Beauty, and Beauty—Truth. Never was the romantic view of the world more profoundly expressed in philosophy than by Schelling. What verifies it in its conflict with the others? He replies: great art and poetry. He expresses a beautiful vision of cooperation between poetry and philosophy.

Then came the greatest philosopher of them all, Hegel, who saw, at the very height of German culture, a tremendous danger, which makes one want to flee back to Plato and Aristotle. If there are several *Weltanschauungen,* there is a danger of a thoroughgoing relativism. What is more, Hegel added the element of history: art in one age is not the same as art in another; neither is religion or morality. Hegel tried to solve the problem and overcome the danger with mind-boggling boldness, namely by transcending all *Weltanschauungen* and putting them into a synthesis.

That was the greatest moment in German intellectual and spiritual history, and Germans recognizing the fact called themselves the *Volk der Dichter und Denker.* But, as I used to hear intoned by every *Privatdozent,* when I was a student in Germany: "The Hegelian system has collapsed." I wondered what they meant by that. I wondered whether it was not the capacity of people to understand Hegel that had collapsed. Be that as it may, subsequent history bore the *Privatdozenten* out; Hegel's synthesis broke up. But what the *Privatdozenten* didn't tell me was that from that time on the decline of Germany began.

The most ominous of the figures of decline is Richard Wagner. However one understands Hitler, there is no denying that one of his inspirations was getting drunk on Wagner's music. Add to this an interesting footnote concerning a miserable Frenchman, Count A. Gobineau, and a still more miserable Englishman, Houston Stewart Chamberlain. The one was a protégé of Wagner; the other became his son-in-law. Both had a *Weltanschauung;* neither got anywhere in his native France or England. In Germany, however, they had a tremendous following. Germans were ready for *Weltanschauungen.* But all usable standards for judging between them had already collapsed.

This sort of thing makes one shiver. In the Germany of my youth, for a person to have a *Weltanschauung* meant to be "somebody." I remember one incident in the classroom before 1933; I was about fifteen years old. I would say that about 75 percent of the class were old-fashioned nationalists who wanted the Kaiser to return; there were three Weimar democrats, of whom I was one, and there were two or three Nazis. The discussion dealt with the fact that the Kaiser violated Belgian neutrality in World War I, and that his government later apologized publicly. We democrats tried to argue that the Kaiser should never have violated Belgian neutrality. Of course, we didn't get anywhere. The Conservatives who loved the Kaiser also lost. But the three Nazis who said that the Kaiser lacked a consistent *Weltanschauung* won. What should he have done? He should have violated Belgian neutrality and blamed it on the Belgians! (That's exactly how Hitler started World War II, except that the first victims were the Poles.) For the first time I understood the tremendous power that a *Weltanschauung* had in Germany, no matter what it was.

Now I ask myself the big question, the terrifying question. What had a *Weltanschauung* come to, by the time of the Nazis? It still had to be coherent, and it was. If the Nazi says that every Jew, no matter how nice he is, is the poisoner of the world, that is consistent—the facts don't matter; they are of no relevance to coherence. Isn't the nice Jew just covering up? Or, if not, is he not betrayed by his blood?

Now comes the crucial question: is all this cosmic? Non-Germans don't understand this, nor do Marxists, who may have less understanding of the Holocaust than perhaps anybody else. Hitler wrote in *Mein Kampf:* "If, with the help of his Marxist creed, the Jew is victorious over the other peoples of the world, his crown will be the funeral wreath of humanity, and this planet will, as it did thousands of years ago, move through the ether devoid of men."[10] And then, as if to help us along, Hitler corrects this in the second edition: not thousands, but millions of years ago. In every country except Germany, people would say that this fellow belonged in a straight-jacket. But in Germany, it was a *Weltanschauung,* and it was respected. Even the Weimar history textbooks that dealt with the 1923 putsch did not say: Hitler was a criminal. They said: Hitler was a "hothead."

The ultimate question is not, Why did Nazis murder children? The answer is that children grow up to be adults and soldiers and, in the case of Jews, poisoners of the world. And other criminals have murdered children before. The ultimate question is, My grandmother's best friend, a spinster, was the most inoffensive person I ever knew; why didn't they let her die in bed? The answer is that they had a *Weltanschauung*. They had to be thorough about it; there had to be not a partial but a *final* "solution." This is the best answer I can find to explain why Eichmann continued with the trains to the concentration camps, and why the SS had their death marches, and why Hitler ended up with his last will and testament. A big task still remains for historians—the exploration of the history of *Wel-*

tanschauungen, and of when and how things took a turn leading to the unprecedented disaster.

In an essay I have written on the subject, I ask two more questions. The first is, Did the Nazis really believe their *Weltanschauung?* This is an enormous and mind-boggling question. I will quote this short paragraph.

> Did Hitler believe his own *Weltanschauung?* Some say that nobody dies with a lie. A dubious thesis, in Hitler's case this may be wholly false. An actor, Hitler was a nobody who became a somebody when he found his *Weltanschauung.* In order to die as somebody, he may well have played to the end a role in a tragedy that he himself had had the main share in writing. If so, the Holocaust, unique in any case, is also a unique tragedy. Like other tragedies, it inspires terror and pity—terror because of the criminals, pity because of the victims. But acted on no mere stage, it offers no way for us, no mere spectators, of purging these emotions.[11]

Is that the end of the matter? Not quite. There is one more question, necessitating an epilogue. When Hitler died, did German *Denken* come to an end? Though this might be an understandable reaction, it offers no way out, because the specter of Hitler, his Reich, his Holocaust, continues to haunt the world and will keep on haunting it. The times, therefore, call for a new generation of *Denken* who can only be German, who will not escape into rarefied realms of being or generalized revolts against transcendence, but rather assume responsibility for their history and ponder the history of German thought from its bright beginning to its catastrophic end.

Notes

1. This article refers in part to my earlier published "Holocaust and *Weltanschauung:* Philosophical Reflections on Why They Did It," *Holocaust and Genocide Studies* 2, no. 2 (1988): 197–208.
2. I. Trunk, *Judenrat: The Jewish Councils in Eastern Europe under Nazi Occupation* (New York: Stein and Day, 1977). This is, of course, not to say that Trunk's immense work was not needed in order to establish the facts by a scholar.
3. Three vol., rev. ed. (New York: Holmes and Meier, 1985).
4. Gitta Sereny, *Into That Darkness* (London: Andre Deutsch, 1984).
5. See George Mosse, *Toward the Final Solution: A History of European Racism* (London: J. M. Dent, 1978); *The Crisis of German Ideology: Intellectual Origins of the Third Reich* (New York: Grosset and Dunlap, 1964).
6. Bruno Bettelheim, *The Informed Heart: Autonomy in a Mass Age* (New York: Avon, 1971).
7. William H. Dray, *Laws and Explanation in History* (London: Oxford University Press, 1957).

8. R. G. Collingwood, *The Idea of History* (London: Oxford University Press, 1957).
9. Eberhard Jaeckel, *Hitler's Weltanschauung* (Tubingen: R. Wunderlich, 1969; English trans., Middletown, Conn.: Wesleyan University Press, 1972).
10. *Mein Kampf,* p. 65.
11. "Holocaust and *Weltanschauung,*" p. 206.

A Response to Emil Fackenheim

STEVEN T. KATZ

MY remarks are to be considered provisional, because I think that all philosophical discussion, especially as regards a historical event, *must* be provisional. We don't yet know all that we need to know. As we are talking about the philosophy of history, we have to know what that history is about. We must be careful to engage in philosophy and history, not in theology.

I concur with Professor Fackenheim that the functionalist and other forms of historical explanation are unsatisfactory as a full accounting of the Holocaust. I might explicate and analyze the epistemic status of Hempel's covering law theory somewhat differently, but I would come to the same conclusion, namely, that it is a dead end.

I also think that the recourse to insanity as an explanation for the Holocaust is unsatisfactory, as is the recourse to psychohistory, which is so popular. It is important to shy away from psychoanalytic and psychohistorical explanations if one is going to make some real, explanatory sense of this extraordinary event.

In response to Fackenheim, I will offer, first, several ideological comments in the form of a philosophical analysis of *Weltanschauung*, and then apply my analysis to the historical material. Regarding ideology, I think that Fackenheim's presentation, and Jaeckel's presentation on which he draws, is the starting point. But it remains for all of us to go further, because we have not yet adequately explored the *Weltanschauung* of Hitler and Nazism. It certainly was a hybrid of pestilential racism and Manichaeanism that made Hitler's antisemitism into a *Weltanschauung* and, as Fackenheim emphasized, it was cosmic, that is, it pretended to explain the universe. Those who do not understand that Hitler was trying to explain not only empirical phenomena but also the rise and fall of nations, the nature of history per se, macroorganic as well as microorganic or microbiocentric phenomena, really do not comprehend his *Weltanschauung*. And, to talk of racism as if it meant blood in some empiric sense, is to misunderstand it altogether; blood is the incarnation, the shorthand of metaphysical principles. What is particularly interesting and needs deciphering is the peculiar way Hitler envisions how transcendental principles become incarnate in history through biological means. Race is not only a cause of difference; race is also a carrier of values.

If these brief observations are correct, the issue is then translated into a biometaphysical architectonic of the universe that has many implications. Sometimes this structure is pictured in biological, genetic, or biocentric terms—"healthy" or "diseased"—we all know the language. But Hitler's material, and that of his fellow travelers, also contains a good deal of metaphysical language that draws on traditional kinds of Manichaean terminology—Good and Evil, Redemption and Corruption; even Male and Female, God and the Devil, Children of Light and Children of Darkness, and the like.

I would say that the uncompromising and noncontrovertible nature of Hitler's antisemitism stemmed from the fact that he did not think that he was consolidating subjective elements; he believed that he had discovered the fundamental principles of politics and metapolitics, nature and metanature. I would agree with Fackenheim that historians who think they can explain the Holocaust with economic, Marxist, or sociological arguments can't really do so. Hitler may not have been a very profound metaphysician or ontologist, but the fact is that he was reading and being tutored in this form of pseudohistorical explanation by people like Eckart and Rosenberg. He was also reading the work of Houston Stewart Chamberlain and the like—a strange concatenation of Hegelian, Kantian, and other principles.

One should really understand Hitler as possessing, in his view and in the view of his followers, a kind of gnosis that saved. You see this very clearly in his table talk; here is just one quotation as an example:

> The discovery of the Jewish virus is one of the greatest revolutions that has taken place in the world. The battle in which we are engaged today is the same as the battle fought in the last century by Pasteur. . . . How many diseases have their origin in the Jewish virus![1]

This type of argument was seen by both Hitler and his followers not as mere rhetoric, but as having a soteric significance. This is what made him the Führer. When he made this remark he was talking to an intimate group, and he may, of course, have felt the need to impress them. But he truly believed that there was clearly a fundamental dualism between the Aryan and the Jew. For Hitler, the Jew represented alienation, negation, and death; conversely, the Aryan represented all of the positive and healthy values of existence, culture, and history.

It was on this putative intuition of what Hitler considered to be the riddle of the universe that the whole of the Nazi system (and of his authority) was based. In terms of positivist legal theory, Hitler is a metajurisprudential figure; he does not have to bend to any positive law, because he is in touch with and intuits certain fundamental factors of the universe. What makes Nazism so special is that it is a revolution, not just in a political sense, but in one's categorical understanding of the world. Hitler really thought, and others thought as well—Schmidt, for example, and even Heidegger—that when one held this Nazi view one had a new metaform of knowledge that explained the Whole. Thus, this kind of reconceptualization was crucial. In a post-Hegelian universe, however, this was not envisioned as it was in medieval gnosticism where, having analyzed a problematic circumstance, one awaited its solution only within an eschatological framework. Now one was required to enact those principles (i.e., one's categorical, racial antisemitism) in time and space. That is what gives Nazism its ferocity, its genocidal characteristic. It becomes immanent and, therefore, unlike classical gnosticism, it insists that the salvific circumstances must emerge from the particular. There cannot be a repression of the active and the physical; rather, it is within the active and the physical realm that the hoped-for biocentric salvation takes place. That's a very interesting reversal of the traditions on which this type of dualistic ontology draws.

I would now like to test this provisional thesis. I would suggest that the way to do so is not with crude empiricism a la A. J. Ayer or the verificationists, but rather in the way all historical postulates have to be tested, that is, to see if they make sense of the event we are trying to decipher.

If one considers two examples of Nazi behavior in particular, the importance of my type of hermeneutic emerges. The first is Nazi behavior in Eastern Europe in general, which I think was blatantly ideological in nature, as compared with its behavior in Western Europe (which was also, of course, ideological). The second should be viewed within the context of the war in the East; one should make a close comparison of the treatment of the Jews in Eastern Europe, with that of the Poles, Ukrainians, or the other nationalities there.

The differences brought to light by such comparisons can only be accounted for by recourse to the kinds of metaphysical principles we have been discussing. Despite Yehuda Bauer's claim that the Polish situation was a case of genocide, I would respectfully suggest that while it was certainly a terrible instance of mass murder, what actually took place in Poland and what was intended for the Poles in the Nazi scheme of things, was cultural genocide within a form of colonial regime, and not physical extermination. In all of the Eastern European states, the decimation was roughly eight to fourteen percent, with the elite classes overrepresented, so that, as a consequence, these nations could be controlled in a colonial fashion.

The case of the children, mentioned by Fackenheim, is even more interesting as a test of the ideological factor. Since women and children frequently are grouped in one broad category, let us consider the treatment of women in the Holocaust compared with other occasions of mass murder and genocide. Compare, for example, the medieval witchhunt, which only became mass hysteria when it was turned from witchcraft in general, against women as witches. Note also that in the ideological framework of late-medieval and modern Catholicism (and, from the sixteenth century on, within Protestantism as well), the social environment of the medieval world created institutions on the basis of its misogynistic ideology. Essentially, the family and the nunnery played a role in limiting the "danger" represented by women. But these were institutions to domesticate women, not to exterminate them.

If I have calculated correctly, between 1450 and 1750 less than one percent of all women were killed as a result of the witch hysteria—hardly "gynocide," to use the phrase of Mary Daly in her book *Gynecology*. The fact is that Daly is wrong. It is not gynocide, for the reason that Christian ideology saved most women. The roles of Mother, Wife, Nun, and Virgin Mary domesticated the natural "lustful woman" with her savage passions; and the institutions of home, family, and church controlled the social reality. Through these socioideological mechanisms, women were safely and usefully reincorporated into the larger sociopolitical fabric.

The abhorrent institution of slavery presents another comparison. We know that slavery resulted in an immense number of deaths; roughly 12 to 17 percent of the slaves exported from Africa died during the ocean crossing. But note that fewer women were exported than men, which meant that fewer women died. In general, women also fared better than men within the institution of slavery because childbearing was a financially significant factor in the economic system. If you read the slave manuals of the time you will see that the slave-owners are urged to be reasonably humane to women, to encourage them to procreate, and to help them form families—not out of any moral concern, but because of prudential and utilitarian reasons: more profit was made on the offspring of slaves than on cotton or tobacco. That is to say, the ideology of slavery was non-genocidal. There is simple proof of this: 400,000 blacks were imported into America; and on the eve of the Civil War there were four million blacks in the United States. Obviously, ideology (e.g., the paternalism that was part of slavery and of the mixed capitalist structure) had something to do with that tenfold increase in the black population.

Coming closer to our own time, let us consider the terrible persecution of the Armenians during World War I. One aspect of this very complicated case is dealt with in Lepsius's classic book on Germany and Armenia.[2] In a footnote, he says that 200,000 women and children were saved because they were incorporated into Turkish harems. This cannot be considered as a desirable fate—but the fact remains: the lives of 200,000 women and children were spared. There is a great debate about the number of Armenians in Turkey in 1915, but if we assume that there were 1.5 million, we must bear this extraordinary factor in mind, namely, that ideology changed the fate of these women. Put more explicitly, the Turkish onslaught against the Armenian population did not require the murder of all Armenian women and children.

Other examples of ideology accounting for the peculiar fate of women and their higher rate of survival, largely because of gender, occurred in the Gulag, or among lesbians in Nazi Europe (the case of Gypsies is more complicated). Consider, however, the fate of Jewish women during the Holocaust. I suggest—and this is an idea on which I am still working—that this was the first time in human history where being a woman constituted a death sentence, because the ultimate crime was to bear a Jewish child. Therefore, every Jewish woman who was pregnant, and every Jewish child under a certain age, were sent to their death. The fate of Jewish women serves to indicate that Nazism was an ideologically driven concept. The designation of the Jewish woman as criminal par excellence reveals the salience of ideology in the Nazi *Weltanschauung*.

Fackenheim spoke about the pillars of the Nazi ideology. I would add that Hitler did not remain on the level of conceptualization; he tried to change the world to fit his ideology. Whether the target was the mentally retarded or epileptic, homosexuals, Jews, Gypsies—their fate within the Nazi orbit was ideologically determined. These groups represented certain kinds of deformation or sickness, unhealthy beings that had to be destroyed or otherwise contained.

The death camps, the struggle in the East, were efforts to re-create reality; it is in this way that one must understand Nazism. It was an effort to remold reality to conform to a world view, whether on a strictly political level (to destroy democracy, to eliminate Marxism), or on a more fundamental genetic level where one tries to destroy unwanted types on the basis of a eugenic or racial program. Nazism was a fundamental empiric effort to locate ideology in history.

That strikes me as the driving force of Hitler's Nazism, and the only way one can really understand what took place between 1933 and 1945.

Notes

1. *Hitler's Table Talk, 1941–1944: His Private Conversations,* trans. Norman Cameron and R. H. Stevens (London: Weidenfeld and Nicolson, 1973), no. 156, p. 332.
2. Johannes Lepsius, *Deutschland und Armenien, 1914–1918* (Potsdam: Der Tempelverlag, 1919).

A Response to Emil Fackenheim

ZE'EV MANKOWITZ

I would like to express the reactions of a historian and, more important, a teacher of history. If it is true that Nazism cannot be subsumed under any laws, if it is also true that it defies the process of Collingwoodian reenactment, we are led, once again, to a dead end, to something that defeats us. I think that many of us, having attempted to ask the "big" question and to account for what the Nazis did, find that when we have finished, our answers pale into insignificance. The best question that I am asked after the eight to twelve classroom lessons that I devote to the question, How was the Holocaust humanly possible? is raised by the student who asks, Excuse me, but how *was* the Holocaust humanly possible?

This question of uniqueness is one that I attempt to unravel with the students, and I certainly welcome Professor Fackenheim's emphasis on the perpetrators, for the simple reason that we operate with a strange distinction. Whereas in terms of history and the making of history, the focus is on Germany and on those who do the murdering, who organize it and provide the infrastructure that makes it possible, the emotional focus of uniqueness attaches to the victims and not to the perpetrators. It is a strange distinction in the thinking of the students and, quite frankly, it took me a long time to understand that it was central to my thinking as well.

Therefore, the first question that I ask in attempting to unravel the question of uniqueness is the following: does the uniqueness of the Holocaust have its source in something existential, that is, in one's being Jewish, or in being a committed Christian with a certain relationship to the Jewish people by way of faith? Or is it something of general significance that stands beyond one's personal connection? This uniqueness of the Holocaust must be demonstrated; it cannot be assumed as a result of personal involvement.

The second question concerns the context of this uniqueness. Does it relate to World War II? Does it relate to the twentieth century and to totalitarianism? To Western history? To all of history? Or does it relate primarily to Jewish history? What is the comparative context of this uniqueness? Steven Katz, in his work on intentionality, has broadened the canvas to include almost all of known history.

Closely related to this is the third, and more difficult, question, namely, the *level* of uniqueness. Does the uniqueness of the Holocaust derive from a consideration of the historical evidence; or is it a metahistorical uniqueness, which is assumed through faith? In the latter case, the evidence is dealt with as a theologian would deal with human experience, in an attempt to bring it into line with his or her theological assumptions.

It seems to me that some approaches to the uniqueness of the Holocaust are indeed metahistorical; they do not start with the evidence, but with something else. Certain Orthodox Jews begin with a commitment to the belief that the Holocaust is as unique as is all of Jewish history, and from that point of view it is not especially unique. Elie Wiesel arrives at a metahistorical uniqueness derived from his personal testimony. It is not something that he ever attempts to demonstrate; it is only something that he articulates. Emil Fackenheim is most problematical for all of us; I have never been able to decide where he stands in this regard. My guess is that his is a metahistorical position, that his claim derives from "something else" and can only be dealt with ultimately as a question of faith.

Among those for whom the uniqueness of the Holocaust is historical rather than metahistorical, there seem to be three basic approaches.

1. The Holocaust is not mysterious; it is open in every way to human investigation. On the other hand, it is certainly sui generis. But that is a historical argument and is open to historical refutation. For example, uniqueness might relate to the perpetrators: who they were, what they were like, where they came from. Perhaps the most dramatic formulation of this approach is that of Richard Rubenstein: "The Holocaust only became possible when it was taken out of the hands of the ruffians and the hoodlums, and put into the hands of decent bureaucrats." This is a radical and very difficult statement that challenges many of our assumptions; but Rubenstein is certainly very close to the truth.

2. The most widely shared approach, articulated by Steven Katz, is that of intentionality. The intentions translated into ideology—in Fackenheim's formulation, the *Weltanschauung* of the Nazis—in many ways mark the uniqueness of the Holocaust.

3. The approach of historical uniqueness may also relate to the consequences of the Holocaust. The Jews were the only group of people who were not able to rehabilitate themselves in Europe. In

their case, the Nazis succeeded. Hitler was victorious in his war against the Jews, at least in its European phase.

Let us return to the emphasis on the perpetrators. This emphasis is very salutary in a number of senses. It avoids many of the questions faced by students when they focus on the victims. In its most vulgar form, the uniqueness of the Holocaust is perceived in terms of degrees of suffering, and not in terms of the intention of the perpetrator.

My question for Fackenheim is, How does one move from the proper focus on the perpetrator to Jewish identity? This move seems problematic; it creates a chasm that I am no longer able to bridge except by a notion of opposition and defiance—*not* by building on the uniqueness of the Holocaust. In other words, the most appropriate response, from a Jewish perspective, to these events would seem to be the classic Jewish formulation of "may their name be obliterated and wiped out." It is bad enough that, as historians, we spend so much of our time in the company of these low, degenerate, worthless human beings. To build this into our identity is something that I find, after many years, impossible—and undesirable.

There is another problem facing the historian. For the person who starts from history and arrives at uniqueness in history, and for whom uniqueness then integrates into identity, views of history keep changing. But identity persists. It is impossible for a person to start from history rather than metahistory, and to build history into identity.

I would like to make one last observation relating to Fackenheim's argument for the uniqueness of the Holocaust. Differentiating between ideology and *Weltanschauung,* he argues that an ideology is not cosmic; it is confined to history. Such crimes as Stalin's murder of the peasants, and the Cambodian genocide, for example, shatter the imagination, but remain within the limits of intelligibility.

I am not attempting to "flatten out" the Holocaust, but I would like to suggest another approach to the "big" question. It comes from Jean Amery's "At the Mind's Limits." As a survivor of Auschwitz, he describes his torture, and speaks about administrators of torture, people who were given power that made them into demigods. He writes: "If one thinks upon it, they were bureaucrats of torture. And yet they were also much more. I saw it in their serious tense faces which were not swelling, let us say, with sexual sadistic delight, but concentrated in murderous self-realization." That is a remarkable phrase—they realize themselves through the act of murder.

In any situation where human beings claim, for one reason or another, to take the place of God or to be sovereigns in the universe, they will substantiate their claim to absoluteness by murder and torture. This applies to Stalin, Pol Pot, Hitler, Torquemada, and others—we can go right through history. They end up murdering vast numbers of people, and that is universal; it is not unique.

Part Five

The State of Israel: Philosophical Perspectives

Political Philosophy and Israel's Civil Society

DANIEL J. ELAZAR

IT is my understanding that the founding of every polity involves, among other things, the linking of certain basic tensions incident to the very character of the polity-in-the-making, within a common framework. These tensions are not fully resolved, but become part of the polity's fabric and persist as long as the polity itself continues to exist—or at least until there is such a drastic change in regime that the polity is no longer the same political entity that it was. Examination of the founding of the State of Israel and, prior to that, of the several components of the Zionist movement, enables one to identify certain tensions that have been built into the enterprise, and that must be reckoned with in both practical and philosophic ways.

In practice, those tensions have been dealt with primarily through a compact among the various movements and groups within the Zionist and, later, the Israeli fold—what is conventionally referred to as a "social contract." Some of the basic agreements, tacit or open, in Israeli society—the religious status quo agreement is one of them—are elements in that social contract. One of Israel's current problems is that parts of the initial social contract that accompanied the founding of the state in 1947–48 need to be renegotiated.

Philosophically, we have not done well in dealing with those tensions. It even may be that an important element of the social contract was that we should not try to deal with them philosophically, except in very private capacities; this was probably a wise decision. Thus, what I am suggesting may not be an immediate task but a future agenda. Nonetheless, I think the time has come to consider whether these questions should be on our philosophic agenda.

A basic tension has been built into the Israeli polity and its civil society from its founding. There are Israelis—and they are found not only in the religious community—who see the relationship between the Jewish people and the Land of Israel as covenantal, that is, derived from the traditional historic, biblical, Jewish covenant; they envision the establishment of a covenantal polity and society in Israel. There are, on the other hand, Israelis who see Israel as "the state of the Jews"; for such a polity it is sufficient to have a social contract to organize relationship among Jews of varying persuasions or orientations, as well as between Jews and non-Jews within the state.

A second tension, of a different order, exists in the organization of the polity, namely, the tension between participation and centralization. From the very beginnings of the Zionist polity in Eretz Israel, it included elements that were strongly oriented toward the idea of widespread civic and social participation; the moshavot of the First Aliyah are an example. It also included strong elements of centralization and bureaucratization—for example, the demands of Baron de Rothschild and his agents for near total control over the economic life of the moshavot they supported.

These are prosaic matters, but they are vital in the day-to-day life of the country; hence, philosophically, they are extremely important. For example, it has been argued that the Sephardim were peripheral in the early days of the Zionist settlement when the main task was to build the central structure of the polity. That is historically inaccurate; but, if one adopts a centralizing model, it is fair to conclude that the main task was to build whatever is defined as the "center"—in Israel's case, the Zionist settlements initiated by Russian Jews. Had one adopted a participatory model, the main task in state-building would have been different. Even at that point, however, the goal would have been to build a matrix or mosaic of multiple centers, each capable of contributing to the whole (which is what the various groups were actually doing). Hence the choices that were made need to be understood in terms of the political theory behind them.

A third tension exists between the religious and secular elements in the polity. Even though most of the population does not fall clearly into one or the other category, this is an all-embracing tension because the cutting edge of the debate over the character of the state revolves around the conflict between religious and secular visions. Much of the population, of course, is not philosophical in its thinking and does not see the two as necessarily contradictory.

A fourth tension has to do with what Werner Dannhauser has referred to as "fraternity," and which one can refer to less felicitously as particularism versus a kind of cosmopolitanism or universalism. In my view, this is a tension that exists not only in Israel, but is built into the Jewish people as a whole and into its political tradition. Nevertheless, it acquires a special character in an embattled country with a relatively small population, in which the tendencies toward particularism are naturally reinforced. Fortunately, the tendencies toward fraternity, which is one of the glories of Israeli society, have also been reinforced.

Particularism leads to self-concern and to a parochial view of the larger world. Ironically, the striving for universalism or cosmopolitanism has tended to manifest itself in Israel as an imitation of those elements of contemporary civilization that are deemed by Israelis to be the most universalist or the most cosmopolitan; these are, in particular, American popular culture and the views dominant among American intellectuals. In Israel, some will argue that until the country is modeled after the United States or Western Europe, it has not achieved "democracy," whereas others will hold that there may be alternate ways to achieve democracy other than a commitment to hedonistic, liberal individualism. This tension also enters into the religious-secular vision, and the covenant-social contract relationship.

A fifth tension, with two dimensions, exists between subcommunities within the society: the tension between Sephardim and Ashkenazim, and between Jews and non-Jews (the "minorities"). I think the first will be relatively short-lived, and the second more enduring. Whatever the case, the problem of intergroup tension is built into all societies in the Middle East, where peoples or subgroups (we might call them "publics") tend to be longer-lived than states.

Political boundaries in the Middle East, whether of imperial provinces or independent states, tend to change very frequently. Even during the Ottoman period, the boundaries of provinces changed repeatedly; none of the present boundaries in the Middle East is even a hundred years old. Historically, states come and go, while ethnoreligious communities exist seemingly forever. Consequently, the tension between ethnoreligious communities and state structures will be a continuing one. I do not believe that there is any likelihood of it disappearing, even if there is formal peace that minimizes some of the present expressions of that tension.

Modern political philosophy, which developed in the West, does not recognize group rights except as a very secondary, even tertiary phenomenon; it certainly does not relate to ethnoreligious communities that take precedence over states. Western political thought is not adequate for this situation—if, indeed, it is adequate for the postmodern West, which has witnessed a resurgence of primordial groups. Jews, Arabs, and other peoples in the Middle East will have to work through these questions philosophically for themselves.

The tension between vision and ideology has frequently been discussed. Zionism has produced highly specific ideological doctrines and has sought to implement them; it has also expressed a broad vision and allowed a great deal of openness as to how that vision is to be pursued. Both approaches are encompassed in the Jewish state of today. In the Zionist movement, the tension was manifested most directly, but not solely, in the struggle between the ideologues and the pragmatists. It was also apparent in the difference between the Zionism of redemption, which predominated among Sephardim, and the Zionism of revolution, most prominent in Ashkenazi circles. The Sephardim saw the Jewish resettlement of Eretz Israel as an expression of traditional Jewish life; the Ashkenazim saw it as a means to revolutionize the Jewish people in ways that rejected the Jewish tradition of the past. While the differences may have been temporary, and a consequence of where each group was in its modernization process, they have contributed to perpetuating a tension in Israeli society.

This, in turn, leads to the tension that exists between accommodation and intransigence in Israeli politics. Israeli politics has frequently seemed to be a politics of intransigence; but I think that is a misreading of the Israeli political scene. It is true that Israeli politics at its highest decibel levels emphasizes intransigence, but in fact it has a substantial accommodationist dimension. The Zionist movement, with two exceptions (the minor exception of the Territorialists, and the somewhat larger and important exception of the Revisionists), has remained united despite the great ideological diversity and conflict that accompanied it from its earliest days, even before the first Zionist Congress in Basle.

To remain united, the Zionists invented accommodationist institutions and processes—for example, proportional representation, which gives everybody a fair share of the pie (and that is currently under attack), as a means to keep potential intransigents together. The enunciation of exclusivist ideological demands was balanced by institutional devices related to the shared vision of Zionism. This still operates in Israeli politics; frequently, what appears to be endless interparty, often most unaesthetic, wrangling in the Knesset, suddenly results in substantive measures being enacted, the result of many years of carefully negotiated consensus. An understanding of the relationship between what seems to be a high level of intransigence, and a substantial degree of accommodation, should be an item on the agenda of political philosophy.

Finally, we have the tension between the pursuit of the messianic and of the prosaic. I would suggest that this, too, is a tension that Israel has inherited from Jewish history. All of Jewish tradition is essentially a tension between the prosaic and the messianic, between the minutiae of practical daily halakhah and the expectation of the

Messiah bringing redemption. This tension is a source both of consolation and of difficulty. It has enabled Jews to survive under the most difficult conditions by concentrating on prosaic acts, in the hope that these would bring the Messiah. Unfortunately, occasional spasms of messianism led to collective catastrophies that have had long-range implications for the Jewish people. Confronting this tension is, perhaps, the primary task of political philosophy. To the extent that political philosophy is skeptical about divine claims and forces us to examine unexamined assumptions, it enables us to stand back both from the prosaic and from the messianic, and look at the relationship between them. In this respect it can add a salutary, sobering element to a political system that can either be easily overheated, or sink into the pettiness of power struggles.

Are these questions being dealt with in Israeli universities? In my opinion, the answer is dismal indeed. Beyond the fact that there may be a social contract not to raise these philosophic issues publicly, even those who raise questions of political philosophy in their classes show a notable lack of attention to such concerns. By and large, the political philosophy taught in Israel follows the traditional historical approach that is partial to Marxist or Jacobin views of what is important, with occasional excursions into other aspects of modern political philosophy. Little serious attention is given to ancient or medieval political thought, to the ancient classics; almost no attention is paid to American political thought. There seems to be no awareness of the existence of interesting questions to explore other than those that came out of continental Europe. At the most, one can point to a certain liberal strand that concerns itself with Hobbes, Locke, and the English philosophers as a source of teachings about liberty.

Worst of all, there has been almost no recognition that Jewish political thought exists. While it is now just beginning to become a subject for study and teaching, it is not yet used to address questions of concern in Israel; rather, it is taught in the spirit of the historical uncovering of a forgotten and neglected tradition.

However, in a Jewish state marked by the resurgence of the Sadducean tradition emphasizing a civil religion focused on the state and its institutions, political philosophy is more than ever a necessity. It becomes a further necessity if the social contract that was accepted for forty years now requires some renegotiation. The application of Jewish political philosophy is also relevant to the current situation in which the moral issues of power and powerlessness have been raised both in Israel and in the Diaspora.

In that connection, I would suggest that moral judgments only begin to be meaningful when there is a sufficient level of moral choice. The Jewish people were not more moral when they were powerless; they were simply outside the realm of moral decision making as a people when they did not have political power, when they were less than fully human. It is only when Jews have sufficient power to make choices as a people that one can even discuss the question of political morality in a meaningful way. The Jewish state is now in that situation. It may have insufficient power for all of its security needs, but it does have sufficient power for the questions of political morality to be relevant. Therefore, political philosophy becomes relevant for Jews as well.

The Jewish Return into History: Philosophical Fragments on the State of Israel

EMIL L. FACKENHEIM

Stateless Jewish Philosophies

IN 1916 a controversy took place between Hermann Cohen and Martin Buber. One was the most articulate anti-Zionist Jewish philosopher of the time, the other the most profound Zionist thinker. Cohen took the highest view of the state: it was "the hub of all human culture." Buber's view of it was lowest: it was a mere "power structure," almost always "trifling." The two, good Jews and good philosophers both, had little in common. But they shared one view—neither wanted a Jewish state. Their Jewish philosophies, in 1916, were stateless.[1] So was the thought of Franz Rosenzweig. According to his *Star of Redemption,* history is made by nations and states, in peace and especially in war. As for the Jewish people, while it may be *in* history, it is in no way *of* it. Jews are "the eternal people," covenanted to the God of Eternity. Rosenzweig sketched his magnum opus in the trenches of the Great War, doing military service in his capacity as a "German citizen of the Jewish faith." But in his capacity *as a Jew* of the Jewish faith, he "knew nothing of war."[2]

Between them, these three are the greatest Jewish philosophers of the early twentieth century. In today's hindsight, this philosophical consensus provokes thought, if one considers what occurred in the rest of the century, which took a course as dreadful as it was unexpected. Soon the word "stateless" came to mean "unprotected," and it became evident, for all with eyes to see, that while its power structure makes the state the source of vices, at least one of its functions is virtue, and not a trifling one. The first duty of the state—what even minimally makes it a moral entity—is the protection of its citizens. In normal times it is easy to forget this, even sneer at it; not, however, when the most valuable possession of a person is a valid passport.

And what if even a passport is not enough? By the time the century was less than half done, it was revealed with shocking clarity that Jews, singled out for an attack without precedent, were nakedly unprotected. Possession of a German passport had become a grim joke, and this quickly became true also of Austrian, Czech, Polish, Dutch, Belgian, and other passports; and, as if not wishing to be found wanting, the list was joined by passports issued by Vichy France. For all it mattered, the Jews of wartime Europe might as well have been stateless; the combination "Jews" and "unprotected-as-if-stateless" had emerged as the century's most characteristic curse.

Jewish hostility to Jewish statehood is not without powerful antecedent. The first time a Jewish state appears as a genuine issue, in the Book of Judges, it is firmly rejected. Judges come, uniting the people in times of danger, but when danger is gone, the judges go also; the people disperse and go back to doing what is good in their own eyes. This happens again and again. Something new occurs, however, when the people ask Gideon to stay and rule permanently—he, his son, and his grandson. They are asking for a state. But Gideon replies: "I will not rule over you, and my son will not rule over you: the Lord will rule over you" (Judges 8:23).

The piety of Gideon and the Book of Judges notwithstanding, God does not always protect His people: the biblical text is nothing if not realistic. Hence, as the theme of statehood occurs again and again, a different outcome emerges. The ruling prophet Samuel is getting old and weak, and the people ask for a king, for a state. They want to be like all the nations. This is a recurring theme in Israelite—in Jewish—history, and why not? Neither the early Israelites nor Jews to this day are an assemblage of saints or monks. They are flesh-and-blood people—men, women, and children, saints, sinners, and ordinary folk.

Even so Samuel is shocked, and so is the God of Israel. "They have rejected you," He says in His wrath, "they have rejected Me from being King over them" (1 Samuel 8:7). And this, after all He has done for them! But having got this, as it were, off His chest, and having warned the people of abuses whenever humans wield power over humans, the God of Israel relents. An Israelite state—subsequently, a Jewish one—is, with reservations, divinely accepted. The centuries of theocratic anarchy are over.

But that was back in the eleventh century B.C.E. In the early twentieth century C.E., in contrast, the "downfall of the Jewish state"—referred to as the second destruction—was called by the philosopher Hermann Cohen "the best example of historical theodicy." And while Jewish statehood is "trifling" for Martin Buber, Jewish existence is raised by Rosenzweig above history altogether and hence, ipso facto, above statehood. All this happened in the realm of thought, just a few years before—in the realm of life—to be Jewish and stateless meant to be doubly unprotected. During a twelve-year nadir—the worst in Jewish history, and arguably the worst in human history as well—Jews, for the most part, were expendable. Of course, even a state of their own—had there been one—could not have given Jews the necessary protection. But there are many ways in which it would have made their abandonment less total, their defenselessness less naked.

Cohen's "theodicy," then, if ever, more than a mere chimera, was smashed by events soon after his death, as was—or should have been—Buber's disdain of Jewish statehood. As for Rosenzweig, his thought raised Exile- or Diaspora-Judaism—that is, stateless Judaism—to its most sublime heights ever, wholly above history, just before (he died in 1929) monstrous events began to occur in history that brought it to a violent end.

The failure to anticipate the future, on the part of these Jewish philosophers, ought to cause no surprise, for it only bears out a teaching of G. F. W. Hegel: philosophy cannot anticipate the future; it can cope with and comprehend what has ceased to be the future and has become past and present. And if, of all things historical, Auschwitz is the least predictable and least comprehensible even after it has become present and past, it endorses, in ways Hegel could never have dreamed of, his most famous saying: "When philosophy paints its grey in grey, then a shape of life has grown old. By philosophy's grey in grey it cannot be rejuvenated but only understood. The owl of Minerva spreads its wings only with the falling of dusk."[3] The question remains, however, whether after Auschwitz the owl of Minerva can fly at all.

The Jewish Return into History

Jews have a four-thousand-year history; have they ever been out of it? For Gentile thinkers, the answer, for the most part, is yes; they are a "fossil," fit for "euthanasia."[4] For Jews and their own thinkers, the answer, for the most part, is no; even in exile they remained both alive and in history. The talmudists, the kabbalists, the hasidim, these and numerous others were alive and kept the Jewish people alive. And while locked away into ghettos by others, they themselves believed, prayed, and studied as though their prayers, their study, their piety were of historic, nay, even world-historical import. If all

Jews ever observed just one Sabbath in perfect purity—such is a well-known rabbinic view—the world would be redeemed. The kabbalists went even further: "An effort from below calls forth a response from above." With this view of the ties between the human and the Divine, they practiced *tikkun olam,* a "mending of the world," meant to call forth—*meant to force?*—a divine response. Their prayers, their study, their good work, all in desperate intensity of spirit, were meant, minimally, to avert calamity and, maximally, to speed redemption. And perhaps they achieved, at times—whether with or without a divine share—at least the minimal.

But then the others came, and murdered the young and the old, the innocent and the guilty, the simple and the wise, the ignorant and the learned, the godless and the pious and, among the last-named, the kabbalists and their *tikkun.*

Murdered their tikkun? They did. Some Jews survived, their spirit unbroken. Some kabbalists survived, their *tikkun* with them. But we dare not forget those whom it is most necessary to remember. The six million. The survivors refer to those who did not survive as *kedoshim,* "holy ones." Jewish philosophy has yet to address itself to this testimony of the survivors.

If absolute power is the prerogative of the Divine, then the gods of Auschwitz were Adolf Eichmann who did the procuring, Rudolf Hess who did the administering, and Dr. Josef Mengele who did the selecting. There are times in history when spirit is broken and impotent, and when all that counts is power. But what is power? Money is power. So is influence. So is prudence. So is genius. Jews in their centuries of statelessness have used all these attributes, and sometimes one has helped, sometimes another. But during the Nazi regime none of them counted. The plain truth is that during the twelve years of the Third Reich, that were like unto a thousand to its Jewish victims, only one form of power counted, and that the Jewish people lacked. In the first period of the twelve years—persecution, expulsion—Jewish victims needed havens, but those only states could provide. In the second period—mass torture and murder—only a state that considered Jewish lives to be a top priority could have mustered planes, bombs, armies, and the other implements of state power that could have made a large difference.

It was therefore an act of world-historical significance when, on 14 May 1948, David Ben-Gurion, on behalf of an ad hoc government of the Jews of Palestine, proclaimed the first Jewish state in 1,878 years. Which date, this one of 29 November 1947, when the United Nations voted for a Jewish state, was historic? The answer makes a big difference. The UN date would make the Jewish state the gift of a world conscience stirred by the Holocaust, and thus—an obscenity often heard—Hitler would be its godfather. The proclamation date would have the state created by Jewish decision, and its godparents would be such as the resistance fighters of the Warsaw Ghetto. In the first view the Jewish people, an object in history without a state, remains an object still, with a state born of the world's charity. In the second view, it becomes, through an act of collective self-determination, a subject in history. On 14 May 1948, *the Jewish people*—not only Israelis—returned into history. As Ben-Gurion was subsequently to put it: "We did not fight in 1948 to establish the state. We fought to defend it. The UN gave it international sanction and then ran away. We brought it about ourselves."[5]

The date of 14 May 1948 marked the Jewish return into history. It also marked an act *in* history—an awesome act, for its consequences were unknown and dangerous. So radical was that step that, not surprisingly, some Jews wish, even now, that it had never been taken. For the anti-Zionist ultra-Orthodox right, a Jewish state is against God, who alone will restore legitimate Jewish statehood, and this not until the messianic days. For the extreme liberal left, a Jewish state is against man, for only by espousing none but non-Jewish causes can Jews aspire to true humanity. Both these reactions to Jewish statehood were always predictable. Both make the Holocaust into an episode: the one in the history of a God-imposed exile, the other in the history of man's inhumanity to man. Both are uninteresting and uninstructive.

Another reaction *is* instructive. "Has Jewish statehood not diminished the moral purity of Judaism?" I was asked this question a few years ago, by Jewish academics at Frankfurt University. When a state in Palestine was impending, a group of morally concerned Jews called "Ihud" (Martin Buber was a member) felt that, if a state were unavoidable, in justice to the Arabs it should at least be binational. It would have Arab-Jewish parity, in population as well as in rule, so that, except by an unlikely Arab consent, Jewish immigration to Palestine would halt once Arab-Jewish parity was reached.

What if Ihud's binational state had become fact? Countries that had shut their borders during the Nazi regime were opening them wide after its demise. The binational state would not have limited Arab immigration; it might also have accepted some non-Jewish "DP"s. But at the moment when other states were opening their borders, the Jewish-Arab state, and it alone, would have imposed on Jews, and on them alone, a *numerus clausus*. This morally scandalous implication caused the binational state idea, never taken seriously by the Arabs, to die a quiet death among Jews.[6]

With this, too, the purity of Jewish statelessness showed itself to be a moral luxury that could no longer be afforded. The state was proclaimed; the Jewish return into history was begun. It would be undone, however, unless the armed Arab onslaught were warded off, and only Jewish arms could do that. Not a moment was to be lost for replacing the old moral luxury, with a new moral necessity, the "purity of arms." The old moral luxury was easy. The new moral necessity was hard, for by virtue of its "power structure" a Jewish state, like any other, is the source of many evils, especially in times of war.

With the act of 14 May 1948, the Jewish state had assumed leadership of the Jewish people; with the 1950 Law of Return, it confirmed it. Jewish exile would continue to exist in many places. Antisemitism, persecution of Jews, discrimination, second-class citizenship—the Jewish state lacked the power to end these. It did have the power, however, to open its gates to Jews willing to come, able to come. By virtue of being Jewish, *all* Jews—except for wanted criminals—were eligible for admission to Israel, and for citizenship. The age of stateless Jews was over. In the grandest manner conceivable, the decision of 14 May 1948 was vindicated, barely two years later.

But is it vindicated even now when, almost half a century later, the Jewish state is still not at peace? Would not the wiser course have been to accept UN trusteeship, and postpone Jewish statehood until a more opportune time? In 1948 Chaim Weizmann, sick in bed in New York, telephoned. "Proclaim the state," he said, "now or never."[7] Weizmann was right, as were Ben-Gurion and his associates. Can anyone imagine the UN implementing its 1947 resolution now? As a rule, one hesitates to speculate on what history would be like had crucial decisions been different. (What if Chamberlain had said no at Munich?) In this case, however, speculation is superfluous. Had Ben-Gurion and his colleagues not seized the moment then, the Jewish people would still be stateless.

And the present Jewish condition? On this too it is safe to speculate. Yemenite and Ethiopian Jews, exiled still, would be without hope and forgotten. Jews from Arab countries, in their old homes still, would be recipients of varying degrees of toleration, but always at the mercy of winds of doctrine and whims of rulers. Russian Jews would wish to emigrate in large numbers, but increased immigration would be in proportion to a decrease in opportunities; the sorry spectacle of the 1930s would be repeated. The Jewish condition in the West? Jewish illiteracy, identity crises, assimilation, childlessness, Jewish self-hatred—all these manifestations of lack of Jewish purpose and failure of Jewish nerve that now exist would pale in comparison. Jewish ultra-Orthodoxy is currently experiencing a revival that, after the mortal blow in Eastern Europe, is astonishing. (It flourishes in the Jewish state, which elements within ultra-Orthodoxy do not recognize.) If the state did not exist, even Orthodoxy, normally the last holdout in times of crisis, would be just a shell of its former self, running out of explanations of the Holocaust. And the Yishuv? It would be a small ghetto in Palestine, ever cautious lest it rock the boat.

The proclamation of the state—whether consciously intended or not—was of religious as well as political significance, to Judaism as well as to Jews. This is nicely shown in Israel's Declaration of Independence. Despite the haste of the hectic days prior to the end of the Mandate, a debate took place on whether the name of God should be included in the Declaration. The debate was serious, for just as the religious signatories could not conceive of omitting the name of God, so the secularists would resort only to conscience and not expediency. So prolonged was the debate, and on both sides so serious, that the text was approved barely two hours before the official ceremony. The compromise reached was *Tsur Yisrael,* the Rock of Israel. But was it really a compromise? It would seem that no meaning can be attached to that sacred, time-honored term other than "God of Israel."

The Jewish Return to Jerusalem

The Jewish return to Jerusalem's Western Wall on 7 June 1967 was unexpected. Had there been no war, or had Jordan, as urged by Israel, stayed out of it, the momentous event would not have happened. Under its impact an Israeli officer said that he was "astonished" and that, while he could explain the military moves by which his men had reached the Wall, this did not diminish his astonishment. Abiding astonishment, Martin Buber has taught, characterizes a miracle. Jews at worship twice daily recall the miracle of the Exodus at the beginning of their history, and remain astonished millennia after—by it and by the fact that they, Jews of today, still exist to recite the prayer.

The Jewish return to the Wall in Jerusalem on 7 June 1967 was the most profoundly religious collective Jewish experience since the beginning of the exile. The experience rivaled that of the "dreamers" of the first return, whose mouth had been "filled with laughter," their tongues "with singing" (Psalm 126). In some respects it even surpassed it. The first exile had lasted less than the prophesied seventy years; the second, nearly two millennia. As exiles go, the first had not been overly harsh; the second had climaxed in nameless horror. And, as the throngs moved through the narrow streets of the Old City towards the Wall, for worship during the 1967 Shavuot festival, it had been, to cite a witness, "only a week" since they "sat in their shelters and prayed to the Creator" to save them "from the killers." The witness goes on:

> Who had ever imagined then that in but a few days we would be making this pilgrimage to the most precious relic of our Sanctuary? . . . I looked into the eyes of the people, the great throng rushing to reach that place of hopes and wishes. And I saw a kind of exalted, heavenly longing, a heart's desire of holiness that rose from a pure source, from wellsprings of purity and innocence in the spirit, which in these few days had become refined and cleansed in the furnace of fear and terror, to reach a most sublime state of holiness and clarity.[8]

What is "precious" about any relic, and about this one in particular? Does holiness attach to stones, even if hallowed by memory? One answer is provided in a midrash. When the people went into exile, and the *Shekhinah,* the spiritual presence of God, went with them, the land lost its holiness; earth and stones can be holy, but only when the *Shekhinah* dwells with them. However, while it left the land, the *Shekhinah* did not leave the Wall, and there alone, it has remained, waiting for the Jews to return.[9] On 7 June 1967 they did.

In Tel Aviv, 14 May 1948, one comes face-to-face with the political; in Jerusalem, 7 June 1967, one cannot evade the theological.

In another, more militant midrash the theological becomes theopolitical. A destroyed Jerusalem inspired the belief that there is another, indestructible Jerusalem in heaven. The belief is Christian as well as Jewish, but with a big difference. The apostle Paul directed his followers to the heavenly Jerusalem, abandoning the destroyed one on earth (Galatians 4:26). The Jews, refusing to abandon terrestrial Jerusalem, staked all on its future rebuilding. In the midrash that startles in its bold, theopolitical militancy, God refuses to dwell in the heavenly Jerusalem until He can reenter the one on earth.[10]

Through the ages Jews acted as though they were informed and inspired by the theopolitical midrash, for despite all attempts—first pagan, then Christian, and later also Muslim—to make Jewish life miserable in the city or to keep Jews out altogether, Jerusalem never was without Jews. On 7 June 1967, did God reenter the heavenly Jerusalem?

It must not be thought that the theopolitical 7 June 1967 Jewish return to Jerusalem is only for "the religious" and not "the nonreligious." The distinction between *dati* ("religious") and *lo dati* ("nonreligious") may be sharp in Israel; but there are issues which transcend it, or very nearly so, and foremost among them is Jerusalem. Was that officer, who was astonished on reaching the Wall in 1967, *dati*? *Jerusalem of Gold,* the song catapulted into fame by the event, is second only to the national anthem in Israel's civil religion. But what, in Israel, is "civil religion"?

The *dati–lo dati* bond with Jerusalem preceded the 1967 return to the city. Nineteen years earlier, when in the War of Independence Israel's existence hung in the balance, the "nonreligious" (but by no means antibiblical) Ben-Gurion told his military people that the just-proclaimed state could survive the Arab onslaught if the Jews held two of Israel's three cities, but only if one of them was the militarily insignificant Jerusalem. Nine years earlier yet, after the synagogues were burning all over Germany, the "religious" (but by no means either Orthodox or antisecular) Martin Buber, chafing at Mahatma Gandhi's reduction of "Palestine" to a metaphor, rejoined that "Zion" would be a "poor metaphor" if Mount Zion did not actually exist.[11]

A consensus is not easy to come by in Israel. But when, barely three weeks after the return to Jerusalem, the Knesset declared united Jerusalem the eternal capital of the Jewish state, nay, of the Jewish people, the Israeli consensus was complete. This consensus has thus far found no acceptance, neither in Arab opinion nor in world opinion. There is a harsh conflict regarding the Jewish return to Jerusalem.

It is possible that a compromise will eventually be attained. But there are also two extreme possibilities. One is that Israel will tire, give in, or be persuaded or forced to give in. This would be the terminal Jewish catastrophe. The Jewish people could endure waiting for a return to Jerusalem for nearly two millennia. They could not endure, having reached Jerusalem, to leave it again. The loss of Zion—whether because of weakness within or superior force without—could not be survived by Zionism, by the Jewish state, by the Jewish people. Even a surviving Judaism would be too spiritless, demoralized, and depressed to remain a living religion.

A possibility exists also at the other extreme. If the Jews had remained in exile in Babylon—if the first Jewish return to Jerusalem had never occurred—would either Christianity or Islam, daughter religions of Judaism, have come to existence? Of course not. Yet this fact is rarely part of either Christian or Muslim consciousness, even more rarely remembered with gratitude. As for the second return to

Jerusalem, this is as yet unacknowledged by either Christians or Muslims and, for the most part, is treated with hostility.

But what if turning took place within the "daughters" toward the "mother"? Peace—true peace, peace at the most profound religious level—will come to Jerusalem, if Christians and Muslims come to worship in the city; not despite the fact that the Jews have returned, but because of it. They may do so more readily if they come to understand the cost of the return to the Jews. Abraham J. Heschel has written.:

> I did not on my own enter the city of Jerusalem. Streams of endless craving, clinging, dreaming, flowing day and night, midnight, years, decades, centuries, millennia, streams of tears, of pledgings, of waitings—from all over the world, from all corners of the earth—carried us of this generation to the Wall.[12]

Jewish Philosophy Today

It has become evident that, after what has occurred in this century, Jewish philosophy cannot remain stateless. There is need for a Jewish political philosophy, or even a political dimension in Jewish philosophy as a whole.

But the same events that have made such a philosophy mandatory also give rise to the question of whether, at this time, it is attainable. Rosenzweig's *Star of Redemption* is decisively "confirmed" by Yom Kippur, in the experience of "eternity" by the "eternal people." The core of Hermann Cohen's philosophy of Judaism, the messianic idea, is related to history, but is not in or of it, for it is the ideal end.[13] Even Buber's philosophy—the most history related of the three—is ultimately not bound to it, for whereas the Sinai event is located in history, indeed, is a caesura between the before and the after, it is recoverable; since God speaks constantly, no generation is cut off from it.

As we have seen, the 1948 Jewish return into history was also an act *in* history, that is, one whose consequences, uncertain until they had fully unfolded, were certain to spell danger. Did this descent into uncertainty pull Jewish political philosophy, as it were, with it? Perhaps at no time in the brief history of the Jewish state has this question been posed by events as clearly, as severely—and, with regard to philosophical pretensions, as soberingly—as by the ongoing Israeli-Arab peace process that began with the Oslo accord and the Washington handshake. This process, held to be irreversible, leaves Israeli opinion radically polarized. Setting aside lesser issues—

all issues are lesser compared with survival—approximately each half of the Israeli electorate believes that the policies pursued or advocated by the other half lead to war, and that war could threaten the state's very survival. No further or more radical evidence is required to the effect that the action taken on 14 May 1948—the Jewish return into history—is still, in its consequences, incomplete.

In this polarization, each side has reasons for its belief. Philosophers may side with the reasons of one, or of the other, or may waver between them. But they do so only as citizens, not as philosophers. It would be an unwarranted presumption for them to act as if philosophy could give them a privileged insight or furnish them with a higher point of view. They cannot produce a mediation; that can be brought about only by the parties themselves.

Yet even in this sobering, humility-inducing situation, philosophy is not reduced to total impotence. The extremes "seek each other and flee each other . . . I am the struggle between them." This Hegelian dictum, put forward in a different context, fits the present one perfectly.[14] That the extremes in current Israeli opinion flee each other is obvious, not least of all to themselves. That they also seek each other arises, or ought to arise, from the fact that they are engaged in a shared project, the core of which is survival of the state. But whereas philosophical thought preserves and endures the tension between the two aspects—the fleeing each other and the seeking each other—this is not necessarily true of combatants. Philosophy lacks the power to avert the catastrophe of potential civil war and, climactically, of national suicide. But it has some power, and it would be an error to underestimate it.

Religious–Nonreligious Polarization

The Hegelian "flee each other . . . seek each other" and the philosophical stance between them, may be brought to bear on other aspects of present Israel, including the profound and, in its extreme form, intractable religious-nonreligious relationship and tension.

The unique Law of Return stipulates that the state accepts all Jews; it cannot exclude even Jews who, on grounds of Judaism, refuse to recognize it. This is the case with a section within ultra-Orthodoxy for which a Jewish state—until restored by the Messiah at the appointed time—is anathema. What mediation can there be between Israelis serving in the state's armed forces, and those who, while enjoying its protection, refuse to recognize that state?

While a mediation is not yet available in thought, fragments of it are discernible in life. The war waged by Egypt and Syria against

Israel in October 1973 began on Yom Kippur, the holiest day of the Jewish year. Few, however, want to think about the reason for choosing that date. Pragmatic cunning, to catch the Jews unawares? But just on that day it is easy to mobilize the military, most of whom are in synagogues; and just on that day the roads, otherwise clogged, are empty. Was the date pragmatic, and the war against the Jewish state? Or was the date blasphemous, and the war against both the Jewish religion and the Jewish state? Perhaps both answers are possible, but it is difficult to reject the second.

Some ultra-Orthodox Jews, at worship that Yom Kippur in Jerusalem, must have taken that view. The sirens were sounding and the soldiers were rushing to their units. On their part, these ultra-Orthodox Jews interrupted their prayers, ran into the streets, tore pages from their prayer books, and gave them to the departing soldiers. They seemed to know that some Jews must pray so that others can fight, and some must fight so that others can pray.[15] Not all religious Jews in Israel reject the state; most embrace it. Between them and nonreligious Israelis a relation has existed ever since their representatives compromised on *tzur yisrael* in the Declaration of Independence. Sometimes it is, as it may have been then, a mere compromise. But in times of crisis it is a disagreement that at the same time bespeaks a close bond. In times of crisis one wonders why nonreligious Israelis do not leave Israel, and why religious Israelis do not join the extreme ultra-Orthodox. When the struggle seems endless or hopeless, why do not both groups abandon the state, the secularists for America, Canada, or Australia, the religious for a God who, alone, is the Rock of Israel? But just then one discovers that the "nonreligious" act as though they believe in God, and the "religious" act as though they could not count solely on Him. Looking on, a philosopher wonders whether, once the Jewish return into history will have fully unfolded, a new chapter will be in the making in the four-thousand-year-old religious-secular history of the Jewish people.

Sovereignty and the Land

Even during the period when there is talk of peace, hope for peace, promises of peace, the four pillars of Zionism and the Jewish state—the land, the state, the Law of Return, and Jerusalem[16]—are still far from secure. The land? Even Hamas wants peace, provided Jews move somewhere else. The state? The PLO has yet to repudiate its Covenant, which demands the overthrow of the Jewish state. The Law of Return? Let water get short and Palestinian refugees return, and that law may die a slow, committee-style death. Jerusalem? Just prior to Jerusalem Day 1994 a clever writer penned "Al-Kuds Day 2044," celebrating half a century of reconquest of the Muslim (but also Jewish and Christian) holy places in Jerusalem; after some U.S. State Department arm-twisting of Israel, the new facts had come about peacefully and had been accepted quickly by the world.[17] The world had never accepted the fact of a united Jewish Jerusalem; there are many more Arabs and Muslims in the world than there are Jews.

Of the four non-negotiable commitments of the Zionist enterprise, Jerusalem is the most profound, but the land is the most basic. Without it there is no state, no Law of Return, no Jerusalem. How can one justify collective sovereignty over land? The question can find no deeper answer than that given in the Bible: the land belongs to God.

The biblical God does not inhabit land. He gives it to Adam and his descendants, and promises the Land of Israel to the children of Israel. So Jews have believed through the ages, on scriptural authority. But philosophy cannot base itself on authority. Authorities clash with other authorities, without hope of mediation; arid conflict is inevitable, between Jews, Christians, and Muslim, but also among Jews themselves. Unable to submit to authorities, philosophy must avoid so arid a conflict. So must Jewish philosophy, at least if it is political. The state, if it were a theocracy, would break the terms of the religious-nonreligious contract enshrined in the Declaration of Independence; also, it would suffer an early collapse. To be sure, Jewish political philosophy cannot ask Jewish citizens to abandon their authority-based Judaism, but it may and must ask that, in the context of political philosophy and its goals, such a faith be privatized.

This point was made by Martin Buber, in a response to Mahatma Gandhi to which reference has already been made. The context was the so-called *Kristallnacht* in November 1938. Some Jewish supporters tried to arouse Gandhi's conscience, asking him to react. Gandhi did, but they must have wished that had never asked him, for the statement the great Indian leader published was not helpful, to put it mildly. He advised German Jews to follow Indian teaching and use "soul-power" against the regime, as if less than half a million Jews pitted against millions of Germans, had a chance comparable to several hundred million Indians pitted against British colonizers, and as if SS stormtroopers were comparable to British officers and gentlemen.

Gandhi was no more helpful in his comments on the "cry" for a national Jewish home, a sanction of which, he claimed, "is sought in the Bible." Politely but sharply, Buber denied it:

> No, that is not so. We do not open the Bible and seek sanction in it; rather the opposite is true: the promises of return . . . which have nourished the hopes of hundreds of generations, give those of today an elemental stimulus, recognized by few in its full meaning, but effective in the lives of many who do not believe in the message of the Bible.[18]

Buber did well with this response to Gandhi; he did better still with yet another response. With a "simple formula"—"Palestine belongs to the Arabs"—the Indian leader had settled what Buber called a complex "existential dilemma." Buber reacted: "You obviously mean to say that a people, being settled on the land, has so absolute a claim to that land that whoever settles on it without the permission of this people has committed a robbery." Then, after showing the regard for Arab rights that was characteristic of him to the end, Buber points out—a tedious necessity—that the Arabs themselves had conquered Palestine and settled it with a view to possessing it. He concludes as follows: "You would be compelled, not at once, but after a suitable number of generations had elapsed, to admit that the land belongs to the usurper."[19]

For a Zionist, Gandhi's "simple formula" would lend support to a project more radical than that of even the most extreme position of the Israeli right—to stay put on every inch of the land, to import more and more Jews with the greatest speed, and to transfer Arabs, nicely if possible, somewhere else, anywhere else, so that the land would "belong" to the Jews, "after a suitable number of generations has elapsed." The world's most famous advocate of peaceful resistance had given the Jewish people, as far as a national home in Palestine was concerned, the choice only between abject surrender and total war. Buber wrote what he did with great respect, for he admired the Indian leader. But Gandhi never replied.[20]

Buber began a philosophical exploration that is greatly needed, but he never completed it. Philosophizing, by his own admission, "no more than necessary," he never pursued the subject of sovereignty and land in the systematic way that it requires. But neither, so far as I know, did anyone else at the time. What political philosopher—American, Canadian, Australian, to say nothing of European—questioned, in 1939 and long after, whether the land "belonged" to those presently claiming sovereignty over it? Even Marxists, self-appointed critics of the rapacious capitalist world, were sure that the land belonged to the postcapitalist, industrial proletariat—and ignored everybody else.

Only recently has it become respectable, even fashionable, to stress the claims of the land's original inhabitants, pitting these against its latest or most successful conquerors. But this too fails to produce a "simple formula" devoid of "existential dilemmas." Who are the earliest inhabitants? Those who managed to avoid being slaughtered by later conquerors but had managed to kill off their predecessors? Jewish claims to the Land of Israel, if made in these terms, would have to be entirely in terms of an uninterrupted Jewish presence in the country. Indeed even in Jerusalem, Jewish history was never completely interrupted, despite Hadrian, Constantine, and Justin Martyr.

Quite possibly these Jews, or the few untraceable descendants of them that may be extant, are the oldest inhabitants of the land. But the case for them will never be heard, for history, cloudy enough in itself, is hopelessly vitiated by ideology. The first attempt to delegitimate the Jewish claim to the Land of Israel was made in the second century by Hadrian, when he renamed Judaea Palestina, the land of the Philistines, and Jerusalem "Aelia Capitolina."

Attempts to relegitimate original inhabitants may get somewhere in Canada, the United States, or Australia; as regards the Arab-Jewish embattled land, they are hopeless. In the end, arguments along these lines will always come up against the fact that, except for the few Jews always present, Palestinians (then named Arabs) were in the land before Jews came in large numbers. It is true that the Jews, like the Crusaders, came. (In the Arab view they came and conquered.) However, whereas the Crusaders came (and left), the Jews *came back*.

In my considered opinion, political philosophy will not do justice to the State of Israel until it introduces "return" among its legitimating categories. It may well be a category with just one member, but this would be no reason for disallowing it. To disallow it a priori would be to make bias into a system. To allow the category of "return" is merely to be open to the possibility that there is a member to fit it. The Jewish people have been driven twice from the land, have returned twice, and—this is crucial—in nearly two millennia of exile and Diaspora they have consistently refused to renounce their claim to it. It would seem that there is no theory that legitimates collective sovereignty over land, that is untroubled by "existential dilemmas." If the Jewish return to the Land of Israel will ever be viewed fairly by political philosophy—if it allows "return" as a legitimating category—the Jewish return of our time, which is also the Jewish return into history, will not fare poorly in a comparison with all the other claims to sovereignty over land that are made in the present age. But that is for the philosophical future.

Having returned into history, having returned to Jerusalem, all Israel—right and left, "religious" and "non religious"—must unite in being open to the future and also unite in remembering the past. At the exit of Yad Vashem, the Israel Holocaust Museum in Jerusalem, are written words by the Baʿal Shem Tov, the founder of Hasidism: *Forgetfulness leads into exile, but memory leads to redemption.*

Notes

On this subject see also my *A Political Philosophy for the State of Israel: Fragments* (Jerusalem: Center for Public Affairs Pamphlet, 1988). In important respects the present essay goes beyond my earlier effort.

1. The Cohen-Buber exchange may be found in Paul Mendes-Flohr and Jehuda Reinharz, eds., *The Jew in the Modern World* (New York: Oxford University Press, 1980), pp. 448–53.

2. For my views on Rosenzweig, see *To Mend the World,* 3rd ed. (Bloomington: Indiana, 1994) pp. 58–99, and "The Systematic Role of the Matrix (Existence) and Apex (Yom Kippur) of Jewish Religious Life in Franz Rosenzweig's *Star of Redemption,*" in *Der Philosoph Franz Rosenzweig,* W. Schmied-Kowarzik ed. (Freiburg: Alber, 1988), 2:567–75.

3. See the end of the preface of Hegel's *Philosophy of Right.*

4. The first expression is the view of the soon-to-be-forgotten Arnold Toynbee; the second is that of no less a philosopher than the unforgettable Immanuel Kant.

5. Cited in Bernard Postal and Henry W. Levy, *And The Hills Shouted for Joy* (Philadelphia: Jewish Publication Society, 1973), p. 119.

6. On Buber's concern for Arab rights, to the end of his life, see Paul Mendes-Flohr, *A Land of Two People: Martin Buber on Jews and Arabs* (New York: Oxford University Press, 1984).

7. Cited in Postal and Levy, *The Hills,* p. 193.

8. M. M. Kasher, *The Western Wall* (New York: Judaica Press, 1972), p. 63.

9. See texts listed in ibid., pp. 16–23.

10. See Talmud Bavli, Taʿanit 5a.

11. See "The Land and Its Possessors: An answer to Gandhi," in *The Writings of Martin Buber,* ed. Will Herberg (New York: Meridian, 1956), p. 281.

12. Cited in Alice L. Eckardt, *Jerusalem* (New York: University Press of America, 1987), p. 240.

13. For my views on Hermann Cohen, see my *Hermann Cohen: After Fifty Years* (New York: Leo Baeck Institute, 1969).

14. *Werke,* 2d ed. (Berlin: Duncker & Humblot, 1840–47), 9:64.

15. My friend, the late Pinchas Peli, has vouched for the accuracy of this incident.

16. See "Pillars of Zionism," *Midstream* (December 1992): 13–15. I use the term "pillars," for if one collapses, so does the whole structure.

17. See *Jerusalem Post,* 6 May 1994.

18. Herberg, "The Land and Its Possessors," p. 282.

19. Ibid., p. 285.

20. See further on this episode, Mendes-Flohr, *A Land of Two People,* pp. 111 ff. There is a possibility that Gandhi never received Buber's letter.

Part Six
Afterword

A Retrospective of My Thought

EMIL L. FACKENHEIM

1. From Halle to Berlin

I completed high school in 1935 in Halle, the German city in which I was born. Then I moved to Berlin, to study Judaism at the Hochschule für die Wissenschaft des Judentums. I begin this retrospective with that move to Berlin, for with it began my concern with Jewish thought, which was to determine much of my life. What started with a move to Berlin ended—perhaps better, culminated—with a move, in 1983, to Jerusalem.

Why did I go to Berlin? With much hindsight after all these years, this is no easy question to answer truthfully. The liturgy of the German-liberal synagogue; the reflective piety of my mother; the rather more simple piety of my father who, busy lawyer though he was, never failed to recite the lengthy morning prayers, and this despite the fact that, while able to read Hebrew fluently, he understood little of it; a dry but knowledgeable and thought-provoking rabbi: all these doubtless had a share in my wanting to become a knowledgeable Jew. (To become a rabbi was only vaguely in my mind, if at all.) However, if there had been no Nazi regime, I might never have left home, and eventually might become a professor of philosophy at the local Martin Luther Universität, or perhaps of classics. My Greek teacher at the Stadtgymnasium, Adolph Loercher, had been a powerful influence, and on leaving school I still listed among my plans for academic study both Jewish theology and classical philology.

But Hitler had come to power in 1933. By 1935 I understood Nazism as an unprecedented assault not only on the Jewish people but also, and for me especially, on the Jewish faith. I went to Berlin, then, in search of an answer. And, odd or even dubious though this may seem to today's reader, of another time, at other places, crystal-clear in my memory is this: before I ever got to the Hochschule I was convinced that what I was looking for was to be found in the sources and resources of Judaism.

That conviction may well be the best clue to my Jewish thought ever since: I *brought it to* the study of Judaism, and it has never left me, not to be destroyed even when holding fast to it became precarious. Midway in my life as a thinker and writer, the bond between the Jewish present and the past faith was made precarious by the Holocaust. A "614th commandment" reaches Jews from Auschwitz, forbidding them to give Hitler posthumous victories: this was my first, much quoted (and also misquoted) statement, when in 1967, having evaded for so long what the Holocaust really was, I could evade it no more. Some readers have viewed that "commandment" as tantamount to replacing Judaism with what one of them has called "Auschwitzism." They did not read carefully: a 614th commandment—not a "new-and-first," all previous "tablets" having been "broken" or crying out to be broken (Nietzsche)—can only be added to 613 others, and these are traditionally said to reach Jews from Sinai.

What did I find in Berlin? Good teachers and lifelong friends, but the teaching I looked for came from three thinkers who were not there. What if—so I found Leo Strauss ask—premodern Jewish philosophy were more truly critical, hence more truly philosophical, than that of modernity? The latter typically comes on the scene as an "autonomous" critic of all things, hence also of all Jewish things. But what if this rules out ab initio the possibility that *some* Jewish things—Torah—are *min ha-shamayim,* "from heaven," divinely revealed? What if that possibility were done greater justice when premodern Jewish philosophy, *self*-critical as well as critical, was prepared to subordinate philosophy—for most philosophers no more than the word of man—to Torah, received as the Word of God? Strauss called for a reopening of those "dusty old books" of medieval philosophy, on behalf not merely of scholarship but also of truth. For the next decade I was to focus much attention on Augustine and Aquinas, al-Farabi, Ibn Sina and Ibn Rushd, Judah Ha-Levi and Maimonides. I even published an article on the *Ikhwan as-Safa,* the—putting it mildly—rather obscure Muslim "Brethren of Purity."

My concern with medieval philosophy did not last. The concern with revelation, in contrast, has been lifelong, and over decades I was to follow in the footsteps of Martin Buber and Franz Rosenzweig, both of whom I first discovered in Berlin. I remain indebted to them to this day: "The theme of the Bible is the encounter between a group of people and the Lord of the world in the course of history."

This teaching of Buber's is basic to my *The Jewish Bible after the Holocaust: A Rereading* (1991).

As for Rosenzweig, in the long run the more profound influence, without his *Star of Redemption,* my own *To Mend the World* (1982, 1989, 1994) would have had to be a different book. And if, *with* the *Star,* it is a book quite other than Rosenzweig's magnum opus (*To Mend,* such as it is, being my own magnum opus), the break with Rosenzweig is by no means due to this or that idea that has appeared in the half century between him and ourselves, but *to that half century itself.* Were Rosenzweig alive in the age of Auschwitz and of the Jewish return to Jerusalem, he would have had to write a quite different *Star of Redemption*—if indeed he could write any such work at all.[1]

2. Sachsenhausen

I knew from the start that I would not have the six years required by the Hochschule curriculum. During my first week in Berlin the Gestapo arrested my father. Having thus begun, my studies ended three-and-a-half years later, with my own arrest by the Gestapo. (This was after the November 1938 *Kristallnacht,* during which they burned synagogues, smashed Jewish store windows, beat up a great many Jews and murdered quite a few, and carted into concentration camps thousands of Jewish males, of whom I was one.) The time between the beginning and the end of my Hochschule days thus made Nazi Berlin the most absurd place for the study of Judaism—and the most appropriate. At the time I was asked by my cousin Lisa how I could study under these circumstances. "We know that we are sitting on a powderkeg," was my reply, "but we must be calm enough to smoke a cigar while sitting on it." I told that story to a neighbor, over half a century later, when the Scuds were falling on Israel, but added that there were two differences now: I was no longer smoking cigars, and I had no intention of running from Jerusalem.

Some lessons of the three months in Sachsenhausen were to become part and parcel of my thought. The concentration camp first taught me to dislike theologies (Christian as well as Jewish) that are concerned with the fate of Judaism but are indifferent to—or so high-minded as to be above concern with—that of Jews. "What is the point of mere Jewish survival?" a theologian asked at a Jewish conference held in the Quebec hills in the mid-1960s. Milton Himmelfarb exploded. "After the Holocaust, let no one call Jewish survival 'mere'!" I have thought fondly of Milton ever since.

At a Tel Aviv conference in the late 1980s—on the film *Shoah* yet!—Yeshayahu Leibowitz asserted that what mattered was the survival of Judaism, not that of Jews. Claude Lantzmann, the guest of honor, was scandalized. He would ask just one question of the professor but would have nothing more to say to him after that: "Where were you during the Shoah?" Leibowitz replied that he had been in Palestine, with Rommel at the gates, and that if the Shoah had also wiped out the Yishuv he would think no differently. With Lantzmann not saying any more, it fell to me to answer and this, I felt, should be in behalf of Judaism as much as of Jews. "If Professor Leibowitz says that Judaism would survive the murder of the last Jew he cannot be serious. He is joking about a desperately serious subject." I was booed by his supporters, and the two of us have not spoken to each other since.

I learned something else in Sachsenhausen: to love *amcha,* ordinary Jewish folk, their courage, decency, and good humor in adversity, but also, and especially, their wisdom. Decades after Sachsenhausen a reviewer wrote that my views would be liked by "Jewish shoe salesmen and taxi-drivers." This delighted me, for *amcha* has in fact often understood me better than quite a few theology professors. Professor Michael Wyschogrod once disposed of the possibility of posthumous victories for Hitler as follows: "If a mad dictator wanted to kill all stamp collectors, one would have to stop him, but this would be the end of the matter; there would be no posthumous consequences." Over two decades later he is still being quoted by other professors.[2] No member of *amcha* of my acquaintance would fail to notice that there has been no bimillennial tradition of people trying to kill stamp-collectors—or that post-Hitler antisemitism exists both in spite *and because of* Hitler.

I learned yet a third lesson in the concentration camp, but this one I am fully conscious of only now, as I write these lines. Three Hochschule friends shared my fate in Sachsenhausen, Karl Rautenberg (later Rabbi Charles Berg in England), Heinz Fischel (later Henry Fischel of Indiana University), and Hanns Harf (later a rabbi in Buenos Aires), the first now deceased, the other two retired and friends to this day. The four of us met often if hastily, exchanged views and jokes, and doubtless here and there talked about Judaism. But never once did any of us ask how God could let this happen to us.

As I reflect on this now, I am not sure what to say. Our Jewish faith was unaffected; for me the experience, if anything, confirmed the view toward Nazism that I had held since 1935. But was it from friends we all had among *amcha* that we rabbinical students learned to focus on two things—that the unscrupulous enemy would shrink from nothing, and that we must husband our strength for the task of survival?

Of one thing I am sure: ask how God can let this happen to you—*to you personally*—and the danger is that you will end up feeling sorry for yourself; and once you give in to self-pity in Sachsenhausen—to say nothing of Auschwitz—you are finished.

3. The University of Toronto

"I am sorry I am so late," I said to Dean G. S. Brett of the University of Toronto Graduate School when I arrived at his office at noon on 15 December 1941. (Released from Sherbrooke internment camp, I had arrived in Toronto four hours earlier.) "I cannot expect to get credit for this academic year." "You can show what you can do," the dean replied. "There is another problem," I went on. "I have no academic degree, only a rabbinic diploma, but on the basis of that, Aberdeen University admitted me to their Ph.D. program." "What is good enough for Aberdeen is good enough for us," was Brett's reply and, having huffed that he wished to be done with all that stuff and nonsense, he launched on a discussion of Aristotle, and I felt that I had never left home.

The University of Toronto was to become a new home—not, however, without either delay or one significant interlude. I was released from Sachsenhausen on 8 February 1939. After this came a hair-raising two months until, having passed my rabbinical exams at the Hochschule with breakneck speed, I got out of Germany on 12 May one week or so ahead of the Gestapo. (I still owe the Hochschule one of two theses, the one on rabbinics, but I like to think that my writings on Midrash would do.) Then came Aberdeen, Scotland, a year's quiet study before the war that was sure to come, and after that some twenty months of internment first in Britain, and then, and mostly, in Canada—a country that was then far less prepared to welcome such as me than, subsequently, its own University of Toronto.[3]

These were the delays. The interruption was five years (1943–48) as a rabbi in nearby Hamilton. The worst years of the Holocaust were included in that period, and the most powerful memory that remains is an overwhelming sense of Jewish impotence. There were long meetings of community representatives nearly every night, with one speech after another, either on trifling subjects or with trifling results. There was no mistaking the depth of *amcha*'s concern or of its sense of impotence. Once I thought I could do something, so every Shabbat I prepared a prayer for the Jews murdered during that week, and read it at services. After a few weeks of this the congregation's president, Jack Mandell, himself of Polish origin, asked me to stop it. "We all know what is happening. Why twist the knife?" I reflected on this as a serious young rabbi would, and at length followed Jack's advice—but to this day do not know whether I did right.

The texts of the great Western philosophers are inexhaustible: this was the principle of philosophy at Toronto at my time. (In some ways, this principle resembles the rabbinic stance toward the Torah.) The theory had its praxis: staff members would take their time eyeing subjects for graduate teaching and, once they knew what they wanted and succeeded in obtaining it, they would keep on teaching it. (But who are the "greats" among Western philosophers? My colleague Bob McRae once chose British empiricism, got tired of it after three years, then turned to Descartes, Spinoza, and Leibniz, never to get tired again.)

Luckily for me, no graduate course on Hegel was being taught when I joined the staff, so after biding my time I gathered my courage—I needed to take on Hegel but hardly less to take on F. H. Anderson, the formidable head of the department and its *spiritus rector*—and asked to teach German idealism. "Do you understand Hegel?" Anderson asked. His question was more like a bark. "Yes," I lied, and began my career of teaching Kant, Fichte, Schleiermacher, Schelling, and Hegel for the coming decades.

Mostly I taught Hegel's *Phenomenology of Spirit*. "The time is ripe for philosophy to become *Wissenschaft*"—what a promise in the opening pages! Philosophy acknowledges the facticity of what-is, but at its boldest seeks to rise to comprehension of it. A philosophy-become-*Wissenschaft* would acknowledge all past philosophies, view them as partial comprehensions of what-is, and rise above all partiality to all-comprehensive totality. And as for the ripeness-of-time for this monumental achievement, this would be the work of history, with the *Wissenschaft*, being *in* history but, having risen above it, also not *of* it. The reader even slightly familiar with my work will detect my own involvement in these themes, and above all in the theme "Metaphysics and Historicity."[4]

I had heard lecturers mention Hegel before, and had read surveys of his thought in histories of philosophy. But when I first opened a book of his—for me his greatest, the *Phenomenology*—it bore little resemblance to any of that. This happened during an unforgotten, unforgettable Berlin evening, when a few of us, invited to the home of the former Husserl-assistant, Arnold Metzger, pondered Hegel's preface to his work deep into the night. During that evening I did not understand too much of the text; but it gripped me at once, and with it came an inkling that, if ever I were to be serious about philosophy, I would have to struggle with that book. And how could one be serious about Jewish philosophy without being serious about philosophy? That evening in the Metzger home was all the Hegel instruction I ever got; but soon after, in Aberdeen, I spent one hour every day studying the *Phenomenology,* alone.

What makes the work unique in German idealism—in philosophy!—is not its opening promise or even its unfolding plan, but the fulfillment of the promise, the "labor of thought" through which the plan is carried out. And the labor is unrelenting until the "absolute knowledge" necessary for *Wissenschaft* is reached.

In my own labor with the text, I never exhausted Hegel's, thus tiring as little of the *Phenomenology* as my colleague did of Descartes, Spinoza, and Leibniz. Hegel begins by immersing himself in a consciousness barely emerged from animal life, to see it (to-be-human is more than to-be-animal!) dissipate and transcend itself; then moves on to a higher, next-emerging form, at length to self-consciousness, only to watch the self-dissipation and self-transcendence of *that;* and moves on patiently, relentlessly, in ever-richer contexts, until a goal is reached that *is* goal because to go beyond it is neither possible nor necessary.

To follow the *Phenomenology*'s road, however fragmentarily, is forever to discover new byways, and often to see why some are taken and others not.

Hegel's own dialectical move toward absolute knowledge is necessary, inexorable, unstoppable. But famous readers, in protest against the purported necessity, have often stopped at junctures significant to them, jumped off, and gone elsewhere on their own. In my earlier years of teaching I was often tempted to do likewise. Were these earlier, famous, influential readers wrongly deficient in philosophical patience when they jumped off? Or, on the contrary, did they jump off rightly, and move rightly on to different goals? Søren Kierkegaard quips that Hegel's *Wissenschaft* is a castle in the air, with the flesh-and-blood Hegel living in a mud hut on earth. In my earlier years I often quoted this quip in class.

In Hegel's necessary progression that begins with consciousness and ends with absolute knowledge, what happens to existence? The following is what Karl Marx saw happen when he came to Hegel's master-slave dialectic (having seen, he jumped off and went on ways of his own). In extremis, the *Phenomenology*'s slave loses his fear of the master and transforms his forced labor into self-activity: with this revolution he liberates himself, attains free self-consciousness, and paradigmatically becomes Stoic who is free whether (like Marcus Aurelius) he sits on the throne, or (like Epictetus) he is in chains. Slavery is overcome, has become irrelevant. For Marx, however, slavery was not overcome, was not irrelevant. He stopped reading on, or acted as if he had, when he sided with *actual* slaves *still existing*—the proletariat—whose liberation he saw as requiring a revolution, not of consciousness but of existence.

If Marx invoked existence against Hegel, so did Kierkegaard, for me always more powerfully because I have always considered him the deeper thinker. Hegel's free self-consciousness becomes "unhappy" when, discovering Infinity (equaling Divinity) and with it its own finitude, it acts to surrender itself in worship; and when, by its very acting, it reaffirms the very finite self-consciousness it would surrender, against Infinity. In its ongoing dialectic the *Phenomenology* sees this self-division overcome in a "Reason" that reconciles finite and infinite self-consciousness; but Kierkegaard protests in behalf of the "existing individual"—*is himself* the existing individual—who, with his task of "becoming a Christian" ever precarious, ever yet ahead, continues to stand, in solitary fear and trembling, and "edified" only by the knowledge that vis-à-vis God, humans are always wrong, *over against* a divine Other *that remains* Other. Kierkegaard too stopped reading on in the *Phenomenology,* or acted as if he had.

Over the years of teaching Hegel's work, my own philosophical patience deepened. Hegel's absolute knowledge, even as it transcends all less-than-absolute knowledge, must contain and preserve all *within* itself, lest some finite knowledge, uncontained and unpreserved, lash out *against* it, destroying its absoluteness. That culminating standpoint having been reached, the *Wissenschaft* for which "the time is ripe" can hope to accomplish its monumental task only if it *preserves difference* within unity—nay, to go further, preserves *even discord and disharmony* within the all-comprehensive harmony. Hegel's nutshell formula is an admittedly mind-boggling "Union of Union and Non-Union." Right-and left-wing Hegelians never allowed their minds to be boggled, the first making light of "non-union," the second, of "union." But in my own work in philosophical scholarship, no harder, time-consuming, patience-demanding task was ever mine than to lay hold of, not let go of, not lose, *Hegel's own middle.*[5] The "left" discord, struggle, historicity, earthbound secularity of "non-union" must be acknowledged: Hegel is no less concerned than Marx with liberating still-existing slaves. To be acknowledged too is the "right" harmony, eternity, heavenly religious "union": Hegel is no less a Christian than Kierkegaard. But the power of Hegel's unique, mind-boggling thinking is concentrated on the "middle" that is the union of both.

To grasp that Hegelian middle was the chief work in my career as a scholar of philosophy. Most fortunately, I completed it just before the turmoil of the Six-Day War, for with this the period of tranquillity in my life, with the University of Toronto as home, came to an end. The restlessness that has followed ever since has left little leisure for detached scholarship.

As a scholar I sought to understand the Hegelian middle; as a philosopher—indebted to Hegel but never a Hegelian—I concluded that Hegel's absolute knowledge is fragmented, that the Hegelian middle is broken. I had reached that conclusion prior to 1967, the year of turmoil that forced me to face up to the Holocaust; thereafter, the conclusion was confirmed, but with a wholly new dimension.[6]

In a way, I may be said to have dwelled in the broken Hegelian middle ever since. While Hegel's enterprise was perhaps always foredoomed to failure, the entire Western tradition—both philosophical and religious, both reason and revelation—amounts to a demand that it be attempted. Moreover, the attempt having been made and failed, it has dialectical consequences. Fragments remain, and these, as Hegel himself might have put it, seek each other and flee each other, flee each other and seek each other. Rosenzweig rightly spoke of an age *post Hegel mortuum;* but perhaps he did not live long enough—or was not concerned enough—to pay sufficient heed to the secular fragments. As for such as Marx and Kierkegaard, in retrospect I regret their impatience with the *Phenomenology.* Had they suspended their protests and kept pondering to the end of the work, Marx might still have sided with the proletariat, but without an atheism that put the proletariat in the place of God and justified its dictatorship. His philosophy might have understood itself as a secular fragment seeking a religious one, even while finding itself obliged to flee the latter. As for Kierkegaard, he might still have sided with—himself have been—"the individual" existing over against a divine Other that remains Other, without committing himself to a one-sided fideism that made him all-but-indifferent to secular society, even to his moral duties toward it, as a Christian.

I reached these views regarding Marx, Kierkegaard (and others) while still in Toronto. But not until I had moved to Jerusalem, and had lived in the city long enough to attempt a sketch of a political philosophy for Israel, did I find myself—to my surprise and in unexpected ways—plunged once more into something resembling the broken Hegelian middle. The extremes of Israeli political life—right and left, "religious" and "nonreligious"—I understand as fragments that flee each other and seek each other. Any journalist can see and report that the extremes flee each other, and the Israel-bashing press delights in dwelling on the fact. But the extremes also seek each other, for in rebuilding a Jewish state, in returning to Jerusalem—after nearly two millennia of statelessness, of only praying for Jerusalem—they are committed to a shared undertaking.[7]

Only once in my career in the academy was I overcome during a lecture, so much so that for a few moments I could not go on. In Toronto, I had lectured on Kant and Fichte, Schleiermacher, Schelling, and Hegel, giving only passing attention to Jewish philosophers and lay people whose love for German philosophy was never really returned. In Jerusalem, I lectured on the same period in philosophy, but now with emphasis on these Jews. I came to Schleiermacher's *Addresses on Religion,* and to the astonishing fact that this great and liberal-minded Christian theologian was helped in the composition of his work by Henriette Herz, an intimate Jewish friend. She was a proud Jewess, but her education in Judaism had been sterile, and eventually she was to undergo baptism. With her consent, Schleiermacher wrote that, once a living faith, Judaism was long dead.

> "Those who yet wear its livery are only sitting lamenting beside the imperishable mummy, bewailing its departure and its sad legacy."

I cited this passage in class, and an incident flashed into my mind. The twentieth-century American-Jewish thinker Will Herberg had been a secularist and a Marxist. Having become disillusioned with both, and being of religious bent, he sought out the Christian theologian Reinhold Niebuhr with the request to be baptized, only to be sent by Niebuhr back to study Judaism, of which Herberg was ignorant, and eventually Herberg became a major Jewish thinker. What a tragedy that the liberal-minded Schleiermacher did not give similar advice to Henriette Herz! What a flaw in German philosophy in its golden age—its ignorance of, even contempt for, the vital continuity of Jewish tradition. Might German-Jewish history have become different if such as Schleiermacher had anticipated Niebuhr?

4. On the Road to Jerusalem

In the early 1970s, Rabbi Yechiel Poupko, then of the Ann Arbor Hillel Foundation, repeatedly invited me to share Holocaust seminars and observances with him. We had much the same convictions as to what was possible and necessary with regard to the Shoah. But then one day he went on a pilgrimage that took him first to Jerusalem and then to Auschwitz. In 1970, my wife Rose and I joined Bergen Belsen survivors on their own pilgrimage, first to Belsen and then to Jerusalem. On this issue, how could the survivors be wrong?

That question has been important in our personal lives. After the 1970 visit, our second to Jerusalem, Rose refused to go on any third visit to Israel without the children, and once we started taking Suzy and David—and, after he was born in 1979, also Yossi—the process had begun which led to our eventual move.

A Jew visiting Israel cannot but relate its present to the Jewish past. The Jewish state and heroes: in 70 C.E. Titus destroyed Jerusalem, its Temple, the Jewish state; but Masada fell only after a heroic defense of another three years. That was then. Now, "Masada shall not fall again" is the vow of Israeli soldiers, aware as they are of enemies who would follow in Titus's footsteps if they could. The Jewish state and martyrs: in 135 C.E. Hadrian, having defeated the Bar Kochba revolt, sought to destroy the Jewish religion as well and made its practice a capital crime; but such as Rabbi Akiba defied him, were caught, tortured to death, and through their martyrdom gave Judaism a new lease on life. Without martyrs, then, Judaism would not have survived in exile; and without heroes—the memory of old ones and the reality of new ones—there would be no Jewish state now.

Can one fit the Holocaust into this Israeli history of heroism and martyrdom? Perhaps it was in protest against such attempts that Poupko took the route he did on his pilgrimage, and as such it would be right. Titus waged a Roman-Jewish war: Hitler's assault on the Jewish people is improperly described as a war, for it was unilateral, and the Jewish people was defenseless. Again, in outlawing the Jewish faith Hadrian, if unwittingly, created martyrs: in making birth—and not actions or beliefs—into the Jewish crime, Hitler set out to murder, along with Jews, Jewish martyrdom. This then is the scandal of the Holocaust: heroes and martyrs have choices; the first between surrender and resistance, if necessary unto death, the others between apostasy and death; but in the Nazi assault on the Jewish people the overwhelming aim was choicelessness, beginning with paragraphs in law and ending with Jewish death.

At Bergen Belsen we heard an address by Norbert Wollheim, a leading figure among the Belsen survivors. He spoke in German, the language of the enemy, and his and my own mother tongue. "Spottgeburt von Dreck und Feuer," "monstrous offspring of filth and fire": thus Goethe once described the devil, thus Wollheim at

Bergen Belsen described Hitler. His words continue to resound in my ears, well over two decades later. Filth and fire, feces and fire, monstrous offspring of both: can there be anyone who ever seriously thought about the *Führer*—his mind, his life, his spell over millions, the murder camps as his ultimate self-expression—who does not understand Goethe's terse description as chillingly accurate? I understood it the moment I heard it at Belsen. What I do not understand to this day is how, well over a century earlier, the greatest of Germans had found the right description for the most depraved. But then, the task of understanding is not really mine, but much more appropriately that of German philosophers.

For another word in Wollheim's address—this of a wholly different order—I also lack adequate understanding. *Kedoshim,* "Holy Ones": thus he, a survivor, referred to the millions who did not survive—young and old, religious and secularists, saints and villains. That even villains among them were innocent is obvious, for they were murdered because of birth, not deeds; and birth, even if Jewish, is innocent. But *kadosh*—that there is a connection between *kedoshim* and the monstrous murderer one recognizes, is haunted by?—for what the devil hates above all, wants to destroy above all, is holiness. But further than this I have not come, in the more than two decades since the Belsen visit. At length a letter to Wollheim got this reply: *Kedoshim* was the name given those who did not survive by those who did, by the *she'erit ha-pleitah,* the "remnant of the devastation." They, the survivors, were in their own eyes a remnant, but not a holy one. *As name for the murdered millions, then,* kedoshim *is a legacy bestowed for explication by* amcha *on future theological thought.* I can think of no more sacred task for theologians, Jewish, Christian, Muslim.

5. Philosophy and the Shortness of Life

At Toronto I was friendly with a classical scholar. His name was Wallace. (We called each other by our last names, so I have forgotten his first name.) On his fiftieth birthday he invited me to his house for a few drinks. "I want to tell you something, Fackenheim," he said to me. "The most striking thing about life is that it is so short." He was dead before he was fifty-one.

I have written retrospectives of my thought previously, but this is the first one that is permeated with a sense of the shortness of life.[8]

In 1958 Rose and I, recently married, visited Martin Buber in his temporary Princeton home. Our conversation of three hours or so touched many subjects, but only in one did we get into an argument.

We had talked about Kant and Schelling and, using them as examples, Buber argued that, in old age, philosophers question everything all over again. With this I took issue. But I was then forty-one years of age, whereas Buber (as I, now) was in his seventies.

I cannot believe that Buber, even in old age, called into question his most basic teaching—the I-Thou doctrine; the published record shows only that he subjected it to ever more radical tests. For my part, having most recently inquired whether, in reading the Jewish Bible in the light of new realities—the Holocaust and the State of Israel—Jews of today must not shift the book's center from Exodus to Esther,[9] I now ask a more radical question by focusing on Ecclesiastes. To focus on Esther is radical enough, for it permits a secular reading of the Bible as well as a reading for which Sinai is the core. To focus on Ecclesiastes is to question Sinai itself, if not to deny it outright. "There is nothing new under the sun": what about Sinai? In response to this question, of extreme awkwardness to any orthodoxy, its traditional defenders may resort to Platonizing, affirming as they do a prehistorical Torah that is above and not under the sun. But for Jews in the age of "the Jewish return into history"[10] this is an evasion. Why, for the Jewish reader who lives in the age of Auschwitz and the Jewish return to Jerusalem, is Ecclesiastes in the Jewish Bible? Whatever the answer, it must contain the possibility of radical doubt built for them into the Bible itself.

If granted the strength and the years, I would wish to explore this theme in the future. I cannot predict or anticipate the outcome of the exploration, but it would not surprise me if I would find myself once more located in the broken Hegelian middle. Hegel's own middle will surely remain broken, with what he called his "absolute Idea" shattered. Of the absolute Idea, Hegel himself writes:

> The absolute Idea may be compared to the old man who utters the same religious doctrines as the child, but for whom they signify his entire life. The child in contrast may understand the religious content. But all of life and the whole world still exist outside it.[11]

Past experience assures me that fragments of the absolute Idea will continue to remain for me.

Notes

1. See my *To Mend the World* (Bloomington: Indiana, 1994), part 2, chs. 3, 4; and also my "The Systematic Role of the Matrix (Existence) and Apex (Yom Kippur) of Jewish Religious Life in Rosenzweig's *Star of Redemption,*" in *Der Philosoph Franz Rosenzweig,* vol. 2, ed. W. Schmied-Kowarzik (Munich: Karl Alber, 1988), pp. 567–76.

2. Most recently by E. B. Borowitz, *Renewing the Covenant* (New York: Jewish Publication Society, 1991), pp. 79–80.

3. On the unique internment operation of which German Jews such as myself were victims, see Eric Koch, *Deemed Suspect: A Wartime Blunder* (Toronto: Methuen, 1980). On Canada's immigration policy for Jewish refugees between 1933–48, see Irving Abella and Harold Troper, *None Is Too Many* (Toronto: Lester and Orpen Dennys, 1982).

4. See, for example, my *Metaphysics and Historicity* (Milwaukee: Marquette University Press, 1961).

5. *The Religious Dimension in Hegel's Thought* (Chicago: University of Chicago Press, 1982; originally published 1967), took me ten years to write. On Hegel's "middle," see especially the crucial ch. 4.

6. For my Jewish thought in relation to Hegel's broken middle, see *Encounters between Judaism and Modern Philosophy* (Northvale: Jason Aronson, 1994; originally published 1973), ch. 3; and *To Mend the World,* ch. 3.

7. See my *A Political Philosophy for the State of Israel: Fragments* (Jerusalem Center for Public Affairs, 1988).

8. The best known of the previous ones is "Jewish Faith and the Holocaust: A Fragment," *Commentary* (August 1968): 30–36. See also "The Development of My Thought," *Religious Studies Review* (July 1987): 204–6.

9. See *The Jewish Bible after the Holocaust: A Re-reading* (Bloomington: Indiana University Press, 1990), pp. 87ff.

10. See my book of this title (New York: Schocken, 1978).

11. Hegel, *Enzyklopaedie der philosophischen Wissenschaften,* no. 237, Zusatz.

Contributors

JOHANAN E. BAUER, University of Tübingen

RICHARD A. COHEN, Isaac Swift Distinguished Professor of Judaic Studies, University of North Carolina, Charlotte

DANIEL J. ELAZAR, Department of Political Studies, Bar-Ilan University; President, Jerusalem Center for Public Affairs

EMIL L. FACKENHEIM, Distinguished Professor Emeritus, Department of Philosophy, University of Toronto; Institute of Contemporary Jewry, Hebrew University of Jerusalem

GERSHON GREENBERG, Department of Religion and Philosophy, The American University

RAPHAEL JOSPE, The Open University of Israel

STEVEN T. KATZ, Department of Near East and Jewish Studies, Cornell University

ZE'EV MANKOWITZ, Melton Center for Jewish Education in the Diaspora, The Hebrew University of Jerusalem

EPHRAIM MEIR, Department of Philosophy, Bar-Ilan University

MICHAEL L. MORGAN, Department of Philosophy and Jewish Studies, Indiana University

GILLIAN ROSE, Department of Sociology, University of Warwick

ANDREY V. SMIRNOV, Institute of Philosophy, Russian Academy of Sciences, Moscow